Private Lives of Ministers' Wives

PRIVATE LIVES OF MINISTERS' WIVES

Liz Greenbacker and
Reverend Sherry Taylor

NEW HORIZON PRESS
Far Hills, New Jersey

Copyright 1991 by Liz Greenbacker and Reverend Sherry Taylor

All rights reserved. No part of this book may be reproduced or transmitted in any form whatsoever, including electronic, mechanical, or any information storage or retrieval system, except as may be expressly permitted by the 1976 Copyright Act or in writing from the publisher. Requests for permission should be addressed to New Horizon Press, P.O. Box 699, Far Hills, New Jersey 07931.

Library of Congress Catalog Card Number: 91-66360

Liz Greenbacker and Reverend Sherry Taylor
   Private Lives of Ministers' Wives

ISBN: 0-88282-100-8
New Horizon Press

To Bud, the steadiest keel through any stormy sea; and to Nathan, who, though wiser than his years, still ate too many breakfasts alone.
Liz Greenbacker

To Harry and our sons, Joshua and Matthew, who have, so far, survived life in the fish bowl.
Sherry Taylor

Acknowledgments

First, Annie Smith. Without Annie's patience, openness, and willingness to share the lowest moments of her life, this book would have been impossible. Her life, with its richness of both joy and sadness is, in its success, an example I choose to follow. To the many women who answered our survey without knowing us, without references, without any assurance that we would not hurt them again, I send my heartfelt thanks. To the many women who encouraged, supported, prodded, and propped me up, through the International Women's Writing guild and my friends, I give a thank you greater than they can ever know. And this book would not have been possible without my Administrative Assistant and Late Night Cheerleader, Stacey Comstock.

My thanks to my agent, Alice Orr, for a large dose of patience. And, I want to thank Joan Dunphy, editor, and New Horizon Press, for their even greater dose of patience.

Finally, to my collaborator, Sherry Taylor, whose experience, wit, and wisdom added immeasurably to this book, I thank you.

Contents

Introduction
xi

**1
Annie**
1

**2
And Baby Makes Six**
5

**3
In the Beginning**
17

**4
Goody-Two-Shoes**
33

**5
Does She Play the Piano?**
47

6
Filthy Lucre
63

7
Home Sweet Home: Ours? or Theirs?
79

8
How Methodist Do I Have to Be?
99

9
Going (or Going Back) to Work
117

10
Who Ministers to the Minister's Wife?
137

11
And Baby Makes Three. Or Four. Or Five . . .
155

12
Who Created This Hell?: him, her, or Him?
169

13
Cleaving
187

14
Clergy Bashing
209

15
Get the Hell Out of Here!
225

16
Take This Career and Shove It!
247

17
Divorce
269

18
If I Knew Then What I Know Now . . .
285

Epilogue I
303

Epilogue II
311

Appendix I
The Survey
315

Appendix II
The Survey Results
319

Bibliography
327

Introduction

She's unsophisticated, plain, dowdy, selfless, unassuming, timid; the perfect wife, mother, and church member—the ultimate goody-two-shoes. She's the minister's wife.

But is she really that perfect?

Private Lives of Ministers' Wives bares the secret lives of women who love and hate, marry and divorce, support and abandon, men who are ministers. This book reveals the women of the parsonages as imperfect personalities with real problems and prejudices.

On no other occupation does public scrutiny focus as intently on the family as it does in the ministry. Every action or deed, their smallest, innocuous statement is watched, heard, and analyzed. Despite this fishbowl existence, the congregation rarely gets to know the real human being who is the minister's wife. They see her as the stereotype, because she creates a public image that is often far different from her real personality. She assumes the role of the role model whether it fits her or not. By doing so, she reinforces the congregation's belief that she is, and all other ministers' wives should be—perfect.

The divorce rate for clergy couples is almost double the national average. According to G. Lloyd Rediger, author of *Cop-*

ing with Clergy Burnout, fifteen percent of all ministers will seek divorces. Yet, figures from the U.S. Census Bureau show that only 7.8 percent of United States citizens are divorced. Loneliness is one of the most-voiced complaints among clergy wives.

Our interviews reveal a sharp contrast between how the women say they live their lives—each professing to be individual, independent of her husband's profession—and how they actually live. They temper their words, restrict their activities, and assume unwanted responsibilities so as to showcase their husbands. Many don't see this contrast or admit, even to themselves, that they are playing a role.

Originally, we believed it was the congregation that forced this role upon the minister's wife. Instead, our research indicates an unwitting partnership. The false role many ministers' wives assume reinforces the myth of perfection in the minds of the congregation, who, in turn, continue to demand it. This circle remains unbroken because ministers' wives believe that their actions have a direct bearing on how well their husbands are perceived to be doing their jobs.

Whether she turns into Mrs. Goody-two-shoes or rails against the stereotype, the demand for perfection, perceived or real, internal or external, controls her life. *Private Lives of Ministers' Wives* reveals and examines the conflict created by this control and the choices made by these women to alleviate the emotional pressures it creates.

The book documents the changes in the women, in their lives and in how they view themselves, and in their marriages caused by the unique pressures of the ministry: unrealistic demands from parishioners, society, and themselves coupled with constant public scrutiny. The book's structure follows the chronological steps in these families' lives: interviewing for a pulpit, moving into a parsonage, getting to know and work with the congregation, making friends, becoming disillusioned with the pulpit and moving on—or out. Broad topics covered are

Introduction

child raising, sex, infidelity, divorce, clergy bashing, burnout, finances, and friendships.

Their stories are told in two threads. One is the dramatic story of several women. One, Annie Smith, was driven to attempt suicide, twice, in large part because of her husband's workaholism. In addition to Annie's story, we include the in-depth personal accounts of six women whose experiences illuminate a specific aspect of life with a minister. Analysis of many more wives, based on our research and interviews with experts, is also included.

So pervasive is the image of the traditional minister's wife—unsophisticated, selfless, unassuming, timid, and perfect—that our early research for this book concentrated on finding a 'modern' minister's wife, a task assumed to be difficult. Like many assumptions, this one proved wrong. Soon our problem was to find a woman who lived, and liked, the traditional role. However, very few of the women interviewed professed to embrace and enjoy the stereotype. Even those women who did, realized their choice made life difficult for the 'modern' wives who followed them. In order to get pastors' wives to share their real feeling on subjects such as finances, sex, infidelity, and divorce, these women are then extensively and intensively interviewed. We are able to build an empathetic rapport with our subjects because first, we're both active in the church—one as a minister's counsel and the other as a church activist and therefore not outsiders; and second, we're good interviewers as well as good listeners. This combination allows our interviewees to talk more freely with ministers too.

A congregation's demands are subtle, yet persistent. A strong need to please may eliminate a minister's wife's ability to distinguish the difference between a real cry for help or abuse of the pastor–parishioner relationship. For the minister, his wife and family the question is: What is the ministry? Is it a job? A profession? A calling? Do those who see it as a calling confine themselves to a role that costs them their individuality? Do

Introduction

those who see it as a job retain their individuality but diminish their service to the church? Or to God? If the ministry is a profession, who comes first? God? The church? The family? Can there be a balance between the three? What compromises are required, or demanded, to maintain that balance?

In addition to talking to many ministers' wives, we prepared a twenty-five question survey and sent it to ministers' wives all over the country. They were easy to find. Almost always the phone listings are followed by their husband's title: Reverend. Accessibility is important in a minister's job and it extends past the church office and into their homes. So, we went to the phone books and found over three hundred names. Over one hundred women were referred to us by the women who answered the survey, or by other people we met who knew we needed to contact ministers' wives. We received one-hundred-nineteen responses representing an almost twenty-two percent response rate.

Therefore, behind every one of the stories, anecdotes, and responses quoted in this book stands a real woman. Because the subject matter is sensitive, we gave anonymity to the women who requested it—and about fifty percent of them did—and changed some names. The constant repetition of "not her real name," would become exceedingly boring. So, any time we used a first name that is not connected, within the space of a paragraph or two, with a surname, that woman chose anonymity; and even that first name is not her real one. In rare instances their town or denomination were changed to further protect their identities. Otherwise, the accounts given are exactly as the women told them to us with all their contrast, contradictions, and compromises.

Picking up the strands of the life of a minister's wife turned out to be as slippery as chasing tiny pearls of quicksilver dropped on a mirror; elusive—as though each drop had an agenda of its own. As we attempted to reassemble the drops together into a whole, we found that, in too many cases, the

Introduction

minister's wife chooses to create a public image that is often far different from her personality. This false image reinforces the myth of perfection in the minds of the congregation who, in their turn, continue to demand perfection. By choosing to either emulate or contradict it, the myth of the perfect minister's wife dogs their footsteps as relentlessly as their own shadow and still controls their lives. How they get trapped in this role, how they rail against it, and the consequences of either choice, is revealed, in their own words, in this book.

This is also a book about choices. As it illuminates a life normally walled off by an intense and deliberate quest for privacy, *Private Lives of Ministers' Wives* offers insight and concrete examples of the choices others make to balance their lives, preserve their marriages, families, even their sanity. Ultimately, this book speaks to all people who, for whatever reasons—work, marriage, friendships, responsibility—are trapped in a false public identity or a role they no longer find satisfying. Through these stories, the reader will find examples to emulate and avenues to avoid.

1

Annie

Annie chose a heavy plastic bag. It wouldn't do to have a thin, weak bag that she could easily tear with her fingernails. It had to be strong. She waited until Harvey was home. While he sat in the living room trying to release himself from the emotional tensions of his ministry, Annie went to the bedroom. She sat on the side of the bed and carefully unfolded the heavy-duty, plastic bag.

To Annie there seemed nowhere to turn. Annie knew she needed professional help, but she knew that scandal would sweep through her husband's congregation when they learned that the pastor's wife was seeing a psychiatrist. There'd be talk. Plenty of it. People would say: he can't even keep his own house in order. How can he help us? She knew the people most likely to say those words, to pass them along until the news spread like spilled ink through the congregation. Annie already felt the shame and worry they'd inflict on Harvey.

She'd never done anything that hurt her husband's ministry. He was so very good at it. So dedicated, with a full measure of faith. He could look back at a long list of accomplishments doing God's work. A good man. Annie knew this, believed it. She simply would not do anything to hurt the ministry she devoted her life to supporting. Professional help was out of the question.

There was another path. Much more treacherous but private. Annie took it.

Annie pulled the bag over her head and shoulders. Harvey would be better off without her, she thought. He could spend all his time serving God if she weren't there to interfere. She wouldn't be around to distract him with her constant nagging and fighting for attention, commitment, support.

She wrapped the bag tightly around her, closing up any openings.

She could still breathe normally. She began to analyze her ambivalent feelings. At that moment she wanted to die to help Harvey. Life would be easier for him with her dead. But somewhere deep within herself she wanted to live and be happy. But she now believed the only way Harvey could be happy, was for her to die.

There was still air in the bag. Annie took several deep breaths and felt a rising panic as the bag closed in on her face. Her heart pounded. She put her arms behind her and laid down on the bed pinning her hands under her back. Yes, dying was the only way.

The air in the bag was stale, warm, and cloying. Getting air was difficult. Her breathing became quick and shallow, a reaction from both the lack of oxygen in the bag and her growing panic. The bag was almost tight against her face. She suppressed a desperate urge to rip it away. Her ambivalent feelings towards her own death rose again.

Then she prayed for her husband to find her. Where was Harvey? Didn't he notice the stillness in the house? Wouldn't he question why she wasn't making dinner? Annie rolled slightly, side to side. First toward the pillows, then toward the foot of the bed. The movement calculated to insure that she wouldn't raise her arms and rip the bag from her face. She

Annie

rolled to the pillows. Rolled to the foot. Back and forth, back and forth.

Now she was sure Harvey wasn't coming to help her. She'd be better off dead.

The plastic bag closed in on her face. All she had to do was open her mouth and take one long, last breath. The bag would soon close over her nostrils. The plastic forced down her throat would choke her. Annie steeled herself.

2

And Baby Makes Six

What drove Annie to attempt suicide? Was it pressure on her? Was it pressure on her husband? Through it all Harvey preached Sunday sermons, led worship, baptized, buried, married, visited, administered. In between he was a husband and a father.

In 1971, Douglas was seventeen, Cynthia was fifteen, Keith was fourteen, Christian was eleven, and Gregory, still waiting for heart surgery, was almost eight years old.

Annie was forty-two and pregnant with their sixth child.

This pregnancy was the worst. Annie spent most of it in bed. Keeping food down was impossible. Annie gave credit to her other children for getting her through this last pregnancy. Particularly Cynthia, who prepared countless bowls of hot cereal, loose and runny, for Annie to drink in bed. It was the only way to keep food in her stomach.

On top of the difficult pregnancy was the fear that this baby, like Gregory, might be born sick. The thought weighed heavily on both Annie and Harvey, and the rest of the family as well. Annie's obstetrician, Dr. Becker, ordered total bed rest and decided to induce labor when the time came.

Annie waited, alternating between physical discomfort,

worry over the baby's health, and the joy of having this sixth child in her life.

It felt unusual to have an appointment to go into labor. Annie and Harvey packed a bag and drove leisurely to the hospital. No rushing, no hurrying, no water breaking, no labor pains; just the worry, now that birth was imminent, that this baby would be born sick like Gregory.

Annie was admitted and taken to the labor room. An IV was inserted in her arm and the medication to induce her labor injected into it.

Harvey went home. This was 1971. Hospitals didn't allow fathers to stay in the labor room or watch the delivery. It could take hours for the induced labor to begin and the baby to be born.

After what seemed an eternity, Shane was born. Perfectly formed, perfectly healthy, Shane had red hair just like Cynthia's. Annie was ecstatic. No longer would she have to explain the lone red head in a family of brown-haired children. More important, Shane was healthy. He didn't suffer from any of the complications that had almost killed Gregory. Relief and joy washed over her.

Annie lay patiently on a gurney in the white antiseptic surroundings of the delivery room, waiting to be moved to an operating room for tubal ligation surgery. With six difficult pregnancies behind her, Annie couldn't risk another one. At forty-two, she had already spent ten percent of her life pregnant. Fifty-four months, to be exact. Four and a half years. Her five-foot, one-hundred pound body simply couldn't stand the rigors of pregnancy and childbirth again. Harvey agreed, and they had arranged the surgery at the same time they had scheduled the birth.

An orderly arrived and pushed the gurney along the halls of the hospital. The anesthetist for her delivery stayed with her. He would attend the surgery, too. The three of them bustled down the halls of Brigham and Women's Hospital in Bos-

And Baby Makes Six

ton. When they arrived in the surgery wing, Annie heard the beep, beep, beep of a heart monitor coming from the operating room reserved for her.

She overheard an argument, too, as she waited in the hall. She felt like she was floating. Euphoria, she thought, and felt her spirits lift. Although she couldn't make out the words, she heard Dr. Becker's raised and angry voice. The argument had something to do with the operating room. Annie heard Dr. Becker's voice rise and fall with different levels of anger. She stopped listening. She had other things to think about.

She was suddenly, overwhelmingly tired. She attributed it to the labor and the months of morning sickness and worry. She tried her recently learned Lamaze breathing exercises in an attempt to relax.

Where was Harvey? Surely they must have called him by now. Shane was at least an hour old. Annie tried to ask the anesthetist if Harvey had been called but a tightness in her chest, then shortness of breath made it impossible to speak. The anesthetist stared at Annie. The concern in his eyes scared her. He left Annie in the hall.

He returned with Dr. Becker. Annie's breathing was extremely labored. Her chest heaved with the effort of filling her lungs with air. To Annie it felt like her throat was blocked. After a quick, but extensive, examination, Dr. Becker explained that they would insert a tube down her throat so she could breath. Annie nodded, gasping and gurgling for air.

She never would remember what the doctor told her. Annie was sensitive to medication. A little was usually a lot for her. The pulmonary edema she suffered could have been caused by a reaction to the medication used to induce labor. Or it could have been caused by the spinal tap used to ease her pain during delivery. It could also have been caused by the severe release of emotions Annie experienced over delivering a healthy normal child, or her fears about the tubal ligation surgery. She never found out.

Dr. Becker, aided by the anesthetist and a nurse, inserted the breathing tube down Annie's throat.

It hurt. It felt like fire. Every inch the tube traveled down her esophagus felt ravaged. Annie panicked. The scream of terror that welled up inside her stayed there, blocked by the tube that helped air to fill her lungs. Annie thought she was dying. She knew this wasn't normal. She'd had five babies. This had never happened.

Where's Harvey? Unable to talk, the words repeated in her mind.

Harvey fiddled with the projector. He jiggled the lever, pulled on the film and tried to start it again. The test runs on the projector prompted the ladies of the Women's Association to find seats in the sanctuary pews. It was their annual travelogue meeting and the ladies had turned out in force.

Everyone knew that only the minister could coerce and cajole action out of the old projector. So Harvey fiddled, jiggled, pulled, and tapped on it again. He'd been called about his son's birth minutes before the start of the meeting. The hospital spokesperson assured him that both Annie and Shane were fine. Harvey told them he'd be there as soon as he got the ladies' meeting started. His annoyance at the balky projector grew.

This time he fiddled, jiggled, pulled, and tapped harder. This time the projector started. He showed one of the women how to shut it off and left for the hospital.

It all seemed like a nightmare. The noises, the raised, angry voices, the people scurrying around her. Where was Harvey?

Annie was told to relax, stay still, remain calm, and Annie wouldn't be Annie if she didn't obey if only to make their jobs easier. But a seed of anger planted itself in Annie's heart. And she wasn't surprised to find it there.

And Baby Makes Six

Finally, he was there. Harvey was always there for emergencies, for the important things in their lives. He was there for the school plays, the games, the award ceremonies. He was there for Gregory. He was there to see Annie in pain, to see the misery she felt, to hold her hand and encourage her. Annie was relieved. Harvey was there. Harvey would help her. She relaxed.

But the anger grew. And Annie felt it grow.

"That sixth baby, that sixth one, it was just too much for me to handle," said Annie in a sermon to the Medford congregation. "It was too much. And no longer could Harvey still be on that same track as before, something had to change. We had to do something differently than we were doing. For me to survive. And I still loved him very much, he was very dedicated and I felt very much in conflict about all this.

"It seems I was able to handle pressures of raising six children, being a reasonable decent and loving wife to Harvey, home management, being the wife of a most dedicated minister, being a good listener to my husband, my children, and to our extended church family. A tall order. I guess following the birth of our sixth child I needed my husband in a different way. I needed his friendship, companionship, support, emotionally, to lean on him more. I needed Harvey to be as concerned about my welfare as much as I was concerned about his well being."

Shane was three when Harvey and Annie packed up the Volkswagen bus and the "bug" with all six children, their camping equipment, and supplies for a month's vacation, and left for Canada. It probably would be the last time the entire family went on vacation together. The children were older, some were already in college. But it proved to be too many people in too close quarters. By this time Annie was more than unhappy— she was depressed. Annie already felt like the cook, laundress, cleaner, secretary, telephone operator, and messenger for her family and the church. The camping trip was too much. Annie really needed a break from all the routine matters of family life.

Miserable, Annie felt there was no time for her own needs. The feelings of frustration, depression, the weight of heavy responsibilities, even on vacation, overwhelmed her. She was irritable, miserable, and it seemed she made everyone around her miserable too. Annie began to think seriously they'd be better off without her.

Not far from their campsite, a short distance through the woods, a dead-end road served as a drag strip for the local hotrodders. The Smith's heard them racing, squealing their tires, punching their engines, every evening.

Annie began to think that the drag strip was the place for her suicide. She'd leave the campsite, walk to the road, and sit in the path of the racing cars. They wouldn't miss her. She'd be dead. Out of everyone's way. God and the church could have all of Harvey.

"I had this constant rumble," Annie preached. "It was just vibes. My heart hurt. I literally had an aching, hurting heart. It was real pain. But Harvey would be free of my constant nagging for more time, more attention. He could do all of God's work."

Annie sat, cross-legged in the middle of the road. First, she prayed that a car would come. A fast car. A very fast car. Instantaneous death. No pain. Easy.

Then she prayed that a car wouldn't come. She didn't want to die. She just wanted her marriage back. She wanted herself back. But she couldn't get it. Harvey was committed to God. Annie was in competition with God. The guilt was terrible.

So she cried and prayed that a car would come and run her over.

But no cars came that night. Was it a sign from God? A sign that Annie should live? And keep fighting? She didn't know. Still crying, she walked back to the campsite.

And Baby Makes Six

Life didn't get better. Annie fought with Harvey to convince him her feelings weren't just pure selfishness. She fought for her marriage. But guilt ate at her. Now, sometimes, she even resented the time Harvey spent with the children. That, too, was time away from their marriage. What a terrible person she was. Look how miserable she'd made Harvey. But she desperately wanted their marriage to be a marriage. The fighting always occurred during their one hour or two in a day they were together. Precious time that should have been spent loving, not arguing. Afterwards, exhaustion set in and it would take a week or so for both of them to recover. Through it all they played their roles: husband, wife; father, mother; minister, helpmate.

But this time, Annie's depression was so deep she couldn't even raise her arms to embrace her husband. There was no energy to raise a spoon to her mouth to eat. She couldn't cook, couldn't clean. With monumental effort, she brushed her teeth every morning. She couldn't even comb her hair. Annie thought of cutting the waist-length, brown hair that was her proudest feature, but she didn't really want to. Her family vetoed the idea, too.

Sometimes Annie went to the cellar and sat on the floor in the dampness. She felt she needed to be punished, because she was interfering with God. She couldn't pick herself up by the ears, couldn't throw herself down the cellar stairs. But she could go and sit in the dampness and the cold. It was the nearest she could come to being adequately punished.

Annie couldn't make the decision to get help. She knew she needed it. But she feared the backlash on Harvey's ministry if she admitted her mental health was in tatters. She chose a different route to peace.

That was when Annie took the heavy, plastic garbage bag and went to the bedroom. She placed the bag over her head and prayed for Harvey to find her before she died.

Where was Harvey?

He was in the room, ripping the bag off her head and

body. He held her and told her he loved her. He convinced her that she needed help, counseling. Annie resisted, crying from the terror of her attempted suicide. She couldn't hurt his ministry. If word got out . . .

Harvey said he didn't care. Annie's health was more important. He'd seen this coming for years. He'd expected it. He knew about her childhood, about the shaky foundation. He knew it would be only a matter of time before it took its toll on Annie. His words were balm to her heart. Harvey loved her.

He called a doctor and got Annie admitted to Ruble 1.

"Harvey saw that I needed help. I was really gonzo," said Annie. "I remember going on the elevator and I didn't want to do what I was doing. I did not want to go to the hospital. I didn't want to taint Harvey's ministry. I didn't want to do this to him. I felt very, very guilty and I was doing this, not to myself, but to Harvey, to his ministry. That was utmost in my mind. I was crying. I didn't want anyone to find out."

Ruble 1 takes up one end of a floor at New England Memorial Hospital. Annie shared a room with another woman. They each had a bureau and a small bed.

There were no locked doors at Ruble 1. Community meetings were held at eight in the morning and each patient was expected to be bathed, dressed, fed, and on time. Sometimes patients had to be dragged out of bed to attend the meeting. The patients had varied problems. Some were drug addicts, alcoholics, some had sexual problems, some, like Annie, suffered from depression. At the morning meeting they talked about their responsibilities to each other and themselves. They met in the large living room where the piano stood. They sat in the chairs and couches arranged along the walls and the staff doctors and nurses met with them. It was the large group that heard a patient's reasons on why they were ready to go home. It was this group that decided when each patient would leave the residency program.

After the morning meeting, they broke into smaller

groups that dealt with their specific problems. Then there were individual meetings with staff psychiatrists and psychologists. There were activities, too. Annie still has the leather key chain she tooled her initial on that she made in the Ruble 1 craft class. They took trips to the mall and to a zoo. Annie's responsibility was washing and drying the dishes. Annie stayed thirteen nights.

"I distinctly remember one very restless night. When I laid down at night, when I first went there, I couldn't stay still. My body would just jerk and shake. It's an awful feeling to lie down and not be able to rest. I got up and looked at myself in a large mirror and I couldn't believe what I saw. It was a nightmare. I looked and I said, out loud, in this bathroom, I said: 'Annie is that you? What's the matter, Annie? What's happening to you?'"

"That was the longest thirteen nights of my life. Like it was never going to end. You saw things that I guess you had to see that you'd rather not have seen. One woman was getting shock treatments.

"But we accepted each other because we were all in pain and all hurting. If you could accept each other in love, that's healing in itself. There was no judging, no saying you're this or you're that. Just acceptance. And that's healing."

Slowly, the healing came.

"It was time for Annie to be looked after and time for Annie to look after Annie," she said. "I brushed my teeth. I ate. I listened to my counselor. I did my own laundry. It was so strange to do my own laundry—no diapers! It was time for me to look after me. I had to forget everything else. I had to get back on my feet."

Annie talked with the doctor about her childhood. The doctors and Harvey concentrated on helping Annie sort through the abuse, neglect, and abandonment she felt from her youth. It helped but Annie had her doubts. She wasn't convinced that her childhood was the only problem facing her. But everyone else seemed so sure of it. Harvey was so sure.

Just before Thanksgiving 1976, Annie went home. She felt ready to face the real work of healing: returning home to get back into her life and family. The group agreed that she was ready. Armed with strength and energy, clutching tentatively at her rediscovered identity, Annie went home.

Soon after, Annie preached to the congregation at Medford about her illness. The Medford congregation showed its love for the ministerial couple with an outpouring of support and encouragement. Three other women sought counseling because of Annie's testimony. Annie returned for counseling sessions every month at Ruble 1. But she felt so well, so whole, that gradually she stopped going. Once again, the church was her haven.

In 1977, Harvey was assigned to another church, also in the Boston suburbs. It would prove to be the most difficult assignment of their career. The church was in chaos. Harvey had spiritual healing to do there. Harvey still felt he must fulfill all the expectations of his parishioners. His work was never finished, there was always more to do. Harvey also had his own agenda. Along with his church work, Harvey supported community causes, too. There was always a cause that seemed important all through Harvey's life. He was active in Vietnam War issues, race relations, and helping the needy, sick, and downtrodden in the community. The church held meetings, at Harvey's insistence, for Alcoholics Anonymous, Al Anon, Al-a-Teen; the disabled used the church for indoor sports events. Many in the congregation didn't like the kinds of people who came to those meetings in their building. Harvey wouldn't make waves to ensure that he and Annie had time together, but he always made waves for the causes he felt were right in the community and in the world.

It proved to be an impossible task. Annie watched as Harvey worked himself towards death. She agonized over his

And Baby Makes Six

ashen skin, his drooping mouth, the slow steps. Harvey developed chronic back pain. Annie had her own impossible task. Following her youthful interpretation of Ruth Peale's (Norman Vincent Peale's wife) example, Annie supported her husband by gradually doing more and more work at home, running more and more interference for him at church, answering more and more phone calls at home and handling them herself so that he was free to do his work.

That tentative hold on her identity slipped. She felt, again, that she took second place to Harvey's ministry. All the issues that caused the first depression, supposedly the last, were back. But this time, she was angry as well as depressed.

She wanted her marriage back. God didn't lead her and Harvey together just to make them this miserable. They deserved better than this. She deserved better than this. Though the guilt over competing with God for Harvey's time was back, it wasn't as strong as before. It didn't manifest itself in yet another attempt at suicide. She needed to know, demanded to know, if Harvey felt the same way about her that she felt about him. Yet, a part of her didn't care anymore. The depressed part of Annie just wanted release and peace. Real peace which meant peace of mind. This time Annie decided. Anger won. She sat Harvey down and announced she was leaving him. Harvey remembers it almost word for word.

" 'I can't live with you under these circumstances,' she said," Harvey told us. "She said, 'I'm going to get an apartment. You take care of the children, you take care of the church, and when you're done being a pastor, come find me. I'll never divorce you. I love you. When you're through with the ministry, we can hook up again.' "

It proved to be the acid test of their marriage.

3

In the Beginning

"I don't know why it took me so long to see the problem," said Harvey, the husband sought by this depressed wife in the first chapter. "I thought Annie was playing a game with me, testing me to see if she could get me to give up something in the church and put her first. And when I finally agreed her attitude suddenly changed. If I said 'OK, I won't go to the meeting,' she'd say 'you really should go to the meeting.'

"I manipulated Annie. I would say 'Yes, I'll stay home,' knowing that if I'd just seemed to give in then today, tonight, tomorrow, would be all right. She, in turn, would always come around. So I would say yes knowing I wouldn't have to fulfill that debt.

"The first depression we thought was because of her background. Sure, I was busy, but that's what it's all about in an effective ministry. You are busy. Annie had this really shaky foundation. We had talked about it a lot. I knew the whole terrible story. I blamed that. It had to be that . . ."

Annie Mihran Hougassian was born of Armenian parents on March 16, 1929. All her life she referred to herself as a Depression baby. The term haunted her later life.

Annie's mother was an eyewitness to the atrocities of the Turkish Massacre. Though she immigrated to America, she never recovered from the experiences. She never learned to speak English. When Annie was two, her father took her and her two sisters away from their mother. It would be more than forty years before Annie saw her mother again.

Mr. Hougassian was twice his wife's age. There were only three things Annie remembered about him. His silver hair. His steel-blue eyes. And his cruelty. When he took his three daughters, Hougassian took the oldest two—Sally, eight, and Nancy, six—to their grandparents' house on Douglas Avenue in Providence, Rhode Island not far from the house they had lived in with their mother.

Annie was put in the State Home. At two, she was not yet toilet trained and neither her father nor her grandparents wanted to deal with the problems of training her.

Annie remembered a wall of toilet seats. She was terrified of them, but the sooner she was toilet trained, the sooner she could go back to her father. As an adult, when Annie took her first Rorschach tests, the inkblot pictures looked like toilet seats. That was a first for the doctor.

When she was four, Annie returned to her father and grandparents. But the Great Depression was having its effect on the Hougassian family just as it affected millions of other families in the early 1930s. Annie's father took out his frustrations of poverty on his eldest and youngest daughters—Sally and Annie—the ones who looked most like his ex-wife. All three girls were neglected. They never had enough food. Annie never owned a toothbrush. Her teeth were rotted and her thick, brown hair was dirty, snarled, and matted. Both her father and grandmother beat her.

Then Annie found a Spring Street playground. She walked almost a mile to get to the park. It was a simple routine. First, get out of the house. Then, down Douglas Avenue, past the laundromat, then down a large hill along the train tracks.

In the Beginning

Spring Street Park was inner city and the town hired supervisors for the children. For Annie, life began on Spring Street.

Annie played on the swings, learned how to weave baskets, danced around a maypole. Each day she'd play, then try to brush the soot and ashes blown over the playground by the trains off her clothing. Every day she made the long trek home again, up the big hill, past the laundromat, down Douglas Avenue, and in the house.

Either her father or her grandmother would beat her for going to the park. Her grandmother picked her off the floor, dangling her in the air by holding only her ears. Her father threw her down the cellar stairs. Afterwards, Annie just cried. She'd sit on the kitchen floor and cry her heart out.

The next day, Annie always went back to the park. And, if caught, she always got a beating.

When Annie was three years old something happened in Syracuse, New York that was to profoundly affect her life. Dr. Norman Vincent Peale, then minister at University Methodist Church, had been offered positions at two other churches, one in California and one in New York. The California church was well established with a large congregation. The New York church had a declining membership and was in desperate need of leadership. After a month's deliberation, prayer, and soul searching, Dr. Peale accepted the call from the Marble Collegiate Dutch Reformed Protestant Church of the City of New York. His decision set his future—and Annie's.

Of course, Annie took no note of this momentous occasion, because she was, after all, only three years old. But at four, Annie found a haven to sustain her for the next seventeen years. She attended services at the Jefferson Street Church in Providence. Jefferson Street Church was Armenian Orthodox, very high church. The big cross on the steeple and the swinging censer, the bells ringing, made a deep impression on Annie. She always remembered the thin communion wafers, and the priests in their jeweled crowns and colorful robes. The peace and quiet soothed her. She was drawn to churches for the rest of her life.

Annie's grandfather, who wasn't her real grandfather but her grandmother's second husband, owned a wood and ice business with his stepson. They cut and delivered wood in the winter and delivered ice in the summer.

Sometimes Grandfather conspired with Annie, keeping her out of school to drive the horse and team with him on his deliveries. Sometimes they stopped at a little diner on his route. Horses and wagons filled the yard around the diner. For a special treat, Annie's grandfather would buy a nickel ice cream cone. Grandfather was the one light in Annie's life. He was her only source of love. Annie always claimed she would never have survived Douglas Avenue without her grandfather. He was her world.

Annie's world died in an accident when she was eight. She was never told the details, never knew what happened. Just that Grandfather was dead. After the funeral, a doctor came to Douglas Avenue to examine Annie. She never knew why. They sat together on her grandmother's bed. A roach skittered across the floor. Annie didn't react to it, it was normal to her. The doctor noted her rotted teeth, dirty body, head lice, and her undernourished, forty-six pound weight.

State workers came and took Annie to the hospital. (Annie preached four or five sermons while she suffered from her two major depressions as an adult. The quotes that follow are from those sermons.)

"By age eight, because of malnutrition and child abuse, I was hospitalized," said Annie from the pulpit. "How vivid the memories surrounding this experience. The doctor shaking his head in disbelief. My head being shaved clean. Several teeth extracted.

"Only Miss Toppy, a social worker, came to visit me, and with an ice cream cone. Boy, was that a treat! On her

In the Beginning

second visit, Miss Toppy said 'Let's go for a ride,' and she took me to a foster home which was a complete surprise to me! The endless tears, the heartache, the deep feelings of rejection and confusion. I must admit though, it didn't take long for me to realize that this new home was going to be better. Isn't it strange how we wish to return to what we know, even if it's not good for us! Knowing the misery I experienced at home, I cried all day when Miss Toppy didn't take me home. It didn't last long, though. I was all done crying that first day."

Life with Mr. and Mrs. Charles Hudson was better than living with her father and his mother. The Hudsons lived on Spencer Street in Providence near Federal Hill. The area was known as Little Italy and Annie said she was 'the only Protestant' in sight. Annie was a straight A student at school and was known as the class reconciler, always stepping in to settle disputes between her friends. In her yearbook they wrote: To a brilliant classmate who kept our class together! Annie was valedictorian of her class.

During the week, Annie had school to keep her busy and out of the way of Mr. Hudson, who was an alcoholic. Only attending on Christmas and Easter, the Hudsons weren't churchgoers, so on weekends, Annie spent time at church. She joined the Episcopal Church of the Messiah in Olneyville. Once again she walked a mile each way to get where she wanted to go. Once again she walked along the train tracks.

Annie loved the Church of the Messiah and formed habits there that would set the pattern for her whole life. The youth group put on plays and Annie directed some. She was in minstrel shows and loved acting. She remembered, with pride, actually crying when she played Mary Magdalene. She joined the choir when she was fifteen and she was the superintendent of Sunday school at eighteen. Annie basked in the acceptance she felt at church. She liked it there. It was her haven.

"Through it all there was one stabilizing influence in my

life, the church," said Annie in another sermon. "For as long as I can remember, the Church has been a vital part of my existence. Although I did not realize it at the time it was probably the Church and the people who touched my life through the Church, people who believed in me, who picked me up and pushed me along, that made the real difference in my life."

Life with the Hudsons was better than it had been with her father, but not perfect. Mr. Hudson was a quiet alcoholic. Mrs. Hudson was domineering. Once, when Annie was fourteen, she spoke back to Mrs. Hudson, whom she now called Mom. Mrs. Hudson raised her hand and struck Annie across the face. Annie fell, landing on the threshold between the bathroom and the hallway. She never spoke back to Mrs. Hudson again but the incident resolved her to leave them, Providence, and her childhood far behind her as soon as she could.

At twenty-one, Annie left. She quit her executive secretarial job in Providence and went to Lake Mohonk Mountain House in the Shawangunk Mountains west of the Hudson River in New York. Mohonk Mountain House was an exclusive resort hotel operated by a Quaker family. The hotel had three hundred-five rooms, one-hundred-forty-five with private baths and one hundred-sixty with running water. The dining room fed five hundred guests. There were fourteen public rooms, 11,000 square feet of porches with mountain and valley views, and one hundred fifty-seven fireplaces. The resort also owned 5,400 acres of forest land, eleven hundred acres of farm and pasture land, and eight hundred acres of meadows. Besides Lake Mohonk, the resort offered guests a golf course, tennis courts, hiking paths and bridle trails. In the peak season of 1949, July, August, and September, two guests got meals, lodging, and use of all the facilities for thirty dollars a day. Annie trained at the resort's waitressing school for two weeks and apprenticed with an experienced waitress for one week before she was assigned to her own station in the dining room. Annie made one

In the Beginning

day trip into New York City to take aptitude tests to determine if she had a future in nursing.

While Annie waited tables in the gracious, formally informal dining room of Lake Mohonk Mountain House, a minister arrived with his wife. In exchange for enjoying the golf course, lake activities, and natural surroundings of the resort hotel, the minister conducted daily morning devotions and Sunday worship service. That minister was Dr. Norman Vincent Peale.

Annie was unsure about the rest of her life. She felt she wanted to go into nursing—to help others—but she wasn't convinced this was the right step. She waited anxiously for the results of her aptitude test. While waiting she solicited advice from anyone and everyone who would talk to her. One confidant was a cashier at the resort. He suggested she talk to Dr. Peale.

Never one to pass up an opportunity or to let formalities stop her, Annie approached Dr. Peale and asked if she could talk to him. Annie wrote about what happened in a sermon:

"All right," said Peale. "How about two this afternoon?"

"I'm sorry Dr. Peale, but I must attend a meeting of all the waitresses," said Annie.

"You see I had no idea who he was: world famous minister, lecturer, author, radio–television personality, editor of one of the leading religious publications, *Guideposts* magazine!

"We had an interesting visit in the palatial parlor of the hotel. Immediately he made me feel comfortable, this simple and kindly man. Dr. Peale asked me several questions. 'Do you smoke? Do you drink? What do you want to do with your life?' My response to his last question took some deliberation. 'When I'm old I should like to feel that this world is a little better for having allowed me the privilege to walk through it.' To which Dr. Peale concluded: 'Let me know as soon as you receive the results of your aptitude test.'

"Well, I failed miserably! And no way was I going to tell anyone. My strictly commercial courses in high school left my academic education terribly lacking.

"Then there was this light tap on my shoulder from behind in the hotel's dining room. 'Mrs. Peale and I are leaving today, and we'd like to see you before we go.' This time Mrs. Peale accompanied Dr. Peale. Of course I had to share with them the news of my failure, to which Dr. Peale responded: Maybe God has something else for you to do, Annie!;' adding 'I'd like to have my friend and associate, Dr. Smiley Blanton, study the results of your aptitude test.' " Dr. Smiley Blanton was the psychiatrist who collaborated on some of Dr. Peale's books. Annie sent the tests and promptly forgot the whole encounter.

Annie decided to concentrate on waitressing. She was small, only five feet tall, and thin, but strong. She had no trouble hoisting the heavy trays of food up on her shoulder and weaving her way through the busy dining room of Lake Mohonk Mountain House. She planned to travel the waitress 'circuit,' working at seasonal resorts in Colorado or Florida. In early September she opened a letter from Ruth Peale inviting Annie to live with them and become her personal secretary. The arrangements were simple. Annie would have room and board in the Peales' New York City apartment. Annie accepted.

Ruth Peale was in charge of publishing her husband's sermons and busy writing books herself. Part of Annie's job was to type Dr. Peale's messages after he preached on Sunday. She didn't have to help with dishes after the Sunday meal.

"Immediately following dinner I was at the typewriter transcribing Dr. Peale's sermons from the tape recording. I attended Hunter College two evenings a week for six months. This course helped tremendously in the editing of Dr. Peale's sermons. Headquarters for Foundation for Christian Living is in Pawling, New York, where each month three printed sermons

In the Beginning

were mailed to a list of more than 300,000 people all over the world.

"One day was never like another. Occasionally I worked at the office of psychiatry; or at another office which handled the mailing of Dr. Peale's books; or I collected publications offerings from special boxes around the church; or whenever Dr. Peale was at home, grappling with an idea or an inspiration for one of his writings, he'd suddenly say: 'Annie, will you take dictation?'"

Life with the Peales was exciting. Annie met many famous people of the early 1950s, such as then Vice President Richard Nixon; Fulton Oursler, author of *The Greatest Story Ever Told;* Roy Rogers and Dale Evans; author Catherine Marshall; Governor Thomas E. Dewey; Lowell Thomas; and Carl Erskine, pitcher for the Brooklyn Dodgers. Annie learned how to plan formal dinners, assisted Mrs. Peale at tea parties and became a friend and big sister to the Peales' youngest daughter, Elizabeth.

Living with the Peales, Annie felt a little of the loneliness that was to haunt her later life. In their thirteen-room apartment on Seventy-fourth Street across from Central Park, she was *in* the home but not *of* the family. Mrs. Peale solved that loneliness problem by insisting that Annie attend the Young Adult Group at Marble Collegiate Church.

In her job offer, Mrs. Peale had mentioned she wanted Annie involved in the group. At first, Annie had other plans. Thirty blocks from the Peales' apartment was the Children's Center in East Harlem. It was an orphanage, a state home, similar to the one Annie lived in when she was two. It was institutional with all the beds together in a big open room. Annie went every Wednesday night to tuck the children in bed and to listen. Bedtimes were the worst for Annie when she was little. Her fears crowded into bed with her until it seemed there was no room for her. At the Children's Center, Annie remembered her own childhood fears and let the children pour theirs out to her. She read bedtime stories and she let them talk. Annie needed to be needed, and the children at the Center fed her need.

Harvey Smith also volunteered at the Children's Center on Wednesday nights. Harvey was an executive with Boy Scouts of America at the time and in charge of the Upper West Side of Manhattan. He had a Boy Scout troop at the Center. Annie was attracted to the sensitive young man immediately but felt he would never notice her. She liked how he treated the boys, recognizing in him her own admirable qualities.

Ruth Peale persisted. Annie needed to meet people her own age. So Annie joined the Young Adult group. Harvey Smith was vice-president. Group members ranged in age from twenty-one to thirty-five and came from all walks of life. They met Sunday and Thursday nights at the church. On Tuesday nights the prayer group met. They formed work parties and painted and repaired churches on the lower East Side and in East Harlem. They put on shows, much to Annie's delight, prepared devotionals, went on retreats, went skiing. Occasionally, they went out to dinner as a group.

Annie wanted to make a good impression on Harvey. But she was afraid. Men frightened her, the experiences with her father left their mark. Yet, a romance grew and the secretary and the executive were soon engaged. The Peales advised against the marriage. Harvey had been involved in a near-death encounter with his roommate. His roommate had stabbed Harvey and left him to die. The story hit the papers, even Walter Winchell's column. The Peales felt that the relationship between Harvey and his roommate was not sufficiently resolved.

Annie felt torn between the Peales and her heart. She admired Ruth Peale and followed her advice. Annie spent the night listening in the darkness and silence of the Peales' living room for an answer to her dilemma. At 4:00 a.m. she gave up. She still felt that God was leading her to Harvey. The message was: marry him.

In the Beginning

It was the influence of the Peales, in fact, that led Annie to consider marriage in the first place. She didn't want to marry. Her childhood taught her that marriage was hell. Even as she got older, her friends' marriages ended in divorce at an alarming rate. Marriage was definitely not for her. Living with the Peales changed that.

"Dr. and Mrs. Peale have a very beautiful relationship. They are definitely a team. In spite of their busyness, they managed to keep romance in their marriage. I had previously discounted marriage, but the special relationship between Dr. and Mrs. Peale made me wonder."

Annie and Harvey were married on Christmas Day at 2:00 p.m. in 1952 in the Southern Baptist Church where Harvey had grown up. She was twenty-three years old, he was twenty-eight. They found an apartment in the Washington Heights section of New York City in the left-hand apartment building of a pair that flanked, protectively, the small Washington Heights Methodist Church. It was a small, four-room apartment. Nice, but nothing plush. Annie and Harvey moved in with little furniture, a foldout couch for a bed, and a desk. They used cardboard boxes until they could afford a dining room set. In the study, Harvey worked at the desk Annie gave him as a wedding gift.

They attended the Methodist Church that was sandwiched between the two apartment buildings. Harvey had grown up in Big Springs Methodist Church near his boyhood farm home in Georgia.

Annie had their first baby.

Three years into their marriage, Annie and Harvey went to the movies with their best friends, Marilyn and George Marvel. They paid their money and took their seats to watch a movie *A Man Called Peter*. The movie was based on a book Catherine Marshall wrote about her husband, Peter Marshall. Annie had met Catherine when she lived with the Peales. As the story unfolded in the flickering light of the movie theater, a transformation took place in Harvey's heart, mind, and soul. During the scene where Chaplain Peter Marshall talks to cadets about what they'll face in war, Harvey grasped Annie's hand and squeezed it so hard she gasped. He didn't say a word but sat rigidly at attention, focused on the film. It wasn't until they returned home that Harvey asked Annie what she thought about him leaving Scouting and entering the ministry. They had been considering accepting a promotion for Harvey that would have moved them to Colorado.

Annie didn't hesitate. When she first met Harvey, he struck her as the kind of person who would make a good minister. She was genuinely pleased and saw her role as supporting her husband. She wanted what he wanted. Secretly she thought she might be married to another Dr. Norman Vincent Peale—a great religious leader. And with the Peales' example to follow, Annie set her course. Whither Harvey went, Annie went, too.

They sold everything they owned except the baby furniture and Harvey's desk. They borrowed money from the Methodist Student Fund, a loan that would take years to pay back at the rate of ten dollars a month. They moved to Atlanta, Georgia where Harvey attended Chandler School of Theology at Emory University. They lived in the one frame house among a hundred Quonset huts on a section of the campus known as Mudville. Mudville, the university's married housing area, was literally a sea of mud every time it rained. The huts were build to accommodate the flood of World War II veterans who had inundated American colleges. The frame house where Annie and Harvey lived had an extra room so that they could take in a boarder to help pay the rent.

Annie was pregnant with their second child.

Harvey took a job with Grace Methodist Church on Ponce De Leon Avenue in Atlanta as Minister to Youth. He was there six months when he heard about a congregation in

In the Beginning

Doraville that was starting their own church. The Northwoods congregation was meeting in Doraville's civic center. They needed a minister to lead them spiritually and to spearhead a fund-raising drive to build their own church. They found one. Harvey took the job. He was still in seminary.

Life was hectic. Harvey rose early and took their son on a bike ride each morning. After classes he went home for lunch and then took off again. He had readings and work at the new church for the fund drive, Sunday service, and visitations. In between he studied, wrote papers, and prepared for church. Annie typed his papers and saw many a sun rise over the keyboard of her typewriter. She always referred to that time as when "WE were in seminary." Their time preoccupied with school, family, and church, they didn't go out much. Money was always scarce. Annie remembered taking care of babies for a long time. It felt like she was always pregnant.

While Harvey went to school and ministered to Northwoods, Annie gave birth to their third child.

After graduation, Harvey was assigned to a two-point charge in Danielsville, Georgia. A two-point charge meant serving two churches at the same time. Some ministers have served four-point charges. Their fourth child was only two weeks old when they moved. Annie was weak, tired.

Danielsville was a depressed area. Many of the homes didn't have indoor plumbing. The village was seventeen miles up into the hills of Georgia. The Bishop who assigned them there said he wanted Harvey to get a little mud on his shoes. Northwoods was a big church in an up-and-coming area, prestigious, with plush homes. Danielsville had mud roads. Annie felt the Bishop wanted to humble them and he did.

Annie and Harvey's salary in Danielsville was augmented with food brought by congregants. One day a bucket of figs, another a bushel of corn. Peaches, chickens, and eggs came, delivered to the parsonage by grateful parishioners. Harvey processed the fresh goods and filled the freezer.

Private Lives of Ministers' Wives

Harvey learned to repair shoes. Saturday night was shoe night and he polished and repaired the children's shoes and his own to be presentable for Sunday morning services. Services alternated between the two churches. Each church had a morning service only half the time. On the alternate Sundays, service was held in the afternoon. Harvey prepared and led two services each week.

Annie busied herself raising babies. She wasn't in the ministry too much with Harvey then. She kept the home fires burning, cooking meals, and keeping the kids happy, and getting everyone to church on Sunday looking neat and clean.

Danielsville was the first congregation that prayed specifically for them. "We pray for our pastor and his lovely wife," a deacon intoned every Sunday. They meant it, and Annie remembered it as a precious experience.

In 1961, Annie and Harvey left Danielsville to serve in an inner-city church in Massachusetts. In 1965, they were assigned a church in Augusta, Georgia.

Annie was pregnant with their fifth child.

During all of Annie's pregnancies she was nauseated with vomiting and extended morning sickness. However, Annie took the rest of the pregnancies after her first with aplomb. She drew on reserves of patience and strength she didn't know she had. She modeled her lifestyle from the woman she admired most: Ruth Stafford Peale. Annie supported her husband's ministry as much as he did. She treated the church as her haven.

However, the birth of Gregory, Annie's fifth child was a difficult experience. Within forty-five minutes of delivery, he turned a bright yellow. He needed almost total blood transfusions to counteract RH factor complications. When that was under control, the doctors discovered a heart defect. Gregory's aorta was contracted. Called a coarctation, the pinched artery didn't allow blood to flow adequately to the baby's extremities. The doctors said an operation was impossible until he was older. For eight years Gregory needed almost constant medical

In the Beginning

attention. Harvey and Annie lived with the fear that each trip to the emergency room with their son would be the last time they'd see him alive. Annie tried to be optimistic but enduring the stress of the situation left her tense and subject to depression. Not having her husband share the burden of her son's illness with her because his own ministry was needed elsewhere made her feel isolated and alone. Having to keep up a strong facade for the outside world, she had no close friends in whom to confide. Finally, her alienation left her seeing no way out but suicide.

§4§

Goody-Two-Shoes

What drove Annie to attempt suicide? Why is the divorce rate among ministers twice the national average?

The pressures exerted upon a minister's wife are simultaneously subtle and obvious, covert and overt, passive and aggressive. The stress takes many forms not the least of which is the pressure to be perfect. Here's a composite description of a minister's wife compiled from the answers to our survey. These answers come from women who live with this stereotyped perception on a daily basis:

A minister's wife is conservative in dress, word, and deed. She usually wears a shapeless hat and sensible shoes. She never gossips, maligns, or argues. The minister's wife is supportive, intelligent, diplomatic, and pleasant at all times. She never says or does anything that will make trouble for her husband. She never swears.

A minister's wife excels in some area that benefits the church. She takes care of the crib room during service, teaches Sunday school, or advises the youth group. She is youth choir director, at least, if she is not also the senior choir director in which she also sings. Often, she is the organist or pianist. She is Chairman of the Kitchen Committee, President of the Mothers'

Group, Refreshment Chairman of the Woman's Association, and active in the Couples' Club. But she is always careful to walk the fine line between a follower and a leader. She doesn't presume to do too much.

She creates an exemplary family life as a role model to church members. Her first priority is her husband and family, although she is also a tireless worker for the church. Her home, her husband, and her offspring are immaculate. Her children are well behaved, never a problem in church, always at Sunday school, enthusiastic members of the youth choir who never skip practices. They are never rowdy, overactive, insolent, or fidgety. Clergy babies never cry during the sermon. Her marriage is flawless.

She hosts Christmas parties and invites committees to meet at the parsonage, gives lavish dinners for congregants and holds an annual open house. She maintains the cheerful disposition of a woman with four servants when, in fact, she does all the work herself.

A minister's wife never looks harried, always says yes to last-minute requests to bake apple pies for church fairs and is willing to talk for hours on the phone to a congregant when her husband can't be reached. She knows to keep confidential information confidential. She visits congregants with her husband and regularly makes calls on her own to the sick, aged, and new mothers. She takes messages, intercedes on her husband's behalf, fields comments, questions, and criticisms about her husband and children with aplomb, and fills in for the church secretary. Sometimes she *is* the church secretary, at no pay of course.

The ultimate joy of all: she has a faith in God that equals or exceeds that of her husband, can quote scripture at a moment's notice, and can lead prayer at the drop of a hat.

She's unsophisticated, plain—even dowdy—selfless, unassuming, timid. She's the perfect wife, mother, and church member. She's the ultimate Goody-two-shoes.

Goody-Two-Shoes

And she, this mystical, majestic woman, is the root of the problem. As laughable as the description may seem, as funny as some of the examples may appear at first glance, remember that they are grounded in truth.

"Last Sunday," wrote Lyn Kratz, a United Church of Christ minister's wife, "a woman came up to me and said, 'Say, Lyn, I noticed in our bylaws that the minister's wife is automatically a vice president in the woman's association. How about it?' I told them to change the bylaws."

Donna Lee Fowlie, a United Methodist minister's wife from Massachusetts (the only woman I've ever seen who can curl up comfortably in a blue plastic stacking chair) was seen out in dungarees and was told by a member of her congregation that jeans were not appropriate dress for a minister's wife.

"In every congregation there are some people who are surprised that I don't play the piano and organ," said Mary Weaver, a seventeen-year veteran in her ministerial marriage. "I am sure, too, that there are those who raise their eyebrows when I decline their request to open or close a meeting with a prayer. I'm not comfortable leading public prayer."

In the time between accepting a new pulpit and actually starting work, one minister got happily married. His wife, in her thirties, looked forward to being the stereotypical minister's wife. She made many heady plans to help her husband in his ministry. Within days of moving into the parsonage, still surrounded by unpacked cardboard cartons, she was visited by a contingent from the church. Her visitors told her that they had wanted a single pastor. As long as she was there they could all get along if she followed a few simple rules. She wasn't ever to wear slacks. She was to entertain congregants at the parsonage. She was not to "interfere" at church. They wanted to make it very clear that she was not welcome.

One might ask why, according to our respondents, ministers' wives accept such interference. Many receive unwarranted advice and others, especially younger wives, innocently solicit advice not knowing exactly what is expected of them. How do women become involved with ministers? It starts because they fall in love with a man, not a minister. One man, one woman, and a spark of interest struck by physical, intellectual, or spiritual attraction or by plain curiosity. It begins with a brief encounter, arranged introduction, first date. Two people going about the business of their lives meet, date, and fall in love.

There's no major revelation, no "visitations" by God or Jesus to accomplish the spark. As it does for everyone else, it just happens. And, as it does for everyone else, it happens while our man and woman are busy with their primary activities: college, work, hobbies, or special interests. Almost half (forty-eight percent) of the respondents met their husbands in college. Half of those met at religion-sponsored colleges and universities. Another twenty-two percent met through church-related activities. They were both in the same young adult group, were counselors at church-sponsored summer camps, taught Sunday school, etc.

"I was outreach leader for my singles department," said Glenda Menger, age thirty-nine, married six years to a Baptist minister in Augusta, Georgia. "I went to visit a member who was in the hospital. My future husband was visiting also and it was truly 'love at first sight' although at the time it just seemed like a great attraction. Mutual friends were determined to get us together."

Almost ten percent of our interviewees said that our ministerial couples met through the constant and carefully planned maneuvers of friends or relatives.

"He was receiving room and board from my grandmother who was very anxious to make a match," wrote Shirley Skirvin, now married thirty-four years to her Presbyterian husband. "We were not initially very enthused about each other, but one thing led to another and we were married after about a year of courtship."

Goody-Two-Shoes

Another eight percent met their future husbands while on the job. Most of these were teachers.

Most of the couples had traditional beginnings to their romances but there were a few who met and mated under more unusual circumstances. One couple met at a square dance and were immediately "struck." As teenagers, another couple, now married twenty-nine years, met at a church youth rally in Utah. Racing to get to classes on time, one couple bumped into each other in the stairwell of the Fine Arts building at Boston University. Jean Hinz, married to a Lutheran minister for thirty-three years, met her husband while he worked at Barnes Hospital in St. Louis, Missouri.

"I went in to visit my brother who was a patient at that time. My husband was the orderly who shaved my brother for surgery."

The most interesting meeting took place in China amidst seething social upheaval. Now married thirty-nine years, Judy is sixty-five years old and the mother of four children. Judy's meeting with her future husband was not traditional in the usual sense. The tradition she followed was tracing the footsteps of two generations before her and heading to China. Her great-uncle was the first family member to serve as a missionary there. Following his example, Judy's aunt and two uncles also went to China. Judy's mother went to attend her sister's wedding and ended up in a wedding of her own when she met her husband. They returned to the states when Judy was six months old.

Judy received a bachelor's degree in chemistry from Ohio Wesleyan and then a master's in bacteriology from Kansas University in 1946.

"I was only a few months from my master's degree when the American Board of Foreign Missions of the Congregational Church contacted me about going to China." Judy accepted and spent one year at Yale learning Chinese. She sailed in September 1947.

Meanwhile, her future husband, Peter, was studying at Emory University. He was inspired to teach in China by one of his professors. He sailed in 1948.

Their paths crossed in Foochow in the province of Fukien. Foochow, an industrial city primarily manufacturing chemicals, was also famous for ceremonial paper umbrellas and salt fish. Thousands of people lived on boats in this coastal city just opposite Taiwan. When Judy and Peter arrived, the country was in the midst of the Cultural Revolution, fighting famine and near collapse.

There were two missionary settlements in Foochow. One was the congregational-sponsored settlement that surround Union Hospital where Judy worked. She shared an apartment with a Swiss nurse. Peter lived in the island settlement sponsored by the United Methodist Church and taught at a boys' school. Judy and Peter met at church.

"There was a lovely, stone Anglican church where newcomers, the foreigners, met for Sunday evening services," said Judy. "There were social organizations established for us too. There weren't many single men or women among the missionaries. So Peter and I were constantly thrown together." They married in May 1949 and watched the revolution, too closely, from front row seats. When Chiang K'ai Shek left, they stayed.

"We worked under the Communists until Thanksgiving 1950," said Judy. "Then the Board told us to get out." Arrangements for their trip were made through an organization called Chinese Travel and although Foochow was on the coast, travel by sea was thought too dangerous for the missionaries. Judy, Peter, their colleagues and whatever belongings they could carry were loaded on trucks and driven to Yingatan in Kiangsi Province. They then traversed the three-thousand-feet high mountains by train to Fatshan.

"It was quite a worry," Judy understates. "They stopped

Goody-Two-Shoes

us every day to check our luggage. They wanted to know what we were carrying, making sure we weren't smuggling anything out." On December 7, 1950, they crossed the border into Hong Kong.

Judy, always an independent woman, lived the women's liberation movement thirty years before it happened. Again, she's the third generation of women in her family to do so.

"My mother was a women's libber before me, and my grandmother before her," said Judy. Judy's grandmother, a widow with six children, put all of them through college. Judy's mother completed one year of medical school. Judy's education, the example of her mother and grandmother, and her own independent spirit were enough for her to meet anything life threw at her.

"I didn't do very much reading or studying to be a minister's wife," said Judy. Raised "reasonably religious," her parents taught Sunday school and her father was the school director. "And I had been in that environment in China, with ministers and missionaries. I guess I felt I didn't need it." Peter thought differently. He gave Judy a book. A most inappropriate book for a woman like Judy, but at the time, it was the best to be found.

"It was rather old. A typical male-chauvinistic book. I thought it was disgusting!" Even forty years later, there's still surprise in her voice. "I read it, I think, out of courtesy to my husband. It had all this stuff about taking baths and brushing your teeth. Hygiene stuff. Maybe the book said something helpful, but I don't remember it."

You'd expect that self-help material for ministers' wives would have changed substantially since 1949. Although it's improved, the literature on the subject isn't much help to today's modern woman—if it helped any of them when it was published.

Dolores, who wishes to be anonymous, has been married for thirty years to a United Methodist minister. Dolores is fifty-three years old and the mother of three grown children. She met her husband at a square dance sponsored by the Wesley Foundation while she was a student at Westminster Choir College and he was a student at Princeton. "We were both 'struck.' We both felt that God planned our meeting."

Most of the women with whom we talked were woefully unaware of the realistic problems they would confront as the wives of ministers. What advice they were given or read turned out to be of little help. For instance, *The Underground Manual for Ministers' Wives* by Ruth Truman, published in 1974, has the courage to address some tough issues such as maintaining an adequate sex life, but Truman's advice heaps even more responsibilities upon the minister's wife. For instance, in one important aside she advises wives to accompany their husbands on visitations to parishioners, particularly those to the lonely women among the congregation, as a way to ward off potential assaults on his virtue and their marriage. While this method might be effective, it's impractical if not impossible. Before children, this might be a viable alternative for a minister's wife keeping her marriage assault-proof, and may even give the opportunity to ward off the loneliness so prevalent among ministers' wives. But once the children come along, and if the wife is career-oriented, there is little time left, not to mention little money for baby sitters. It is usually impractical for the minister's wife to accompany him around the countryside visiting parishioners. Aside from the time commitment involved, Truman's advice also ignores the fact that few ministers' wives have the same counseling and psychology training as their husbands, and may do more harm than good on pastoral visits.

The balance of the self-help books are also woefully out of date in advising on clothing: never wear shorts outside, never wear pants in public. They all include advice on spirituality, ways to make faith stronger and more meaningful. However, much advice on spiritual growth for the minister's wife is naive. What these advisers fail to recognize, and what most parishioners

Goody-Two-Shoes

don't understand, is that marriage to a minister does not mean acquiring automatic, absolute spiritual faith. A woman who marries a minister is not automatically endowed with knowledge of the bible, the answer to all her religious questions, or the ability to lead prayer. Some ministers' wives are not religious when they marry, and stay that way. Yet many people assume, because a woman is a minister's wife, that she has an equal share of her husband's zeal and mission.

There are autobiographies on the market, which while they are interesting for comparison purposes as they talk about specific problems in a specific life, what they lack in addressing the issues in a general manner leaves a wide gap in a minister's wife's knowledge of the realities of her future life.

So our books aren't very helpful for these women as they prepare for a life with a minister. Where else can they turn? Wives' meetings? Seminary support groups?

Of the women we interviewed only three attended student wives' meetings while their husbands were in seminary. Moreover, these women reported that the meetings they attended were unstructured, informal social gatherings, not groups that adequately addressed the problems of ministers' wives. The seminaries of husbands of those interviewed didn't include formal activities for spouses or classes for their students on the realities of married life in the ministry.

Our research yielded the fact that not one of the three oldest seminaries in the United States—Andover-Newton, Bangor Theological or Yale Divinity—offer any formal course or school-sponsored support group that addresses the issue of how to deal with the demands of the ministry on marriage and family.

"We probably should be considering the amount of problems they have and the divorce rate among ministers," said a Yale Divinity spokesperson. "But we don't." While all three institutions offer day care programs so that parents can attend classes and study, none have a support structure for married students.

"They get that on an informal basis, as needed," continued the Yale spokesperson. "They can get help at our Women's Center or they can approach a member of the faculty on their own. Ministers are no different from doctors or lawyers. Their jobs are just as demanding and they don't get any training in that area either."

However, the wife of any other professional man is not in the public eye as much as the wife of a minister. A doctor's wife is not driven by the expectations of her husband's patients. People don't compare the doctor's wife to standards of perfection or require her to meet an inner ideal before hiring her husband for medical needs. However, many congregations routinely meet and interview a prospective minister's wife before deciding to offer him a pulpit. In many churches, meeting the wife is still a requirement.

"The congregation does have a concept of the minister's wife and the role she should play in the congregation," said Reverend George True. Reverend True is a Congregational minister serving a moderately sized suburban church in Connecticut. Contrary to popular belief, not all ministers are the sons of ministers and not all wives are the daughters of ministers. Reverend True is the first minister in his family. We asked him why seminaries weren't addressing the issue of the changing role of the minister's wife.

"The seminary sees its role as educational and practical," he said. "There are limits to a seminary's faculty. What's important to them is theology and church history, not the minister's marriage." How then did a seminary student, or his wife, learn of the problems to come and how to handle them? Who told them the facts of married life in the ministry?

"You would be told if you happened to have a relationship with another clergy couple," explained Reverend True. "But even then, ministers like to go on their own. Each believes he's found the best way. Some see themselves as trail blazers." Although seminaries regularly offer courses on marriage counseling, not even these courses address the stresses their own marriages will face. Ministers are trained to help others, but not themselves.

Eighty-four percent of the respondents knew when they met their husbands that those men were going to be, or already were, ministers. Sixteen percent of the women said that they had hoped to marry a minister. Terri, age twenty-nine and married five years, wrote:

"From the time I was in my teens and had decided to dedicate my life to the Lord, to the extent of doing whatever he led me to do, I had in the back of my mind that I'd be most fulfilled if I were a minister's wife." Of course, there were women who had the opposite opinion. Jean Hinz was in that dissident group.

"As a teenager, I always said, 'I never want to marry a farmer or a minister.' But I didn't plan on falling in love with a certain young man." On the other hand, almost half the wives with whom we spoke were happy that the man they loved was, coincidentally, a minister. That's not a surprising figure as it corresponds with the percentage who met their husbands through Christian colleges or church-related activities. Of the balance, twenty-two percent treated it as any other career decision.

"To quote the wife of a seminary professor," wrote Mary Weaver, age thirty-eight from Savannah, Georgia, " 'Marrying a minister was not on the top of my list or the bottom of my list; in fact, it wasn't even on my list!' In all honesty, I married him in spite of the fact that he was going to be a minister.' " These women repeatedly stressed that they had married a man, not a minister.

"I accepted his choice of occupation but mentally treated it as any other profession," said Donna. "I tried not to dwell on the unique characteristics of this profession or his being different from other human beings."

So most women who married ministers knew in advance that it was a stressful profession. How did they prepare for their lives as the wife of a minister?

Basically, they didn't.

"Prepared?" said Mary Jean Miner with a hoot of laughter. "I took out the license and bought a new dress. That's all I did to prepare. My husband told me not to expect to please everyone. That was the extent of my preparation."

These women were no more prepared for the realities of married life than any other couple in love. And they were definitely not prepared for the realities of life married to a minister. Only twelve percent of my respondents did anything to prepare for their life in the religious limelight. Mostly they read the outdated, chauvinistic self-help literature available. Thirty percent said that their upbringing or education prepared them for the future.

"My parents were my prime example for faithfulness to the Lord," wrote Jean Hinz. "I had always been active in church attendance and choir, Sunday school teaching and various positions in our youth organization. But I did resort to prayer that I would be a fit wife for this man."

One woman, who said she made no special preparations to be a minister's wife had a succinct answer to the question: Did your husband offer any suggestions?

"Constantly!"

They were overwhelmingly unprepared, and innocent of their futures. Seminaries still don't include anything in their curriculum about spousal relations to the church community. And the pursuit of perfection, the stereotype of the minister's wife, reared its head early in most of the marriages.

"I was quite young when my husband was ordained," said Jean Parker, married thirty-five years. "I was nervous about being 'the right kind of clergy wife.' "

Goody-Two-Shoes

Prepared or not, religious or not, the realities of life as the wife of a minister come as a shock. Merely by choosing to marry a man who happens to be a minister, she assumes the cloak of the role model. Whether she wants it or not, whether she conforms to it, adjusts it to fit her, or rebels against it, she is still ruled by the stereotype. The specter of perfection relentlessly dogs the footsteps of every minister's wife. To cope, she develops a strategy of secrecy, a strategy we'll unfold throughout this book, that buffers her from her husband's ever watchful, sometimes wrathful congregation. Once burned, and, most ministers' wives have such an experience at least once, most act to ensure they will never experience the fire again.

When is the match struck? It can be as early as her husband's first pulpit interview or as late as midway through his chosen career.

❧5❧

Does She Play the Piano?

Some feelings of alienation begin early.

"I don't know any other woman," said Donna Lee Fowlie, "who is generally required to accompany her husband when he goes on his job interview." It's true. We don't interview the doctor's wife before we schedule surgery. The accountant's wife has no connection to our carefully prepared tax returns. We see only the plumber, electrician, and auto mechanic, never their spouses. But hiring a minister is somehow different.

Although many denominations state the policy that the wife is not to be a part of the interview process, she is still, and probably always will be, included.

"My experience is that wives are not often part of the interview process," says one of our authors, Reverend Sherry Taylor. Sherry is a minister married to a minister. They both belong to the United Church of Christ, Congregational denomination. "However, it is true that they have some interaction with the committee during the process."

As a practical matter, and in defense of the congregation, to some extent she *needs* to be a part of the interview process. Moving to a new church is not an easy matter. Rarely is the prospective pulpit so close by that an afternoon sightseeing trip through the town, past the parsonage, and around the schools will be sufficient for the family to decide that this is a community where they might like to live. Distance prohibits the close look they need to have of their prospective home.

So, when the wife is politely asked to accompany her husband on the interview and gets a guided tour of the parsonage, she accepts. If arrangements also are made for them to stay a few days so the entire family can augment what they've read and heard about the area with first-hand "research" on the community; and, if the rest of the family relaxes together while the minister attends the pulpit interview alone, the ideal scenario would be complete.

However, for some wives, the ideal has never been the reality. Some wives resent the feeling of being "looked over" during their husband's job interview. One wife reported that, to get around the no-wife-at-the-interview rule, their churches held the interview in the parsonage so "your wife could look around while we talk."

The blatant curiosity of the search committee aside, traditional expectations play a large part in "needing" the minister's wife at her husband's interview—at least many congregations think so. These expectations are best summed up by the statistics found in several studies.

The first, a 1977 Presbyterian Panel questionnaire titled *The Role of the Pastor's Spouse in the Local Congregation,* found that seventy-seven percent of all Presbyterian members felt that the pastor's spouse is treated differently from other lay persons at least some of the time. Thirty-eight percent thought they were treated differently most of the time. Of the pastors surveyed, ninety-five percent thought their spouses were treated differently from the laity all of the time, most of the time, or some of the time.

Does She Play the Piano?

Respondents for the Presbyterian Panel were asked to select three ways a pastor's spouse was treated differently. Looking only at church members' responses, sixty-three percent selected as their number one answer that clergy spouses were "expected to be an example of Christian deportment in his/her manner of speaking, dress, childrearing, etc." Sixty-two percent chose that the "pastor's spouse is expected to attend worship services more regularly than others." Fifty-three percent of the members picked, as their third answer, that "the pastor's spouse is expected to be more informed about the lives of members of the congregation than other lay persons." About their activities in the church, forty-nine percent of the members chose the statement that "the pastor's spouse is expected to be involved in more church activities than other lay persons."

In the pastor's responses, seventy-five percent perceived that the congregation expected their wife to attend church more regularly than other church members. The pastors' second selection, at sixty-five percent, was that the pastor's spouse should be more informed about individual members of the congregation. Third on the pastor's list was the statement that the pastor's spouse is expected to be an example of Christian deportment.

The differences in the percentages between the pastors and the members is interesting. Pastors have a greater perception of congregational expectations of their wives than do the members. In each case, the percentage of pastors selecting a response was higher than the percentage of members. This provides some basis for the argument that ministers and their wives place greater expectations on themselves than do their congregations.

It's a weak basis, however, to prove that ministers' wives stew in pots of their own making. Even though the percentages were higher for responding pastors than for members, both groups selected as the top three, *the same expectation state-*

ments. The only differences were in their ranking. Pastors placed spouse church attendance first while members chose deportment. Pastors selected a spouse's knowledge of members of the congregation second while members picked church attendance. And last, pastors thought deportment was important to the congregation while members chose an informed spouse.

The selection of the same three expectations, regardless of their ranking by pastors or members, indicated that ministers' wives who perceive congregation expectations do so out of a strong basis in reality. They aren't making it up, carping and complaining with no basis in fact. The members of their husbands' congregation do indeed expect the wives to be models of Christian deportment, to attend church more regularly than the congregation members do, and to know more about what is going on in the congregation than anyone else other than their husbands.

In the second survey, done for this book, *The Healthy Hectic Home,* Marshall Shelley found that fifty-three percent of the pastors surveyed chose "dealing with congregational expectations" as problems for their families. It was the number two answer, second only to time pressure, chosen by eighty-three percent of the pastors. Shelley asked his respondents to choose the single biggest challenge their families faced in the ministry, and "congregational expectations" was again the number two answer (behind "time pressures") with twenty percent selecting it.

David and Vera Mace, authors of *What's Happening to Clergy Marriages?,* compiled responses from clergy couples through surveys filled out at marriage encounters, group counseling sessions, and retreats. When asked to list the disadvantages of clergy marriage, three separate groups of ministers and their wives listed as the worst disadvantage that their marriage was expected to be a model of perfection. In this case, eighty-five percent of the pastors listed this disadvantage while only fifty-nine percent of their wives selected it. It was still the number one disadvantage for both. Out of nineteen disadvantages, seven of them dealt with aspects of congregational expectations. Third on their list was lack of family privacy. Sixth was that their children were expected to model the church's expectations. Eighth was a feeling of lost humaness by the ministerial couple because of role expectations. Ninth was that the wife felt exploited because her duties were assigned by the church. Twelfth was confusion about the wife's identity and roles. And, sixteenth was the feeling that the family "belonged" to the congregation.

In a paper titled "Married to the Minister," compiled by Roy M. Oswald for the Alban Institute, Oswald assembled twenty wives from five denominations whose length of marriage ranged from one and a half to thirty-four years. Fifteen of the twenty felt that the congregation projected a definition on them of the stereotypical minister's wife. Sixteen said they felt they were being treated as a non-person, being introduced as "our pastor's wife," many times not even using her given name. Fifteen also thought they needed to be more cautious than normal around parishioners. Twelve agreed that they must be models as a family, a couple, and as an individual. And a whopping nineteen out of twenty stated that they need to get involved even if involuntarily. Finally, to reinforce the argument that congregations do indeed expect an extra measure of Christian charity from their minister's wife, we return to the Presbyterian Panel study. When asked to select the one statement that best reflected their congregation's thinking about the minister's wife, forty-two picked: "The pastor's spouse should attend worship services regularly and take part in church activities to a certain extent, being careful not to discourage the leadership capacities of other laypersons."

Over forty percent of church members expect a certain pattern of behavior from their minister's wife. Problems arise because the expectations vary from member to member. Each evaluates their minister's wife according to their own private expectations. How much or how little she can do depends on each individual within her husband's congregation. She's damned if she does, and she's damned if she doesn't do enough.

The tie that binds all these expectations together seems to be the congregation's belief that her husband *is* God. Certainly he is the only physical representation they have of their God.

"The clergyman, at a totally unconscious and very primitive level in the minds of the congregation," wrote Donna Sinclair in *The Pastor's Wife Today* (1981), "represents no less than God the Father." How this translates into expectations of his wife is succinctly stated by Oswald in "Married to the Minister:"

"Can you share the same bed with the resident "holy man" and not have some of that rub off into you?" It is the congregation's perception that the minister's wife is their resident "holy woman" which creates friction between the wife and the church, the wife and the husband, and the husband and his church.

And it all starts at the interview. Dressed appropriately, not too well yet not too shabby, the minister's wife appears at the interview ready to do her part to showcase her husband—as any wife would in a similar situation. No spouse chooses to make their marriage partner look bad. She's asked a few questions, not usually about what she does, likes, or wants, but questions relating to the church.

The most frequently asked questions are about her musical abilities. Our survey asked the wives to describe the traditional minister's wife. In those descriptions, all mentioned some aspect of music: singing in the choir, playing the piano or organ, or both. Musical abilities are so taken for granted by congregations that their question is not "Can you sing?" but, "You're going to join the choir aren't you?" It's not "Can you play the organ?" but, "How often?"

Does She Play the Piano?

Andrea is thirty-four years old. Her minister husband works in the Christian Church denomination in a rural community. In their sixteen years in the ministry, her husband has served at seven churches.

"During the first few years in the ministry the first questions the congregations would ask was whether I played the piano and whether I would speak at ladies workshops and ladies groups," said Andrea. "One church would not consider my husband since I did not play the piano!"

"One time when my husband was candidating," wrote Mabel Victoria, wife of a Presbyterian minister living in Goldfield, Iowa and married for thirty-two years, "a member of the search committee assumed I would play the organ. I can't. I think she felt all pastors' wives played the piano or organ, or perhaps directed the choir." Mabel didn't say how that member treated her later, but Gloria, another minister's wife, told us about an incident in her husband's first church:

"One woman came to me at a gathering very early in our time there," said Gloria. This was one church in a three-point charge in a rural area. "She asked if I was an elementary teacher. I said no. She asked: 'Can you play the piano?' I said no. Well, she turned abruptly on her heel and I never saw her, nor did she speak to me, again. The previous pastor's wife did these things and more, so I was a disappointment to her evidently. Often ministers' wives are valued for what they can give rather than for who they are . . ."

Shaking hands and greeting parishioners at the end of services is another problem for some ministers' wives. Cathy's husband serves a rural United Church of Christ congregation with approximately one hundred-fifty members. Within a week or two of their arrival at this church, their first parish, Cathy came in contact with her first congregational expectation.

"Coming from city churches, I was not prepared to be involved in the custom of walking out with the minister at the recessional, then shaking hands with all the congregation as they file out," said Cathy. "I thought I WAS one of the congregation. An outspoken member of one of the largest church families, who is sometimes a joker, said, 'I'll give you two weeks to stand up there with your husband.'

"I was angry and threatened, and felt forced to comply. From that time to this, I have done it every week. I have made some peace with the custom somewhat, because I am able to gather news, make my own observations which are sometimes helpful, and pass messages on that my husband might otherwise miss; but I will never be completely at ease with it."

Leading prayer and a background in theology are also expectations of the congregation. Many church members seem to feel that a minister's wife receives, with her marriage certificate, instant knowledge of the scriptures and how to apply them. Some of our respondents noted that Bible study and prayer are believed by many parishioners to be the ministers' wives only interests.

"There are also expectations—not necessarily of behavior, but of knowledge—theological, biblical, doctrinal," said Mary Weaver, married seventeen years to her Presbyterian minister husband. "While I am fairly well versed in theology, there is a great deal that I don't know. I don't do anything well in front of a group of people."

Carolyn, wife of a United Methodist minister who lives in New England, has been married for thirty years and still lists public prayer as a disadvantage of being the minister's wife.

"Being asked to pray on the spot," she said. "I freeze without some warning."

Another aspect of the non-person treatment of ministers' wives is the expectation of some congregation members that ministers' wives merely mirror their husband's theology, opinions, and faith.

"I believe many people feel that anything a clergy wife says comes from her husband," said Rosemary Todd of Cheyenne. Her minister husband works in the Episcopal denomina-

Does She Play the Piano?

tion in an urban church of approximately one hundred fifty families. "It makes me sad to be attending a Bible study and be afraid to ask a question or to express my nontheological opinion."

"It is assumed that you reflect your husband's thinking and that it is not your own," said Elizabeth Sweet of Rumford, Rhode Island. Her husband has been a United Methodist minister for more than twenty-seven years. "I was recently elected to head a delegation to the General Conference. People objected —they said I'd only reflect the clergy view."

Why do some wives have so much trouble with congregations? According to our conclusions, it's attitude: theirs, the congregation's, and the attitudes of the women who preceded them into a particular parsonage.

"I feel sorry for the wife to follow me at this church," wrote Carole, a minister's wife, who lives, and loves, the stereotype. "I don't expect every wife to do as much in the church as I do, but I don't want to be stopped from doing what I do either." Her list of activities was long and varied: "typing, filing, phoning members to keep in touch—a sort of go-between for pastor (her husband) who can't afford to sit and chat for longish periods of time, try to attend functions, keep records up to date, set up and keep track of appointments, play for one or both churches monthly on Sundays. Actually it *IS* my career, other than being a mother." This couple, who belong to an Independent Lutheran Congregation, has spent ten years at the same suburban parish.

Cathy, still shaking hands after Sunday services, follows the traditional role but not without pain.

"Various church members have assumed I would play the organ, make the coffee, run the Sunday school, join the choir, host out-of-town guests, pray publicly without effort "whenever my husband is not available . . ." Cathy wrote. "All because I am married to the minister. I have often gone along

Private Lives of Ministers' Wives

with it, so as not to rock the boat, at the price of my own bitterness and isolation.

"I am partly responsible for their treatment of me. It is hard to admit that when I don't question their assumptions, it is even more of a set-up for the next time, or the next person. Sometimes I think of the next person to live in this parsonage, and pity her. I sometimes hope that she is of the old school herself, so she won't have my miseries and may be able to settle here more wholeheartedly and love these people."

Jane, another wife wrote that "in the case where he has been ill, I have conducted the worship. I have also organized the worship services for such occasions as Mother's Day or Children's Day."

With these sterling examples, how can some congregations fail to have high expectations of their next pastor's wife? They are accustomed to a two-for-the-price-of-one ministry, so accustomed they don't realize they need to ask the next wife how much she wants to do in their church. They assume she will take up where the previous pastor's wife left off. If the congregation noted their expectations and made it clear in the interview process that they want their minister's wife to take the traditional role in their church, much disappointment could be avoided. Some congregations are blissfully unaware that the stereotype of the minister's wife is rapidly disappearing. And why would they know that it is? Their minister wife, after all, is, and enjoys, the stereotype.

"Historically, the role of minister's wife offered the chance for full-time Christian service to women who were forbidden to be ministers," wrote Marilyn Brown Oden in a 1988 article in *The Christian Century* about women in the ministry. Today's tradition-oriented minister's wife can find herself in a congregation that wants her total involvement in the church.

"For us a team ministry has been very much a pattern that has worked," Dorothea married thirty-six years to a United Methodist minister, told us. "I always try to let people know I do

Does She Play the Piano?

it because I want to and because I can, not because I must simply because I am a wife. If I had been born forty years later, I would probably have felt called to become ordained, but I doubt we could have done as much in separate ministries as we have done together."

But, as we saw in the Presbyterian Panel study, some church members want their minister's wife involved, but not too involved. The wife who wants to fill the traditional role can find herself in a congregation that blocks her involvement. That wife can be as disappointed and frustrated as the one who feels forced into the two-fer attitude.

Linda is married to a Congregational minister serving a church in the southwest. Linda wants to do more but has encountered only congregations that want to keep her at arm's length. Her frustration is as palpable as those women who bitterly complain about excessive demands placed on them.

"I now embrace what is probably a very traditional notion and struggle with the implications of it in my life," said Linda. "My vision is one of shared ministry, a vision that is often problematic as I struggle with this strange role of 'minister's wife.' I have professional skills I would love to bring to ministry —but he was hired, I was not. I would love to share his life as a co-professional, but so far this seems problematic. I sometimes resent that. I wish more stature could be given to my contributions. I feel I have a great deal I would like to give but that I am required to hold back."

Barbara, a Washington, D.C. United Church of Christ minister's wife, wrote that she experienced the opposite expectation from the wives who felt forced to be theologians and expert at leading public prayer.

"People seem to feel that the real Christian commitment belongs to your husband," she explains. "They do not expect you to have a Christian viewpoint or a sound faith commitment. They are surprised if you know how to pray, know the scriptures, have a sense of direction."

Private Lives of Ministers' Wives

"I was asked to be an Elder by the nominating committee," wrote Mary DeHaven of Cut Bank, Montana. Mary's husband is a Presbyterian minister working in a rural church with two-hundred-fifty members. "Realizing there were poor feelings about it, I said no. They asked me again. When I said yes, and served, it split the church."

Solutions to the two-fer expectations also start with the interview. The most important asset a minister's wife brings to her husband's interview is her own attitude. Many wives rail against the stereotype aggressively. Olivia, who lives in Nebraska said, "any time my service or work is taken for granted I feel angry. Usually I stop doing it." Another wife wrote that even if she was already doing a volunteer job within the church, if a member mentioned that she should be doing it because she was the minister's wife, she'd stop.

Carla Neggers, married to a United Methodist minister, is the author of over two dozen romance and contemporary women's novels. She told us,

"What Joe does for his profession is up to him and has no real bearing on who I am or who we are, together. If he's a minister, fine. If he's something else, fine. I don't define myself by who he is or what he does. And I'm not active in the church. I just do what I do and let the chips fall where they may—which probably has affected some people's notions of ministers' wives."

Other wives, like Linda, the wife who said helping her husband at church was her career and Jane, the woman who conducts worship in her husband's absence, assume the stereotype because they want to. Ever-growing numbers of ministers' wives take an individualistic stand learning how to say no while still supporting and encouraging their husbands in the ministry.

Still, it's an amazing dilemma. The wives who want the traditional role of the minister's wife seem rarely to match up with congregations willing to let them assume all the duties and leadership they want. And wives who want the freedom to choose how much, or how little, they'll do in the church seem rarely to match up with the congregations willing to leave them alone to do their own things. These two attitudes represent two extremes. Most wives fall somewhere in the middle. Wives that fare the best are those whose attitudes convey that they are not the unpaid second helpers of the church but members of the laity. Like water off the proverbial duck's back, these wives shake off the stereotype while still building places for themselves in the church.

How well a minister's wife fares during the interview for her husband's job, and in the new congregation, may depend on how willing her husband is to buffer her from the demands of his congregation. Ministers are learning to make it clear in their interviews that the congregation is not getting two workers for the price of one.

"We both interviewed for the job," said the Reverend Larry W. Osborne. Osborne is pastor at the North Coast Evangelical Free Church in Oceanside California. "Nancy is shy— well, that's not the right word—she does not enjoy the spotlight. I made it clear that I would come and stand in front and answer questions but Nancy would not be interviewed by the pulpit committee or any women's group," he said. "She wouldn't even stand up in front with me. She would stand when introduced. That way people knew right away: 'Oh, give Nancy space.'

"Nancy likes hospitality, she likes people but she's not going to teach or play the piano," said Osborne. "I backed her up on that. I put it all on the table right at the beginning. If they were not going to hire me because of that, I wanted them to know it immediately. I was willing to risk not getting the job for my wife's sake. I'm not willing to be owned by the church."

One Congregational minister said he always asks the search committee before setting up the interview what they expect of his wife. If there are any two-fer expectations, or if they demand that his wife be present, he declines the interview and searches out another possible pulpit.

Mary is an eleven-year veteran of her ministerial marriage. Her husband is a minister in the United Church of Christ denomination. He also acts as her defender.

"He told pulpit search committees that I was an independent, but supportive spouse," said Mary. "He made it clear that this job of his did not include me any more than any other church member's spouse and family are expected to participate. This interview speech re: my participation was very effective. I was warmly accepted and could pretty much make my own rules."

Not all minister husbands are as straightforward, willing or able to defend their wives. A common problem of the minister as nondefender sometimes occurs when wife and church get involved in a dispute over expectations.

Another pastor's wife, Marianne Bahmann described the traditional wife as being like her mother who was also married to a minister: "The wife does what the congregation wishes or needs, she is an unpaid second employee." Marianne tried that role, then rejected it, convincing her husband first.

"We started out that way," said Marianne. "But I exerted some muscle with regard to *my* needs. I told him, if I were to keep him happy, I also had to be happy. Then my husband supported me on occasions when they tried to exert pressure."

Why is it that Marianne escaped the trap that caught her mother in involuntary servitude to the church? Or was her mother really a willing party to the work she did in her husband's churches? Perhaps Marianne's mother, like many ministers' wives before her, actually enjoyed the "holy woman" status she achieved only through her marriage—a status that more and more ministers' wives are rejecting. It's the old question: What came first the chicken or the egg? But in this instance the question may be answered. What came first was the hen in the form of the traditional minister's wife. Whether born

Does She Play the Piano?

of a frustration over being shut out of an occupation because she was a woman, or out of simple love of the man, she married the minister, accepted and lived the traditional role. For today's independent, individualistic wives, she laid the egg, the standard against which all are measured.

Oswald's paper "Married to the Minister" and the Maces' book *What's Happening to Clergy Marriages?*, published in 1980, represent the latest published survey material on ministers' wives until this book. Surely, in the eleven years that have elapsed, some changes have occurred. Not so, wrote Beverly Kaiser, married thirty-five years to her United Methodist minister husband. Beverly's husband is a district supervisor responsible for finding pastors for pulpits and pulpits for pastors.

"My husband has found, as he meets with people who tell them their expectations of their next pastor, that the lay people have not greatly changed in their expectations," said Beverly. "They are quite critical of ministers' wives who are not active in the church."

The results of our survey indicate that the wives still perceive high congregational expectations. The Presbyterian Panel also confirms members' attachment to the traditional role. Only six percent of the church members surveyed chose this statement about the attitude in their home church: "The role of the pastor's spouse has nothing to do with the pastor's ministry or my congregation's acceptance of the pastor. It makes absolutely no difference what participation the pastor's spouse has in the congregation."

Thelma Grinnin has seen it all in her forty-five years of marriage to an American Baptist minister. She embraced the helpmate concept of her clergy marriage.

"I think my husband and I complemented each other in our ministry," she wrote. "More than once we were told it was 'two for the price of one.' I know that some ministers' wives resent this, but I did not. In no other professions is the wife expected to share so much in her husband's profession.

Today's generation of parsonage ladies seem to want to do their own thing and are trying to change that role. Apparently problems are arising over this philosophy."

Whether she accepts the role or rails against it, today's ministers' wives, both traditional or modern, accepting or rejecting, are as controlled by tradition as they ever were. And if their journey from minister's wife to individual personality is a slow one, the other aspects of their husband's job that control their lives are changing even more slowly.

The job interview is survived. Like any interview, all sides, minister, wife, and church, put their best foot forward. The pulpit is won. The delicious anticipation of challenges to come permeates everyone. But only the first hurdle is cleared. How adequately each of this triumvirate meets the needs of the others is assessed in the remainder of this book.

6

Filthy Lucre

Any time you can get seventy-nine percent of any population to agree on an issue, it must be important. But when seventy-nine percent of our survey respondents agreed, emphatically, that their husbands were not paid adequately for their level of education, responsibility, and experience, each of them tacked on a qualifier. If "money is the root of all evil" and pastors should be kept humble (read that as poor), are the watchwords of the people in the congregation who set the minister's salary, "God will provide" is the financial answer for most of our respondents.

Jean, one wife, turned to secretarial work for four years to pay for her children's braces. Another wife, Betty, points with pride to the fact that her husband refused an offered raise because the church budget was short. One couple, Robert and Susan, must borrow—every year!—to pay income and social security taxes.

One of the most plaintive stories came from Terri, a young wife married five years to her United Methodist minister husband. (We met Terri in Chapter Four.) Early in her marriage, Terri decided that she didn't want a career.

"I tried some jobs and schooling," she said. "But I have

come to grips with the fact that I want to be a traditional wife, and eventually mother, pastor's wife, and work the amount that helps us make ends meet." Terri's husband, John, was still in seminary and they had no children. Terri already worked part-time for another church when making ends meet collided with the expectations of their parishioners.

"John has a close friend in the church. This friend has two businesses of his own and is set well financially. Last winter, this friend talked to John about getting a membership together at a Racquet Club, so they could remain active and work on their tennis during the winter. My husband wanted to do this very much, but wasn't sure we could make ends meet if he did. Finally, after about a week of undecidedness, they went to visit the Club. They came home with memberships.

"John felt terrible and tried to justify it, knowing that their time together would be very beneficial." Terri, like the other wives, knows only too well how hard it is to find close friends in a congregation. In fact, friendship (covered in Chapter Ten) is a more difficult issue for ministers' wives than money. John had felt so pressured by his friend that he felt he had to buy a membership, because he was "being cheap" if he didn't.

"Not knowing how to handle the situation, I encouraged him that we would make it and it would be good for them. So I took on an extra cleaning job to help at least a little more.

"Because of our comparatively low income to those of the young couples in our church we socialize with, we have to be very selective in what we do for entertainment and how often," explained Terri, "but it seems that even the nicest of people can have a double standard in their mind of how we should spend our money. It's like they expect that we can go out as often as we wish, but as soon as we convey the fact that it's not a particularly good time for us to do a certain thing, a judgment is set on us." Clergy families often feel pressured to maintain the same level of lifestyles as their parishioners even without equivalent income.

Filthy Lucre

Terri had one hope: that the publication of the church's annual report, revealing their low salary, would "educate" their friends in the church.

"At the beginning of the year, the Annual Report was published, showing all the expenses of the church, including John's meager salary," said Terri. "I thought that perhaps some of our friends who previously were not aware of our low salary would have made some sort of a comment, expressing their surprise in the difference of the level of their salaries compared to my husband's when John has had so much education. But, nothing was said. We have the bill almost paid, but it was a very expensive lesson. It just seems that most people don't realize how careful 'careful' is when we have to survive on what we do." Terri still hasn't given up on the basic humanity of the members of the congregation.

"All I expect is that expectations won't be so high on us having to keep up with the others when we make about one-third or less of what most of the couples our age in the church make." Relying on good wishes of the congregation, and moving to a bigger, higher paying church, is all Terri feels they can do to improve her financial situation.

"We do not want to ever let anyone get the impression that we are ungrateful for our salary," she said, "or that we covet a much higher salary."

While it is the wives who bear most of the brunt of the burden through careful shopping, denial of simple pleasures, keeping gardens, and sewing clothing, they bear it with an enviable aplomb. That isn't to say they enjoy it. Even if money is the root of all evil, there probably isn't one wife that wouldn't want to be blessed with a little more. But most have taken their religion to heart, sob silently and alone over their checkbook, and trust in God to provide them what they need. Lois Farina remembers such a time:

"When the kids were small, our second church was a mission church and our salary was frozen," she wrote. Lois married her United Methodist minister husband thirty-three years ago. "We were very careful in what we spent, didn't go out much, I made clothing for the kids, but we never missed a meal, had our lights shut off or were without a house. One time I got so upset I just cried."

What a minister gets paid may not be easy to determine from a church budget. In some cases, the total cost of the minister is lumped together in one line item so that it looks like he earns more than he does. The total cost to a church to have a pastor does not equal what he's paid. Payments for utilities, travel, books, and sermon resources are not paid but may be included under one line item labeled 'minister.' It's a policy that reinforces the congregation's belief that their pastor is paid enough. Other issues also obscure their actual pay: housing allowance vs. parsonage, paying double social security tax, medical, pension, and other benefits.

How much *does* a pastor earn?

Ask a parishioner how much he earns and he'll often give you his gross salary figure. Sometime his net. Three factors make it unfair to simply compare parishioners' gross pay with that of their minister: years of education, hours worked, and level of responsibility. An ordained minister has a minimum of a bachelor's degree plus three years in seminary. Many go on to earn doctorate degrees. Although it looks like they only work on Sundays, ministers typically work anywhere from fifty to eighty hours a week and are always on call. The minister's salary can only fairly be compared to that of other professionals in his community with the same level of education and responsibilities. Those professionals are middle and high school principals and assistant principals, hospital administrators, social service agency directors—even attorneys and doctors.

Even between these professionals, comparing gross salary alone doesn't reflect total pay. There are benefits: medical plans, employer contributions to pension plans, half of the social security tax, federal and state unemployment benefits

Filthy Lucre

taxes, and workmen's compensation. The average employee not only doesn't pay the full costs of these benefits, he rarely knows what they cost his employer. United States Bureau of Labor Statistics show that these benefits equal 22.1 percent of gross pay. So, if the average individual is earning $30,000 year, the total salary package is actually around $36,600.

Using the figures from a Meriden, Connecticut church and that town's Board of Education, let's compare one pastor's salary package with that of an assistant principal. Meriden is a small town of sixty thousand residents with a labor force of factory, blue collar, and professional and government employees. Connecticut has typically been in the top three highest states in the country when ranked by average annual pay.

The pastor we have selected receives a base salary of $27,000. He, his wife, and two children, live in a parsonage with a fair market rent of $700 per month, or $8,400 per year. The church pays utilities and heat expenses of $1,800 per year. So far, this pastor earns $37,200. In 1989, instead of a raise, the church voted to give the pastor a social security allowance of $4,985. His total income, as defined by the Social Security Administration, was $42,185.

A word here about a minister's Social Security status. For Social Security Tax purposes, all ministers are considered self-employed. Because of that ruling, they pay the entire 15.3 percent Social Security rate: the half the typical wage earner pays *and* the half their employer pays. And, they must pay the tax on the fair market value of the parsonage and utilities because Social Security had defined that as income. On his total income of $42,185, the minister pays $6,454.00 in social security taxes. If we deduct half of that—the half the church would pay if it was considered his employer—this pastor's pay, before income taxes, is now $38,958.

Our example pastor is a member of the United Church of Christ (Congregational) denomination. The Connecticut Conference of the UCC in its *Clergy Compensation Guidelines* issued in July 1990, requires a minimum pension payment of fourteen percent of Salary Basis. Salary Basis is defined as one hundred thirty percent of the pastor's base salary. The salary basis for our pastor is $35,100 (130 times $27,000). Fourteen percent of that is $4,914. A family protection plan which includes life insurance and long-term disability insurance costs another one percent of salary basis, or three hundred fifty-one dollars. Group term life insurance is provided at six hundred dollars per year. Medical insurance is also paid for by the church at $3,130. The total is $8,995.

Because he is considered self-employed, our pastor is not eligible for state or federal unemployment benefits nor is he covered under a workmen's compensation policy. According to the United States Bureau of Labor Statistics, this amounts to 2.7 percent of gross pay benefits available to the layman but not to the minister. Excluding vacation, holiday, and sick leave benefits which almost all full-time employees receive, our pastor's total benefits equal $8,995. This pastor's benefit package is twenty-three percent of his salary before income taxes. Since the average worker gets 22.1 percent of his salary as employer-paid benefits (again excluding the costs of vacation, holidays, and sick leave) our pastor is a little ahead of the average layperson but without the safety net of unemployment compensation eligibility.

So why, if a pastor's salary package is better than that of his congregation, do so many wives feel their husbands are underpaid? For starters, it's that matter of base pay. Our example pastor has a starting salary of $27,000. But with seven year's of education, and often an additional two to four years of study for a doctorate, that level of education doesn't come cheap. Added to his normal family expenses are seven years of student loans. Ministers can take as much as five to ten years to pay off their education. Most wives feel the pastor should be earning what his peers earn. An assistant principal in Meriden earns $57,500 annual salary—more than double the pastor's

Filthy Lucre

base pay. If we add on that 22.1 percent benefit package, the principal's salary package is a whopping $70,300! Even when we add in the minister's benefits, including his entire social security allowance, the principal earns more than one and a half times what the minister earns.

Education and taxes aren't the only reasons that demand we compare the assistant principal to the minister. Both have, at a minimum, a master's degree, it's true, but we must also compare the level of their responsibilities.

Ministers don't work only on Sundays. In fact, they are on call twenty-four hours a day, seven days a week. Doctors don't make house calls anymore, but ministers do. Many postpone or cancel vacations, and routinely cancel social events with their families to help their congregation with emergencies. In one study, thirty-two percent stated that they don't use all their allowed vacation time.

Because they work with a volunteer-staffed organization, they attend meetings in the evenings to ensure the smooth working of the church. Eighty-hour weeks are not uncommon among ministers. One recommendation, supposedly to ease their burden, suggests that pastors contract with their church for a specific number of hours in their work week. A great idea, but the recommendation was for a minimum of fifty to sixty hours per week. That recommendation simply fuels workaholism among clergy, while giving a green light to parishioners to continue overworking their pastors. How this level of clergy commitment and a congregation's expectations contributes to workaholism and abuse is the subject of Chapters Twelve and Thirteen.

Ministers don't only prepare and preach a weekly sermon. Every minister interviewed expressed surprise at the level of administrative duties required in his parish. Many ministers perform parishioners' duties themselves just to get things done in a timely manner. Even if a minister delegates work, he's still the boss and responsible for following up to see that work gets done. If the church is currently involved in a renovations or expansion program, he may supervise architects, contractors, carpenters, plumbers, electricians, and coordinate meeting federal, state, and local ordinances and inspections. One pastor even did all the janitorial work in his church.

He is responsible for evangelism. Responsibility for church growth should be shared equally with of the laity, but traditionally it has been left to the pastor. In some churches, membership growth is the sole criteria for judging the pastor's effectiveness.

Every committee and social group within the church wants the pastor at its meetings. Unless he sets limits, our pastor could find himself out attending meetings every night of the week leaving his wife home, alone, as sole caretaker of the children.

He's the ecclesiastical fireman ruling, with tact and diplomacy, on such weighty issues as the color of the drapes, the length of the altar candles or the proper placement of the creche. He resolves church fights, clears muddy waters, and forges together opposing factions. Studies show that his own goals in the ministry are first to preach and pastor, and to be administrator last. In reality, these administrative duties usually take up forty percent of his time.

Then he does those duties he wants to do; the reasons he became a minister in the first place. Spiritual counseling. Visiting with new members, old members, absent members. Leading new member classes. Interviewing prospective newlyweds. Planning weddings, baptisms, and special church events such as Christmas or Easter. Assisting, planning, and officiating at funerals as well as supporting and counseling family members. Planning the weekly Sunday service by coordinating with Christian education committees, organists, choirs, and whatever special events that need announcing: fairs, suppers, prayer vigils. He teaches confirmation classes, adult bible classes, prepares and leads special Lenten services, and may take on

Filthy Lucre

the task of youth group advisor. He's an unpaid psychologist counseling on marriage, child raising, and family relations.

With the time he has left over, he initiates those programs he feels his congregation needs for spiritual or communal well-being. These can mean new social groups within the church for select segments of its population currently neglected. A care team program to provide services for shut-ins or ill members. Community awareness programs to help the homeless, collect food, lead prayer vigils for community events, scandals, or crises.

In between he uses vacation time to continue his education, taking courses or attending conferences to fill in the gaps in his seminary education to better meet the particular needs of his church.

Only then can he go home, kiss his wife on the cheek, tousle his children's hair, eat supper, determine how to stretch that base salary of $27,000, and fall exhausted into bed.

An assistant principal doesn't have it much easier. No organization head does. Long hours, multiple duties, staff problems, working summers as opposed to having them off as his teachers do. But the assistant principal has an advantage the minister does not: more money. One and a half times more money.

If a pastor works as hard as that assistant principal and has the same level of education, why doesn't he earn as much money? The ability of a congregation to pay its pastor depends of the income of that congregation. Unfortunately, one can't fill a church solely with tithing. Assistant principals can earn $70,200 a year. In our example pastor's church, approximately four hundred members donate a total of $96,550 which is only fifty-eight percent of the budget. Each member, on the average, donates $241.14 per year to the church. This church relies on invested income to make up the forty-two percent difference in its budget not supported by member pledges.

We've compared the salary of a minister who lives and

works in one of the richest states in the nation with his parishioners and with one of his professional peers. If we look at other churches across the United States, our sample pastor is doing OK. He works a little too hard, spends too little time with his family, and he's not getting rich. How do his colleagues, other ministers, fare? In a word, worse.

First, as we saw above, parishioners traditionally do not give ten percent of their income to the church. Even in the middle-class, suburban church we used for our example, members averaged only one percent. That church is larger than most. Average church size in the country is only two hundred fifty-nine members. Average annual pay ranges from a high of $28,008 in Alaska to a low of $14,963 in South Dakota. If percentage of giving remains the same, that South Dakota church receives only $38,000 in member pledges toward its entire church budget! Unless it has investment income, that church won't be able to pay what our example pastor earns.

The Meriden pastor enjoyed certain benefits that many of his colleagues don't. According to a clergy compensation survey done by the Ministers and Missionaries Benefit Board of American Baptist Churches, only 18.2 percent of pastors are paid a Social Security allowance to offset their double taxation. Twelve percent of all pastors receive neither a parsonage nor a housing allowance. Almost half pay their own utilities, including some who live in parsonages.

Over ninety percent of the ministers receive some form of mileage allowance. It's estimated that the average pastor drives 12,500 miles per year on church business. Only twenty percent receive a books and periodicals budget. A scant twelve percent are allowed a discretionary fund for entertaining parishioners or prospective new members, or emergency purchases for the church. Forty percent of all ministers pay for their continuing education. More than half of the pastors who receive an education budget get two hundred dollars or less, far less than the cost of one graduate level course.

Filthy Lucre

Another reason for the discrepancy in what pastors are paid and what would be a fairer wage is that the laity doesn't realize there is much of a difference. In the American Baptist Church survey, both clergy and laity were asked how the pastor's salary compared with experienced professionals in the community. Sixty-eight percent of the clergy felt their salaries were lower or much lower. Only thirty-nine percent of the laity agreed that their pastors were not paid enough compared to other professionals. While twenty-five percent of the laity thought their pastor had a high income, only 7.5 percent of the pastors thought their pay was higher or much higher than community professionals. When asked to compare the pastor's salary with that of his members, 33.5 percent of the pastors felt their pay was lower or much lower. Forty-five percent thought it was about the same. Among the laity, however, 47.5 percent thought their pastor earned more or much more than they did.

Among those pastors who thought their income was lower than their peers, thirty-eight percent thought they could change it and another thirty-eight percent thought it was not realistically possible to remedy the inequity. The most frequent response on how to change the situation was to educate the laity by communicating the pastor's financial needs.

Do they? Do most ministers sit down with their boards or members and explain the financial facts of a minister's life? No.

Earlier in this chapter we observed that minister's wife Lois Farina cried over her checkbook and was frustrated over the prospect of feeding and clothing a family of five and keeping ahead of the bills.

"Each church sets their own salary," explained Lois. "And unless the minister really deals with the issues, he will be given whatever the finance committee decides. Finally Tony realized how tough it was and went to the church board and things improved."

Some wives, along with realistic husbands spurred on

by the strong, yet small voices of such practical-minded ministers as Larry Osborne, have learned that they had to have enough faith in themselves to seek what they needed to live comfortably. Ministers are people pleasers, nurturers, givers. Those traits are not positive assets when it comes to asking for a raise. Most wrap themselves in the 'God will provide' philosophy (remember, thirty-eight percent believe their situation cannot be improved) denying themselves, and their families, even small pleasures of life.

But most ministers don't ask for a salary that allows them to live at least as well as the members of their congregation.

". . . the bottom line is usually a fear of the consequences," wrote Larry W. Osborne, pastor of North Coast Evangelical Free Church in California in a 1987 *Leadership* article titled "Negotiating a Fair Salary." "Some pastors fear getting their heads bitten off; others fear the appearance of greed or a lack of contentment. Some fear breaking the spiritual relationship with their board."

Their dilemma deepens with the controversy over how they view their career. Are they competent professionals, deserving of a professional's salary? Or are they dedicated servants, so dedicated, in fact, that their work approaches servitude instead of service?

Ministers get a "call" from God. It's a subtle, but for many, as strong a pull as any basic life instinct. They know the issues, suffer the sacrifices, but are unable to do anything else. One Baptist minister described it as having a wart on his nose that he couldn't get rid of.

"You ask, 'God, why me?' It was an internal sense, a nagging. I had plenty of reasons not to," and he cited his lack of finances for the additional education.

"I think it's as much that the ministry chooses you as you choosing the ministry," said George True, a Congregational minister. "There were other professions I could have gone into

Filthy Lucre

and been just as successful, but the ministry was the one I had to do."

Because of their strong commitment and noble goal of serving God through man, many ministers take the dedicated servant stance too much to heart. Using prayer, faith, and trust in God, they do and go as they hear the call. If that means a church with a low pay, they and their families adapt. These ministers never let their church know they are financially strapped.

The congregation, on the other hand, seems just as happy to let their minister suffer along with low pay. Almost any other expenditure is given priority over the pastor's salary. A new roof is a necessity; the pastor's salary is not. Being human, parishioners want the most for their dollar and resist paying more than they have to.

"It is a practical mistake to assume that the church will look after its clergy except in a minimal way," wrote Henry Sawatzky, pastor of a UCC church in New Jersey in an 1988 article in the *Clergy Journal*. ". . . when the 'poor church' argument is used, the church suggests that the clergy ought to sacrifice . . . but that its members do not have to sacrifice very much." Capital expenditures spur on aggressive stewardship drives. The pastor's salary increase does not. Because the dedicated servant pastor does not confide his needs, the congregation assumes his pay is adequate.

How do they cope? By sacrificing. One wife wrote that her husband's parents regularly supplemented his salary during financial crises. Another wife once borrowed from their son's paper route money to avoid paying credit card interest. Though she points out that later they put him and two siblings through college, she was never able to pay back that initial loan. She still feels badly about it.

Jacquie Reed is forty-two, married seventeen years to her United Methodist husband. They have two children. She told us: "Our philosophy has always been that we can live on what we are paid, and we have done just fine. We do not own much, our house is furnished sparsely—we have a tiny camera, no movie camera or other items most people own. We try to live simply and we must deny ourselves things or experiences we would like to have because we do not have extra funds. We have always tithed and give generously to many causes. At times, I think we needed to give less so that our finances would not have been so tight. However, we have always had food to eat, and that is what is most important."

As we saw in Chapter Four of this book, most ministers' wives have received or read advice which is unrealistic, patronizing and merely reinforces the pastor-as-servant role. The minister is advised to increase his income by submitting sermon manuscripts to magazines, peddling his services as an after-dinner speaker, teaching, or having garage sales. Just what he needs, more work.

One book, written by a minister's wife, suggested putting away one's pride and buying used clothes for the family; using old wallpaper sample books for Christmas wrapping paper; encouraging the local library to carry the magazines you want and then dropping your subscriptions. She also advised selling the second car and having the kids get part-time jobs to earn their own money. Other solutions for the minister's wife are to plant a garden, put up vegetables, cut her and her children's hair, sew their clothing, and get a job herself.

The number of ministers' wives who work matches the national average of all married women who work. Almost half the population does and most of them do so to earn money for extras. All perfectly normal, highly commendable, and eminently practical. In the American Baptist Survey, ten percent of the pastors who felt resentment over their financial situation stated they would ask their wives to get jobs in order to relieve the tensions. That's instead of asking for a raise or moving to a better-paying church! The same survey showed that when the laity was asked if the pastor's spouse should have to work to

Filthy Lucre

supplement the family income, seventy-two percent said no. Yet when she does get a job, some congregations, and even one article in a clergy trade magazine, advised taking into account the wife's salary when setting the minister's pay. That's like asking the chairman of IBM not only to reveal his wife's salary, but reduce his own because of it!

The United States Department of Labor lists statistics on four hundred thirty-two occupations. Ministers rank with unskilled labor when earnings are compared but their level of education lists them with the top ten earning occupations. The median income for people with a graduate degree is $50,525, again, twice our example pastor's base salary. Congregations need to remember that providing a realistic salary for their minister and his family is the church's responsibility and not his wife's. And the minister has to regard himself as a little less of the devoted servant and a little more of a professional. Whether or not they are paid adequately depends both on the church and how aware the minister is of his needs, tax advantages, and his right to negotiate.

Somewhere in between the million dollar earnings of the televangelists and refusing offered raises from a small church budget lies a middle ground that can only be reached by careful negotiation over a myriad salary and salary-related issues. Rather than bring a secular matter between themselves and their parishioners, most ministers don't bother. The combination of call, obligation, and the need to be needed, thwarts many of them from asking for their dues. Probably the most tragic story concerning the conflict between call and family responsibility came from a thirty-three year old wife in Florida to whom we spoke. Her husband committed to the ministry several years after they were married. He works in the Assembly of God denomination and after completing seminary his call was so strong, he accepted a post as associate pastor at no pay. Linda has had second thoughts. Her advice to ministers' wives:

"I would have preferred to wait to go into ministry until

financial circumstances were better. The church my husband initially worked for as associate pastor could not afford to pay a salary so they provided housing and we sold our house and lived off the equity money for the first year of ministry. We were extremely young and anxious to go into full-time ministry. This very unwise financial decision will affect us for a long time. I wish I would have realized at that young age that you must plan for your future and it is unwise to jeopardize yourself financially."

7

Home Sweet Home: Ours? or Theirs?

Even though the previous chapter painted a pretty gloomy picture of the minister's finances, money, it turns out, is not the primary issue irritating pastors' wives. Our ministry couple may have adapted to a self-imposed or church-imposed vow of poverty, but where they live, or rather, in what they live, is a greater issue to ministers' wives than their husbands' salaries.

"We live in a church-owned parsonage," wrote one sixty-year-old United Methodist minister's wife. "It seems practical in most places we've been. One does feel less tied down. However, after thirty-five years, I'm beginning to WANT MY OWN!"

In the survey compiled for this book, fifty-eight percent of the wives lived in parsonages and more than half of those would prefer a housing allowance that enables them to buy their own home.

The parsonage system has deep roots. Parsonages are as old as the churches that own them. In New England particularly, the manse or minister's house was almost as important a place as the church/meeting house. Visiting dignitaries were put up, fed, and entertained there. The manse often housed the minister's office and it was expected to accommodate church group meetings.

Today some parsonages still serve as the church office. Some are comfortably large and some are woefully inadequate. Absurdities occur such as the childless couple who lived in a ten-room manse while Annie, with six children, made do with a one-bathroom parsonage and sent her boys out to water the bushes in the backyard.

"We have no say about the house that we live in," wrote one wife who wished to remain anonymous, obviously bitter over the system. "Our house is very small for a family of six, but, too bad, because we have to live there anyway."

Some denominations believe in an itinerant system. Itinerancy also has its roots in colonial and expansionist America. In the past such ministers travelled from church to church staying with members and carrying only a few personal items. Material possessions were anathema to these traveling pastors. Although ministers no long ride horseback from church to church carrying their meager belongings in a carpet bag strapped to the saddle, some move more frequently than denominations not grounded in itinerant philosophy. Later, completely furnished parsonage and frequent transfers between charges replaced the old method of staying in members' homes. This preserved part of the itinerant system and all of the belief that material possessions just get in the way of preaching the gospel.

Some churches do supply just the house. Beth, the wife of a minister who travels around, indicated that she couldn't have afforded to buy any of the manses they lived in since, in their denomination, they must provide their own furniture. To their credit, congregations must feel, at times, an overwhelming confusion. In some cases they need to furnish a parsonage for the pastor, in others the pastor wants the furniture stored.

Home Sweet Home: Ours? or Theirs?

Then, the next pastor wants the furniture back. The pastor who follows him doesn't want the furniture or the house but asks for a housing allowance. The next pastor . . . well, who knows?

Furniture presents the first problem for a minister's wife. Some have their own, some don't, and it seems as though the ones that do are hired by denominations which provide furniture while those who have none are hired by denominations that give their ministers only the bare walls. They never quite match up with the congregations they join. Gerry's husband took a year's sabbatical from the ministry and scrounged up enough to furnish a rented house. Katy, another wife, owned too much furniture for the parsonages she lived in.

"Through the years we have accumulated furniture," said Karen, who has moved twelve times in her thirty-seven year marriage. "As an only child (and only grandchild on one side of the family), I have inherited some beautiful antique furniture that holds a lot of memories from my own childhood. This was furniture that was in my grandmother's house, then my mother's and my aunt's homes, and now in mine. Someday it will be in my children's homes.

"The parsonage situations we have got to don't have much room for additional furniture owned by the pastoral family." Karen's husband is a United Methodist minister in Texas and their parsonages have always been furnished. "And some parsonage committees do not look kindly on storing the church's furniture. Guess who that leaves?"

Physical location is another issue. Many parsonages are located next door to the church. In *What's Happening to Clergy Marriages?* by David and Vera Mace, pastors ranked lack of family privacy third on the list of disadvantages of clergy marriage. This goldfish bowl feeling was ranked fourth by the wives.

"The need for privacy is the desire not to be observed by eyes believed to be critical and probing for faults," observed the Maces. The words "believed to be" are important here. As we've seen in previous chapters, expectations of the clergy couple are high—but where those expectations come from is the real issue. Some congregations are extremely critical of their pastor, his wife, and children. Other congregations are sources of great support, encouragement, and sensitivity. Some wives skitter around trying to meet expectations that don't exist except in their own minds while others blithely ignore real demands of their congregations. Perceived or real, the feelings of lack of privacy are most obvious in many a parsonage.

Lisa Chaloner, with only six years experience as a United Church of Christ minister's wife, now owns a home. Her husband receives a housing allowance as part of his salary package.

"Although our church always kept their parsonages in excellent repair, I do prefer our own home," she wrote. "It helps us feel as though we are not controlled by the church. We bought a home seven miles from the church and this has discouraged 'drop in' visitors."

Roy M. Oswald, in a 1984 Alban Institute *Action Information* article titled "Why Do clergy Wives Burn Out?," stated he believed it was living in a parsonage that created the most difficulty for wives. He cited the drop-in visits of parishioners, designed to discover how well their minister's wife takes care of the house. It is usually the wife's responsibility to supervise repairs, starting with hounding the church board to get the work done. This is particularly distressing when the actual work is donated by members of the church. Rather than the leverage held with a paid tradesman, she must work around not only the member's schedule, but their spiritual and employer relationship with her husband. To complain too much about volunteer help can create a controversy within the congregation that can only hurt her husband's position.

Other wives who live in parsonages next to the church reported days when a seemingly steady stream of parishioners came to their doors. Frances, one wife, mentioned she felt as though the members were silently accusing her of hiding her

Home Sweet Home: Ours? or Theirs?

husband. He wasn't in his office, therefore he must be home and she was covering for him. Even when finally convinced that the minister is not in, parishioners expect answers from his wife. Some parishioners expect their minister's wife to be so intimately involved with matters at the church that they should be able to answer any and all questions. The parishioners leave miffed because the answers weren't immediately forthcoming.

"I feel that the congregation feels that they own more of you when you are in their house," said Rosemary Todd of Cheyenne, Wyoming, married to an Episcopal minister for fifteen years. This is Rosemary's second marriage. During her first, she was an Air Force wife and she feels her outgoing personality and entertaining abilities have helped her as a minister's wife. She invites church leaders to the parsonage for dinner or breakfast at least once a year. "I am proud of our home and keep it nice, but there is not much room for creativity when you do not own the house or do not know how long you will live there."

The lack of freedom to redecorate, hang pictures, even paint walls was high on the wives' list of disadvantages to the parsonage system. Betty Sweet, who now lives in her own home, lived in parsonages for most of her twenty-seven years of marriage.

"I like choosing my own place," she wrote, "decorating it myself, pounding nails where I wish, adding decks and doors and gardens without worrying about Mr. X or Mrs. Y whose spouse gave or built or designed it!!" The congregation's attachment to the parsonage was a recurrent theme in our survey answers. Just as her minister husband has as many "bosses" as he has members, so may the minister's wife have as many proprietary landlords. At the very least, she believes she does.

"I never wanted to ask for anything new in the house, because I felt like since we were living there rent free I should be grateful for anything they gave us," said Glenda Menger of

Augusta, Georgia. She'd been married six years to a minister in the Baptist church. "It was never 'our' home," she added.

Betty Jean Souers, a minister's wife from Jacksonville, Florida reiterated this feeling of not being *at home,* while pointing out another invasion of their privacy.

"When I lived in a parsonage I felt as though it was their home and that I should hold meetings and groups there." Opening the parsonage to the parishioners is a hotly contested controversy among ministers' wives. They seem to be equally divided on the issue between feeling expected to open up the parsonage as an additional church meeting room and insisting that what happens in the parsonage, their home, is solely up to them. Here again, the expectations do not always come from the congregation. Sometimes the wife springs the trap on herself.

"My own sense of obligation," wrote Donna Sinclair in her book *The Pastor's Wife Today,* "mingled with my desire to be loving and caring, sometimes landed me in an entertainment schedule that was more than my family—or I—could cope with."

Laura, one pastor's wife, reported that after a visit from some church members, stories circulated that she and her husband were alcoholics because beer cans were noticed in the garbage, and that they weren't taking good care of the furniture because the church members found the dog asleep on the bed.

Dealing with volunteer committees in the church also poses hazards for the minister's wife.

Ideally, all requests, follow up, and hounding should be done by the minister. The parsonage is, after all, part of his pay for his job. If he is not a negotiator, or fearful of being seen as too secular by the flock he tries to lead, he will resist going after what he needs to make the parsonage livable. Even if he does handle all parsonage requests, the minister's wife still deals with a situation similar to creating the world by committee. Decisions can take forever.

Home Sweet Home: Ours? or Theirs?

"Now we are in our own home which I prefer," stated Donna Lee Fowlie, a parson's wife. "I do not have to go to a committee when I want to purchase a new pair of curtains. I do not have to wait weeks to get approval from the Board of Trustees to get the washing machine repaired if it breaks down."

Sometimes, even the simplest requests are regarded as greed. Annie, the wife who became desperately depressed, advises not moving in until parsonage repairs are completed. She once asked for a washing machine and dryer—a family of eight made the two appliances a necessity, not a luxury. After much negotiation, the board purchased and installed them. When Harvey was transferred, he and Annie suggested to the board that they leave the washer and dryer for the new minister. The board removed it and sold them.

We've written so far about work required to the parsonage that is minor or for the convenience of the occupants. But not all parsonages are well maintained. Alice, one young wife with two children, one an infant, inspected an older parsonage and made an extensive list of needed repairs. The requests were expressed in a letter, signed by her husband Todd and sent to the church board. Repairs included a new bathroom and leak damage repaired in the dining room because of the old bathroom; new kitchen sink with cabinet; a used stove to replace the current, inoperative one (even though used appliances are against their conference standards); walls painted, washer and dryer turned side by side; house thoroughly cleaned including windows and carpets; backyard mowed. The letter went on to express concerns about the safety of the parsonage porches. A rotted step on the front porch broke when they used it and the back porch was becoming detached from the house.

"I can't emphasize the concern we, as parents, feel about having our children use the porches."

"In addition," the letter continued, "the loose and

chipped paint on the exterior poses health risks to a child like ours who puts everything in his mouth. We'd like to see the parsonage painted before the condition deteriorates any further. We also would like the leaks in the hall near the stairs and in the pantry repaired, both for the looks of the house and its structural integrity."

We can only imagine, the true condition of this parsonage. Even so, Todd and Alice felt that in order to convince the congregation to do the work, they must promote these repairs not just for themselves, but for future pastors as well.

"We realize this list seems long, but we're concerned about the condition of the house and safety standards for ourselves and our children. Furthermore, since a parsonage is part of the recompense for the pastor, the better its condition the more attractive is the appointment. In order to help recruit and keep good ministers, it behooves the charge to maintain an attractive and safe house."

However, despite this couple's concern when they moved in, the porches were not fixed. When they moved out, the porches were still not fixed. Only the front of the house had been painted.

Unfortunately, Todd and Alice did not fare well in their next church either. Moving into an old dilapidated parsonage, Alice was promised the work on a new parsonage would go quickly. She and Todd tried to be optimistic. They moved in July and were promised the new parsonage before the holidays. A year and a half later, they moved into the new home but without a certificate of occupancy. Most of the work on the modular home was done with volunteer labor from the congregation. The volunteers worked at a very slow and uneven pace. For instance, while still in the old parsonage, the well at the new house was tested and found contaminated. It took two months for the church to solve the problem.

Alice and Todd moved themselves, carrying everything, including appliances, from the old parsonage next to the

Home Sweet Home: Ours? or Theirs?

church to the new one built on land behind the church. Two rooms, built into the basement, to be used at the discretion of the occupants, were designated as a family room and the wife's office. But, there were no provisions for heating these rooms. Back the couple went to the church board to get an adequate heating system installed. When they pointed out that the lack of heat made it impossible for Alice to work they were told: "We have to provide you with a home, we don't have to provide your wife with an office." Nothing has been done about the heat.

Todd is now looking for another church or a job outside religion. Alice has had enough and would prefer he leave the ministry.

Diana Higgs, a minister's wife who now lives in her own home in Las Vegas, summed up the parsonage problems succinctly:

"I like not having to ask a committee if I could sneeze."

Most churches don't quibble over paying for needed repairs—if *they* decide they're needed. Roof repair, new furnaces, exterior painting, leaks, and other major repairs are the responsibility of the church. And most churches include the utility bills as part of the parsonage and pay those, too. The Connecticut Conference of the United Church of Christ advises that "Along with the parsonage, the church pays directly for parsonage utilities (heat, light, water, refuse service, local phone calls, etc.)." Utilities create yet another area of contention between the church board and the pastor's wife. Still, Glenda Menger, a parson's wife, feels guilty if she turns on the air conditioner, even down low, because it might make the electric bill too high. Robert, one pastor, began his search for a new pulpit after he inadvertently started an uproar in the congregation because he asked the church to pay for garbage collection at the parsonage. He asked for it after the church voted to give him an insultingly low ninety-five dollar raise in his *annual* salary.

On the flip side, and in support of the church board, another minister's wife, Rosemary Todd, noted: "We are criticized for the utility bill and rightly so, since I feel we are not as saving as we might be if we paid it ourselves."

But, as we saw in the previous chapter, almost half of the pastors in parsonages pay their own utilities.

"The houses we have lived in have not always been the kind we would have chosen," wrote Jocelyn, a pastor's wife from Montgomery, Alabama. "Some were horrible on utilities which we had to pay."

Lack of freedom to change or redecorate, drop-in visits from parishioners, bureaucratic decision-making, utility bills, the perception, if not actual occurrence of, constant surveillance of all matters, large and small, at the parsonage mask the greater risk of the parsonage system. At some point, the pastor retires. Where does he, and his wife, live then? Scarier still, if he dies prematurely, where do his wife and children go? If they've relied on the churches they served for a roof over their heads, they have no home of their own.

"It scared me when I heard that a wife had such a difficult time moving out of a home she'd lived in for twenty years because her husband died," wrote a minister's wife living in Washington State who preferred not having her name used. "We like the independence of owning our own home. It's also security for me if my husband should die."

The embittered wife who complained earlier that the parsonage was too small for her large family, advocated a housing allowance.

"If we were paid an adequate housing allowance we could buy our own home—our choice—decorate it the way we want and have something to live in when we retire. As it is, the congregation gets to build equity in their home. They keep the home after the pastor retires and house other pastors long after they've paid it off. The retiring pastor has to start at age sixty-five (when he is living on Social Security) to make mortgage payments.

Home Sweet Home: Ours? or Theirs?

"Some people think they are *giving* the pastor a home, but really the pastor is giving the congregation a home."

The clergy family that lives in a parsonage for his entire career, and is not paid enough to save, or had pension contributions made to offset his loss of equity, is in a dire situation indeed.

"Home ownership is advantageous because it allows a minister to build equity in real property and to gain annual appreciation," states the Connecticut Conference of the United Church of Christ. "For married clergy with children, equity is especially important when it comes time to finance a child's college education or to buy a permanent retirement home, and home ownership insures that a minister's spouse and family will have a home and a community in the event of a minister's untimely death." For a widowed clergy wife, the loss of her husband is the biggest, but not the only, life-changing problem she faces. At some point, usually sooner than she is ready, she must leave the parsonage. After all, the church needs it for the next pastor. She must find alternative housing that may be too expensive in her present community on what may be a woefully small pension. Pension contributions are made as a percentage of base salary, as we saw in Chapter Six.

"Where a retirement benefit is based on the dollars the pastor can accumulate by retirement," wrote Manfred Holck, Jr., a Lutheran minister and publisher of *The Clergy Journal* magazine, in a 1990 article for that publication, "higher paid pastors are simply going to have more pension dollars than others. Both Holck and the Connecticut Conference of UCC advise giving pastors in parsonages additional contributions to their pension plans. According to the American Baptist survey, only 2.8 percent of churches that own a parsonage make such an additional contribution.

So then, our wife must move out, sometimes away from the community her children feel is their home town. The untimely death of a minister living in a parsonage triggers sweeping change for the entire family. His wife, if she perceived herself as being in the ministry with her husband, loses not only her community, but her special place within it. "This is our previous minister's wife," is not a phrase members wish to use, nor does she want to hear it.

Finally, in this long list of parsonage system problems, is the underlying feeling of being not quite an adult. Donna Sinclair, author of *The Pastor's Wife Today,* felt making requests to a church board was too much like being a teenager and asking dad for the keys to the car. She refers to the church as a substitute parent constantly protecting the minister and his family from the realities of major repairs and utilities bills.

"It places me squarely back in adolescence, with all the rebellious feelings that are a necessary part of that stage—but inconvenient in this one," she wrote.

Not every wife feels that the parsonage system is bad. Karen, who wrote about her difficulties owning furniture in a denomination that typically furnishes its parsonages, pointed to several advantages in the system.

"In the early years, having parsonages was easier, as no one had enough time or money to search out a living space on appointment changes," she wrote. Karen and her husband now own a house and receive a housing allowance. "Many small towns did not even have a good selection of 'For Rent' houses. Pastors on a 'move every two to three year schedule' would certainly not be into buying their own house each time. So parsonages have their place."

Mary, age forty-two and married eleven years to a UCC minister, lives in a parsonage but would prefer a housing allowance. Even with a housing allowance, it's doubtful Mary and her husband Andrew could afford their own home.

"We have no means of accumulating enough for a down payment," said Mary, who described her husband's pay as "pitiful." "This area (Massachusetts) is extremely expensive and we would both have to work full time in order to make a small

Home Sweet Home: Ours? or Theirs?

mortgage payment. Our flexible time and my time with the children is taking priority over full time work for me." Mary's "advantage" to living in the parsonage is really the congregation's advantage to save themselves, not only the money, but the stewardship work necessary to pay her husband a decent salary.

Mabel Victoria's straightforward manner reassures us that she holds no bitterness toward the parsonage system. At fifty-six years old, married thirty-two years to a Presbyterian minister in Goldfield, Iowa, Mabel has always lived in parsonages.

"Our housing has always been provided for us. At our stage in life, we no longer want property," stated Mabel. "I'm not sure we could have ever raised the money for down payment on housing. My home must be comfortable, but not elaborate. I can live with few closets, if necessary. We do not expect it to be redecorated unless it needs to be. We do expect the congregation to keep up with leaks, etc., so the building does not deteriorate. If we break a window, we replace it. If the furnace goes out, they do."

Many ministers' wives pointed out that the size, style, and situation of a good parsonage would be beyond their means to buy. Ten-room parsonages are not uncommon. Location is also a key factor. Survey answers revealed that some wives didn't think they could afford to live in the neighborhoods where their parsonages were located. Even a minister with what seems to be a high salary might work in an area where housing is beyond his financial reach. On the other hand, Beverly, one wife we talked with, was excited and happy about living in a four-story brownstone parsonage on Manhattan's upper east side.

Beth, a pastor's wife living in Michigan, wrote: "We live in a parsonage now, and I would not want to have had to buy a house in this community, with a stagnant market and flat real estate values, but we might have rented something. As it is, we live on a very pleasant street, close to the schools and across town from the church. In this situation, it was a favor to us to have a house available to move into. However, each house has its drawbacks, and my son's tiny bedroom is on a different floor from the rest of us."

Housing allowances are a relatively new phenomenon in the ministry. Because of the parsonage system, and the traditionally low salaries paid to ministers, the housing allowance accomplishes two things. It increases the minister's salary without calling it salary and it gives the minister and his family equity to finance their children's educations and to provide a home for the couple after retirement, ideally mortgage-free.

As we saw in Chapter Six, the housing allowance as well as the fair rental value of a parsonage, is considered taxable income by Social Security. It is not considered income by the IRS under two conditions. First, the housing allowance amount must be shown as a separate line item on the church budget. Lumping a housing allowance in with salary makes the entire amount subject to income tax. Second, the minister may only deduct as nontaxable income that part of the housing allowance he actually used for housing. That means if a minister is allowed seven hundred dollars per month as a housing allowance and his rent and house expense only equal five hundred dollars, then the balance is subject to income tax.

It's important to remember here that although the minister gets this tax break and, supposedly, gets "free" housing, it is not discretionary income. Neither he, nor his family, gets to enjoy the money for anything other than housing costs. His spendable income is still limited to his base salary even though, when salary and allowance are added together, it seems like he makes more.

Housing allowances depend as much on a pastor's negotiation skills as does his salary. He must know the community he lives in, the area he wants to live in, and the exact costs of living there. No church board is going to arbitrarily set a

Home Sweet Home: Ours? or Theirs?

housing figure and no minister should let them. Yet, there are ministers who will rely on their board to set an amount and then make up the difference out of their already insufficient salary. One recent study showed that the average housing allowance across the country was only $5,000 per year. That's only a little over four hundred dollars a month. A sum not sufficient for a monthly mortgage payment, nor will it even rent a decent apartment in many areas of the country.

In the American Baptist study, housing allowances range from a low of $1,500 to over $9,000. Adding in utilities, the Connecticut Conference of UCC found a range of $12,000 to $30,000 in housing allowances. The amount of the allowance is affected by location, size of home required, and cost of living in the community. Housing allowances simply cannot, nor should they, be generalized.

The forty-two percent of our survey respondents who get housing allowances and own their own home say they not only prefer it, they love it. That isn't to say there aren't glitches in this system, too. One couple currently serves a rural congregation of only one hundred fifty members in Michigan. They are considering taking a new pulpit from several that are available.

"Housing cost is a factor in one situation we are looking at—nothing was available to the last pastor within twenty minutes of the church." The couple has two children. "Another situation we are considering is known to be in an area which admittedly lacks 'starter' houses—and we do not know whether the job comes with a house or not." Availability of affordable housing isn't the only disadvantage.

"We have always had parsonages until coming to Boston," wrote Carolyn, a United Methodist minister's wife. "We had a day and a half to find a home. We now have a housing allowance. This house has needed so much work. Each year has seen major repairs from a new boiler, furnace, new roof, driveway paving, painting jobs, etc. We were spoiled living in parsonages, having someone see to the repairs and the bills." Not only is their safety net gone, but some of their risk taking as well. Carolyn added that they've found it harder to move to a new church after buying their own home.

Mary Joe Dwyer Miller of San Benito, Texas is a Roman Catholic married thirteen years to a Methodist minister. Her objection to housing allowances and owning seems based on a true embarrassment of itinerant preaching.

"I live in a congregation-owned home," she wrote. "I like this situation because I don't want to bother owning furniture and such that must be carted around when we move." Mary Joe and the Methodist itinerant philosophy are a perfect match for the congregation with a fully furnished parsonage.

Lois Farina, the parson's wife from Wisconsin who wept bitter tears over her checkbook, is a staunch supporter of the parsonage system.

"We have always lived in a church-owned home and it has worked out okay. I always treated it as my own house and didn't consider myself in 'their house.' We would not have lived in some of the large homes if we had had to buy our own. And mostly the trustees have been good about fixing things."

Moving presents its own problems when a ministerial family owns a house. If a move occurs during a downturn in the economy it could take months to sell the house in the old parish, necessitating double mortgage payments on an already stretched-to-the-limit salary. Or, it means taking a loss on a house in a depressed real estate market. That happened to Christina and Todd, who were forced to take a $10,000 loss on the sale of their home. Margaret and James made double payments for so long they finally gave their home away to a relative rather than waste any more time, money, or effort trying to sell it.

The last disadvantage to housing allowances may have its root, once again, in the pastor-as-servant philosophy. In reality, it's only a disadvantage to the congregation. Just as ministers accept their low salaries as part of their call, so they accept

Home Sweet Home: Ours? or Theirs?

the fact that a congregation can't afford to give them a housing allowance. The minister permits his church to financially abuse him instead of insisting that they raise the needed monies as they would raise the money for anything else. Ministers' wives follow along with the "poor church" philosophy.

"It would be nice to own our own home," wrote Beverly Kaiser, a minister's wife from Connecticut, "but it would cause a lot of problems every time we moved and would be much more expensive for the church, so I am happy living in a parsonage."

Betty Sweet, another pastor's wife, who has her own home, remembers worrying about offending church members who "gave, built or designed" the parsonage, and also pointed out the cost of the housing allowance to the small church.

"I realize that in many, many small churches, a decent housing allowance is impossible," she stated, "and that many clergy do not have the resources available for down payments, but I prefer the housing allowance. It cannot work for the small congregation, but it would be nice." Betty assumes, like many clergy couples, that although a stewardship drive for a new roof or expanding the Sunday school will meet with approval, the same effort to adequately house their pastor will not.

Does a housing allowance really cost more than a parsonage? The statistics seem to indicate that it does. According to the American Baptist study, almost seventy-two percent of those pastors living in parsonages listed the rental value between $1,500 and $4,500 per year. The largest percentage of pastors receiving a housing allowance was a little over nineteen percent getting $5,001 to 6,000 per year. Only twenty-four percent of pastors with housing allowances got an allowance of $4,500 or less. Sixteen percent receive an allowance of $9,000 or more. And we have to remember that the entire housing allowance is a cash expense to the church. Only taxes and utilities, if paid, represent a cash outlay to the church that has paid the mortgage on its parsonage. Even if the fair rental value of the parsonages are understated, and it would appear that they are, unless there's a mortgage, the parsonage rental value is not a cash expense to the church. Regardless of the increased cost, it seems unfair that a congregation can't treat the housing of its pastor with the same concern as painting the interior of the sanctuary.

In a roundabout way, we've already covered the advantages to the housing allowance by hearing the wives explain the disadvantages of parsonages. With a housing allowance, they can decorate and renovate at will without waiting for permission or prying open the church's purse; they control how many church activities take place in their home; and they are building equity for their children's educations and their retirement.

Betty Jean Souers told us: "It's so nice living in a home where you don't have to ask someone to have everything done. It's nice to be able to paint a room whatever you desire without getting someone's approval. We're building equity so that when we get to retirement we have money to buy in the area we intend to stay."

More than half of the respondents who live in parsonages said they would prefer a housing allowance, making a total of seventy-seven percent of all ministers' wives who would rather own their home. So strong is their desire for ownership that one wife wrote:

"It is best for us, long-range, to get into the capital investment cycle before it's too late. Here again, we will rely on his parents for help." In this case not only is the minister subsidizing his church, but so are his parents!

Parsonage versus housing allowance can sometimes boil down to servitude versus independence. In the worst case, the parsonage system can create a parent–child "owning" attitude on the part of the congregation. In return for "taking care" of the pastor and his family, the congregation demands twenty-four hour, seven-day availability to him as well as the freedom to inspect and criticize the care of "their" parsonage. In the best

Home Sweet Home: Ours? or Theirs?

case, with parishioners who respect the ministerial family's privacy, parsonages truly can be regarded as home sweet home.

Even when congregations don't add to the goldfish bowl feeling of life in the parsonage, more ministers should negotiate for a housing allowance and buy their own home.

As one Ohio wife put it:

"I think it would be fiscally irresponsible not to try to get your own home, if possible."

Now that she's settled, in the parsonage or her own house, many ministers' wives turn to the next test of wills. How active, or inactive, do they need to be in their husband's congregations?

8

How Methodist Do I Have to Be?

"It is like a doctor being married to someone who is opposed to having immunization shots for their children," said Judy, describing interfaith ministerial marriages. Judy is the missionary who escaped from China during the Cultural Revolution in 1950. "I feel very strongly that for a minister and his wife to have a happy home and happy pastorate, they should have similar religious beliefs. For a Protestant minister to marry a Catholic or Jewish young woman is asking for *problems*. She will be subject to lots of comments by members—is she going to change—Why not? If a minister's faith is important to him, after all that is what he is preaching and teaching, how could he have a lasting marriage with someone who had quite different ideas?"

According to the Presbyterian Panel study (Chapter Five), over sixty percent of church members agree with Judy. That is the percentage who expect their pastor's wife to attend church more regularly than they do themselves. In the same study, ninety-four percent of the responding pastors stated that their spouses are members of the church where they work, while only eighty percent of the members' spouses belong to the same church. In our study, which polled only ministers' wives, ninety-four percent of them, the same percentage as Presbyterian pastors, are members of their husbands' congregations. Clearly, ministers and their wives impose a higher expectation for church attendance and membership on themselves. So high, in fact, as to be virtually unanimous. Ministers' wives go to great lengths to ensure that low church attendance is not one of the criticisms leveled at them by the congregation. For one wife, this meant the public repudiation of her birth religion.

It never occurred to Alice that she might meet, fall in love with and marry a Congregational minister. Even when it happened, Alice never intended to convert away from Roman Catholicism.

The person who referred us to Alice described her as slim slight, shy ("When I say shy, I mean SHY!" our contact told us). Alice was a traditional minister's wife who stayed in the background, but was very active in her husband's church. She served on the kitchen committee, and helped with Sunday school. She always attended church. We needed Alice's perspective: a woman who had chosen the traditional role. So far all our contacts assured us they were "modern" wives. We contacted Alice to set up an interview.

Alice didn't want to be interviewed. We persisted and she reluctantly agreed to an interview. A few days later, she called and cancelled.

"Nothing I say will change anyone's mind about ministers' wives," she said. "It would be futile." She sounded definite, but perhaps her natural shyness was getting in the way. We persisted again and she finally agreed to fill out a questionnaire but we held little hope of receiving it.

A month later the complete questionnaire returned. Al-

How Methodist Do I Have to Be?

ice was definitely not a traditional wife. She was, or rather had been, a Roman Catholic.

We called her back. This time she agreed to an interview.

We met in a quiet restaurant in a town that was half way between us. Over our seafood salads, Alice began:

"I was raised in a traditional Roman Catholic family," she said. Alice attended parochial schools through high school and then enrolled in a Catholic women's college. "Until meeting Dan I had relatively no association with anyone Protestant. In fact, I belonged to a Brownie and Girl Scout troop that met in a basement of a Protestant church and it was taboo for us to go into a Protestant sanctuary." She paused and leaned back in her chair.

"This was not an ecumenical era and I led a very sheltered life. My family for generations had always been Catholic.

"Dan was just finished with his first of three years of seminary when we met," she said adding that they were both attendants in a wedding party. "I had just finished my sophomore year of college. I mentally accepted Dan as being a graduate student. I respected his choice of profession but did not dwell on it." Like many Catholic girls, Alice had fantasized about being a nun. "To associate Dan on the level of a Catholic priest would have been a difficult comparison for me to accept. So I simply didn't think of it.

"The first time I saw Dan in his collar was a shock" she said. Three months before their marriage Alice visited Dan at the church where he completed his seminary training working as a associate pastor. "Separate bedrooms, of course," said Alice, whispering the aside statement with a smile. We laughed. "There was never an occasion prior to this that I would have seen him professionally dressed." On Sunday morning both Dan and Alice left their rooms simultaneously. There was Dan in his black suit and white collar. They stared, turned, and silently retreated to their rooms each waiting for the other to go downstairs first. They never discussed the significance or impact of that meeting.

"Meeting Dan was quite a shock for my family," continued Alice. "They then, and still now, think of him as a minister, someone a bit different. They have accepted our relationship but it was a difficult period. And I would not want to relive those times. I made Dan go with me to tell my parents. I didn't want to face them alone.

"I feel sorry for them," Alice said about her parents. "Dan and I didn't see much difference between our two religions but here was their daughter—turning into a Protestant! It was something they didn't understand. Our families have been wonderful to us—my family learning about a whole new world. His family was and still is very kind to me. His father simply wanted Dan to understand what we were facing." Whatever advice, or pressure, her father-in-law dealt his son, Alice wasn't telling.

Their immediate families weren't the only groups exerting pressure on the young couple. Her church added to the confusion. Alice wanted to take her vows in the Catholic church.

"We went to prenuptial classes prior to our marriage so that we could be married in the Catholic Church" said Alice. "Dan was very open to this. But at the last minute, the local priest refused to marry us because Dan would not promise to raise our nonexistent children Catholic." In the early 1970s, requiring interfaith couples to raise their children Catholic was still rigidly enforced in many Catholic parishes. "We were eventually married in Dan's home church. My entire family came to the wedding. Some traveled far distances to attend their very first Protestant service."

The Catholic stance on raising children as Catholics is more lenient now, as are other aspects of the Catholic wedding service for interfaith marriages, but the feeling persists that many Catholics are more authoritarian about their members

How Methodist Do I Have to Be?

marrying "outside the faith." A March 1990 issue of *U.S. Catholic* magazine, attempts to refute that claim. Robert T. Reilly, in his article titled "Mixed Blessings: Ten Lessons Learned from Interfaith Couples," noted that a recent Gallup poll showed "three out of four Americans approve of interfaith marriages, with Catholics demonstrating more acceptance than Protestants." Perhaps that's why Alice and Dan came face to face with more pressure from the members of his first church.

"I was not as active as people would have liked in our former church but their views did not dominate my life," said Alice, again sidestepping our attempts to fill in the details. "They had been used to very traditional ministers' wives and I would not placate them by being someone else." But finally the pressures won and Alice relinquished the public ties with her birth religion.

"I decided to join Dan's church," she said, leaning back in the chair and holding both her hands in her lap with fingertips lightly touching. "A purely social gesture on my part because people could not handle our mixed backgrounds. I could. And Dan could, but society couldn't." How she learned that stays forever Alice's secret. She would not reveal the context, criticism, or events that convinced her to join her husband's denomination.

"I did not give up any religious beliefs and feel that God knows that. Human beings have just complicated God's Word by giving various titles to it. It was just common sense. We didn't see much difference between the two religions. And society seemed to demand it. So why not?"

Somehow, in ways we can only guess, Alice learned the hard way that the knowledge of her past merely blinds people.

"What I say isn't going to make a difference," Alice repeated when pressed for details. "People have already made up their minds about ministers and their wives.

"I have a firm belief that our background is not for public scrutiny. A few friends know but there are still many people who are not so open to accept such information," said Alice. Did our mutual friend, the one who told us about Alice, know?

"No," said Alice.

"Why?"

"Because it would be of no benefit to her or my family if she knew." The firm set to Alice's mouth shut off, again, any possible flow of details. She offered one more insight.

"I am very cautious of my position and rarely make reference to the fact that I am a minister's wife," she said. "Once this fact is known, people react differently toward me—an attitude handicap on their part not mine."

How has all this affected their marriage?

"Throughout this entire experience, I am very grateful to Dan for being so open and understanding," she said. "I don't think that he would have been as happy with a person whose sole objective in life was to be a minister's wife. I suppose we are both a bit radical in that sense. He certainly knew that I must have loved him for himself—not for his title. It's been an exciting time for us and we believe that God brought us together for a purpose. We only pray we can fulfill his plan, day by day."

Statistics aside, we wondered if Alice's experience was an aberration. Through coincidence, or just plain bad luck, did she encounter the one congregation that felt as strongly about the minister's wife's choice of religion as Judy? How did other wives feel about the interfaith ministerial marriage?

One of our authors, Liz Greenbacker, attended a United Methodist ministers' wives' retreat where, quite fortuitously, the subject was discussed at length.

The weekend retreat opened at 6:00 p.m. Friday and ended at 5:00 Saturday afternoon. Their twenty-three hours together contained three worship services, three meals, and three Sharing Sessions with discussion on questions culled from our survey. The Friday evening session ended at 10:00 and most of the women were in their rooms by 11:00. In the

How Methodist Do I Have to Be?

twenty-three hours, their only free time was that last hour on Friday night and a forty-five minute period scheduled into Saturday for personal/packing time. Soon after 5:00 Saturday afternoon, they had all gone home.

Why was this weekend retreat, billed as a time to reflect, relax, and recreate, confined to just those twenty-three hours? Why was there no time to visit, make friends, or be alone? Why was so much packed into such a short period of time? Because these women, who described themselves as independent individualists, undefined by their husband's occupation, planned their much needed retreat, their brief escape from the pressures of the pulpit, to end in time for them to return home and be in their husbands' churches for service on Sunday morning.

Reverend Sherry Taylor, our second author, who was asked to participate in a "weekend" retreat for ministers' spouses, insisted that the program be extended to include Sunday. The organizers of the retreat felt their retreat must end on Saturday evening to allow them to be in church Sunday morning.

"At the retreats where I've been a chaplain," said Sherry, "the weekend did last until Sunday, but a lot of folks left early." Why?

The most telling answers came from the United Methodist wives' retreat during the second Sharing Session. The discussion centered around questions the wives developed about their lives. A panel of four woman answered the questions posed and attendees added their own experiences to those answers. After some questions about parsonages (Do I have to let them hold meetings there?), Barbara, one young wife barely a month into her husband's first pastorate in a small, troubled, rural parish, asked: "How Methodist do I have to be?" The panel's silence was longer than normal. They finally agreed that "it would be nice to be of the same denomination," a sentiment already supported b the statistics in our survey.

Eight percent of our respondents wrote that they changed from their own Protestant denomination to their husband's when they married. One woman, a panelist at the retreat, had changed her denomination when she married.

"But they're all so close," she said. "There really isn't much difference between Protestant denominations."

One of our survey respondents confirmed that opinion.

"I was an Episcopalian," wrote Marianne Bahmann, married thirty-two years to an Evangelical Lutheran Church of America minister. "I still am in many ways. I became a Lutheran because that was where I would be worshipping the rest of my life. The theology is similar; the differences are mainly cultural."

Leaving the topic of church membership unresolved, the group leaped to the subject of church attendance and that brought the United Methodist wives' retreat into agreement. Four of the twenty-four women attending said their churches had special pews set aside for the minister's wife and children. Two used them, two did not. All of the women regularly attended Sunday services with their husband's congregation.

Although the previous Sharing Session had determined that each wife is a person in her own right, free to do as much, or as little, as she chose in her husband's church, attendance at Sunday service appeared mandatory. They cloaked the mandate in the guise that it was sign of a wife's support for her husband. How could a congregation listen to, respect, and follow the teachings of her husband, they asked, if his wife didn't make the appearance of also doing so? How could a wife not go? It was a short leap back to the interfaith marriage question for the group to agree that a wife of a different faith could cause many problems.

"How could they handle it?" several asked at once. "How could they balance it?" Discussion rose to a clamor, then silence as each woman considered the reaction of the not-so-silent partner to their marriage—their husband's congregation.

In a May 1989 article for *U.S. Catholic* magazine, Robert

How Methodist Do I Have to Be?

T. Reilly wrote: ". . . many ecumenical marriages lead to one spouse's conversion to the other's religion. . . ." In our survey, four women were Roman Catholic when they married their Protestant minister husbands. Two changed to their husband's denomination. One of those was Alice and she stated that it was easier on her, her husband, and her marriage to convert. We can only read between the lines and guess why that is true for Alice.

Janet maintained her ties with the Roman Catholic church, raising both their adopted sons in her faith, while her husband worked as a Congregational minister. Her experience was much different from Alice's.

First, Janet's family reacted differently to their daughter's impending marriage. She was one of six children, all raised Catholic. Three married Catholics and three married Protestants. Janet's parents had only one subject to discuss with Bill.

"My parents told Bill if there was ever a problem, our marriage came before his church," said Janet. "They told Bill there would be no divorce. My parents never said another word after that.

"Bill's parents weren't too thrilled. They knew more about their tradition then I did and they didn't think it would be possible. I think they have come to accept it. Seeing Bill in a decent size church, and doing well, I don't think they have any qualms about it anymore."

Bill didn't object to the requirement that their children be brought up in the Catholic faith.

"Both my sons were raised Catholic," Janet said. "That's how I was raised. The way we thought about it, most mothers are responsible for getting the religious training for the children. Our reasoning was that after they were confirmed, if they wanted to change, that was up to them. Bill didn't have any problem with that."

Neither son attended their father's church regularly.

"When they were younger, they went to Bill's church,

downstairs mostly, not to the services much," she explained. "They went with me to Mass. In the Protestant tradition the children don't go to the service much." Neither son, both now confirmed, has changed religious affiliation. "Maybe when they get married they will, but they haven't had a reason to do so yet."

"I've been fortunate that the Catholic church changed at the right time," said Janet. Changes over the years made it easier for her and her Congregational minister husband to participate in Catholic rituals.

"When the kids were confirmed, the priest was nice enough to invite Bill to stand on the altar and take part in the laying on of hands. I know Bill appreciated it and I thought it was great. It certainly looked good to my mother, I know that!" said Janet, laughing. "The Catholic church has come a long way in some respects.

"Over the years I have found that the Catholics have really relied on their ignorance," she said. "They kind of blindly bumble their way through. Protestants know more about their traditions, but are able to change less. It's a different system. Protestants have to make the changes themselves where the Roman Catholics, all they have to do is say, well, we're going to change this and that's the way it is.

"In either tradition members look at the church as the one unchanging dependable thing they can turn to against all the crap that can come their way. For anybody that is religious, they don't want it to change or be subject to change like everything else is."

Janet said her husband's congregations always knew she was a Roman Catholic who attended mass regularly and took her children with her.

"I've gone to both churches for twenty years!" Janet said. "Once in a while I take a Sunday off from my husband's service." Janet didn't feel it was pressure from either the congregation or her husband that sent her to both churches for both services. "I did it for Bill. I felt I would like to support him and his job just the way a lot of other wives do. That's one way I could do it.

"I'm afraid the word traditional no longer really applies to a minister's wife," continues Janet. "I really don't think she is expected to teach Sunday school, sing in the choir, or do anything else except to support her husband as a wife." Janet realizes that other ministers' wives don't share that view. "Perhaps being Catholic has helped me in this respect as the churches we've been involved with have not so much expected me to do things as much as appreciated whatever I did." Janet turned her handicraft skills to good use, starting and operating, out of the parsonage, a crocheted doll house accessory business.

"I usually work on church fairs," said Janet about her involvement in her husband's church. "I also help with suppers."

Janet is unaware of any negative reaction from her husband's congregation about being a practicing Catholic.

"Let me put it this way. If they have, they never bothered me with it," she said after a pause. "If they bothered Bill, he hasn't mentioned it. Oh, I'm sure some of them may have at one point or another but I wouldn't know. I thought it was a plus. Because I was Catholic, they didn't expect much of me. Also, people don't try to treat me like their confessor. They do that more with the church secretary. Bill has a secretary and I'm not it.

"Actually, I know more people in his church than I do in my own. Bill's church has the coffee hours, and its smaller, four to five hundred members. It's been harder to make friends in this particular church because there isn't any woman's group or a lot of things to belong to. I go to whatever I can with Bill."

Bill and Janet discussed the future of their interfaith marriage before they took their vows. If they ever had an argument over her membership in the Catholic church, Janet doesn't remember it.

"Yes, if you plan to have kids at all you have to discuss it. We got that all settled before we got married. We respect each other on our different faiths."

It appeared that Janet had a handle on her dual religion marriage. She seemed confident, secure, and comfortable talking about her marriage, her religion and her husband's career. But like many wives we interviewed, there was an addendum.

"There aren't going to be any real names are there? In the book?" she asked. On her survey, she circled the option of anonymity and we planned to honor that.

"I think it makes it easier," she explained. "I don't want people—let me put it this way—I don't go out of my way to make trouble for my husband. Not that I'm trying to make a name for myself or anything, or that anything I said—I just wouldn't want it to have to come back on Bill and make any difficulty." Janet admitted that nothing she said was particularly controversial. But like many ministers' wives, she's learned that it's the unexpected that can cause problems. And, like Alice, the particulars about why she is compelled to request anonymity remain a secret known only to her.

Mary Joe Dwyer Miller, another minister's wife, also maintains her membership in the Roman Catholic church while her husband, Jim preaches in a two hundred-member United Methodist church.

While working at the American Medical Association Library in Chicago, a co-worker asked Mary Joe if she ever dated Protestants.

"Then she asked if I'd be willing to meet a brilliant New Testament scholar," said Mary Joe. "Then, she gave a party." Their go-between had been Jim Miller's student when he taught at Oberlin College.

Mary Joe had attended parochial schools and obtained a library science degree from a Catholic college. She was the first woman Lector in her Chicago church and had served four

How Methodist Do I Have to Be?

years as the Cantor when her parish instituted that part of the mass. Mary Joe also had served the Eucharist for communion.

In the early 1960s, she had answered Pope John XXIII's call for Papal volunteers to serve in Latin America. The Papal Volunteers were formed six months before the founding of the Peace Corps. She had worked for three years in guerilla territory in Guatemala. Because of her Roman Catholic upbringing and adult involvement in her church, she had no firsthand knowledge of the role of the minister's wife.

"I grew up with nuns in the convent and priests in the rectory," she explained. Even with generations of Catholic ancestors behind her, Mary Joe's family had no problem with her marriage to a Protestant.

"My aunt is a Methodist married to my uncle who's still a Catholic. My mother's first cousin married a Jewish man. Two of my cousins are Jewish.

"In fact in the 1930s when my mother's cousin married, her mother was not happy and invited the old Monsignor from the parish to dinner to meet this fellow. And before the Monsignor came through the door, she stopped him and said: 'Monsignor, my daughter wants to marry a Jew,' and he turned and said: 'My dear Lady,' he said with the brogue, 'y'know,' here Mary Joe lapsed into a creditable Irish accent, 'Our Lord Jesus Christ was a Jew.' And that was all he said! You find out the end of the world doesn't happen. Ecumenism is alive and well in my family and has been for a long time!

"Twenty-five year ago, before Vatican II, my marriage with a minister would have been impossible," said Mary Joe. "When Jim decided to leave academia and return to preaching, I left my pension plan behind and spent all our savings on the move from Chicago to a town of six hundred in south Texas. Jim had to start over at below the minimum salary. Life has been an adventure since then." After teaching for twenty years, Jim went back to parish ministry serving a two-point charge in Victoria County, Texas.

"We had two country churches, two little white frame churches. One had about fifty members and the other had a regular attendance of sixteen or seventeen," said Mary Joe. "It was wonderful. I had the best time because we had to be everything for everybody. That's a sense of service."

Mary Joe kept up her membership in the Roman Catholic while her husband preached at the two little white frame churches, and joined St. Benedict's when he transferred to the First United Methodist Church in San Benito. She does not serve regularly as Lector or Cantor because St. Benedict's already had enough volunteers.

"If they need me, yes, I do it. But I didn't push my way in." At First United Methodist, Mary Joe teaches Sunday school and sings in the choir.

"I just like church, which is nice," she said. "I cannot live without my Mass so if I miss it Friday night, I'll go to Saturday Mass."

Mary Joe, like Janet, has never had a problem with members of her husband's congregation over her membership at St. Benedict's.

"They know that if there's a conflict, like Holy Thursday, I'll be at Mass," she said. "If I can get back to Jim's church for the end of the service, I try. Good Friday is no problem because the services are at different times. His is at noon and mine is in the evening. He goes to the Easter Vigil service with me because it's such a beautiful service and then we go to the Sunday morning service at his church. It's like the Catholic church arranged it all just for me. The Holy Spirit worked out all these times so I could do both.

"I really had no qualms at all," said Mary Joe about the expected reaction from her husband's churches. "My philosophy—it's always worked for me—is you go and love the people and they love you back. I was in guerilla territory in Guatemala. I lived through many bombings. What problems can you have

How Methodist Do I Have to Be?

after that? You just go and love the people and you pitch in to the best of your ability and you be happy where you are.

"We were sent to this little place and the people before us, the woman was desperately unhappy. The people who preceded us by several ministers had not been happy. And I was just happy as a clam. Expect you're hoping to love the people and they'll love you back." Mary Joe stopped for a breath and some time to think. Talking to her is like being tumbled by a wave at the beach. her infectious good humor washes over you leaving you breathless and amazed at her good will and energy. Mary Joe is the only medical librarian working in the Rio Grande Valley. She visits nine hospitals and a clinic between the towns of McAllen and Brownsville and seems to be constantly on the road. She is still considering her effect on her husband's congregation.

"I might have been responsible for one or two members who left . . ." She stopped. In the background was the low rumble of her husband's voice. Mary Joe laughed, then continued:

"No. Jim says No, I wasn't responsible for them leaving the church to go to the Fundy." Fundy is Mary Joe's slang for Fundamentalist churches. "They would have joined the Fundy church anyway!"

Did Mary Joe and Jim ever have disagreements over their different faiths?

"Do you mean doctrinally? Well, there's always the question of the Eucharist. Is Jesus really present during communion? The veneration of Mary is another area. But these are things we can argue for the next two thousand years. The discussions are intellectual, friendly—never an argument.

"It's never been a problem with Jim that I attend Mass," she said. "Jim never asked me not to go to Mass."

"I'm an oddity. I love it. I get to witness the positive joy of ecumenism. I contribute to the ecumenical spirit between Roman Catholics and Methodists." First, United Methodist draws students for their Vacation Bible School every summer from every denomination in the area, including Catholics, because Mary Jo teaches it.

"Jim and his church are organizing a food bank with many of the churches in the area: Catholic, Lutheran, Presbyterian, Christian Brethren," said Mary Joe. "I'm the representative to the food bank from St. Benedict's.

"I work a seven-day week sometimes, but I'm never bored. Seen by others, I suppose I should complain that I'm tired, underpaid and living in a remote, backward part of the country. But, I love it!"

We didn't overlook the possibility of a Jewish woman married to a Protestant minister—we just couldn't locate one to interview. But the three women who told us their stories represent three distinct choices available to the interfaith ministerial marriage. And none of the choices are wrong.

Alice chose, for her own reasons and experience, to convert to her husband's church, although in her heart she never felt she gave up any of her Catholicism. Her secrets remain her own. If she compromised for the sake of her husband and family, it appears to have worked. They all continue to flourish.

Janet chose her church. Denials aside, Janet must also have taken some blows in the past as the wife of a minister. Like Alice, she is cautious about members of her husband's congregation finding out too much. She fears unexpected consequences probably because the unexpected has trampled on her before. In what context, only Janet knows and again, like Alice, she isn't telling. But for Janet, another layer of mystery is added. "I don't go out of my way to cause problems for my husband," she said. Only Janet knows what walking that tightrope costs her.

Mary Jo chose outward and highly visible ecumenism when she chose her own church. Mary Joe and Janet attend both their Masses and Sunday services with their husbands' congregations. But Mary Jo actively promotes her Catholicism, a choice her husband fosters with his own ecumenical spirit. Although she was ready to take the blame for the loss of two Methodist members to Fundamentalist churches, Mary Joe simply has no secrets. Her choice was not made from the pain, parochial attitude, or pure insensitivity of her husband's congregations or society. Scratch her surface and dig within, neither does she walk a tightrope constantly on the watch for any retribution for her actions or statements.

Ministers' wives choose their husbands, their denomination and how much, or how little, they'll do in the church of their choice. For many, more than half, the next decision is leaving the relatively smaller world of the parsonage and parish and moving out into the community. More often than not, ministers' wives expand their horizons while increasing the family income by going, or going back, to work.

9

Going (or Going Back) to Work

"The nurse in me, which was there before I became a pastor's wife, wanted out and I was encouraged by several things to be true to myself." Jessica is married to an Evangelical Lutheran Church of America minister and lives in the Pacific northwest. Jessica wrote that she was the traditional type of minister's wife for about eight years into her husband's career when her individuality took over.

"The children were growing up," she said. The couple's three children are now in their twenties. "I wanted to get out of the home (away from the phones!) and work with professional people again. We wanted to build a cabin, to have something of our own. I read an article at the time—August 1970—in the *Seattle Times* about the interesting jobs pastors' wives were doing, came home from vacation and read an ad for part-time nursing in a local hospital and my friend offered to babysit our four-year-old. It all fell together in one month. But it was hard to go back to nursing after nine year's absence. Many changes had occurred. It was scary but exciting to be valued for what I was rather than for who I was married to. I was responsible now for my own reputation as a nurse." Jessica and her family lived in three parsonages but thanks to her return to nursing and a housing allowance from the church, they built their own home.

Seventy-six percent of our respondents work. According to the *Statistical Abstract of the United States* (1989, 109th edition), fifty-six percent of all women over the age of sixteen in the United States are active workers in the labor force. Employment among ministers' wives is one third greater than the national average. Even the statistics for wives participating in the labor force is only 56.7 percent of all women who work. Since all of our respondents are married and their husbands are present in the home, there are still one third more of them employed when compared with the number of employed married women in the United States.

Since we know that most ministers are underpaid for their level of education, experience, and extent of duties, we could assume that the number one reason so many more ministers' wives work than other wives is solely to augment the household budget. If we did assume that, we'd be wrong. Only eight percent of our respondents stated that they went back to work solely out of financial necessity. Twenty-four percent said they went back to work for *both* professional and monetary reasons.

So why do they go to work? Finances obviously play a part in the decision. In the Maces' book, *What's Happening to Clergy Marriages,* the ministers' wives surveyed listed as the number four disadvantage to life in the ministry "financial stress—wife must seek job." Ten percent of the ministers in the Clergy Compensation survey of the Ministers and Missionaries Benefit Board of the American Baptist Churches said the first thing they'd do to ease financial tensions was to ask their wives to go to work.

According to a compensation survey done for *Leadership* magazine almost a decade ago, ministerial couples may

Going (or Going Back) to Work

feel compelled to join the ranks of dual career couples to increase their lifestyle to a level they perceive as compatible with their leadership role within the congregation. The article poses the question that perhaps embarrassment over inability to reciprocate social events leads many ministers' wives to work. Certainly that question is answered by the wife whose husband joined a health club at the insistence of a member of his congregation when the minister obviously couldn't afford it (Chapter Six). Conditions spoken of in this survey have worsened.

Which brings us to a note about what the survey statistics don't show. As we saw in Chapter Six, many ministers and their wives accept low pay as a given part of the ministry. Time after time the response to questions about low pay is: The Lord will provide. Since ministers are service oriented, eager to please, and need to show a faith in all matters that is greater than their congregation's, we suspect that their answers to salary surveys are clouded by their passive acceptance of low pay situations. In their eagerness to serve, they overlook, ignore, even deny, financial abuses. In the more recent Baptist survey, 51.9 percent of the pastors surveyed said their personal financial situation adversely affected their ministry. Almost twenty-three percent of those said they approached the problem with passive acceptance. In the *Leadership* survey, the pastors' first response to the problem of inadequate pay was passive acceptance: "I knew what I was getting into; somehow we'll make it on what we receive." Not even our survey asked the wives how their families would cope financially without their jobs. Therefore, we believe that the percentage of wives who worked for financial reasons may be higher than these survey figures.

Sixty-eight percent of the wives who responded to our survey work at careers they either trained for or worked in before they married. It is in this figure that the number of wives who must work for financial reasons overlaps those who also want to work. Luckily for them, they work in their career of choice, enjoy it and don't consider their jobs as only money producing. Many, like Jessica, go back to work to find their own sense of self. Others work to avoid the unrealistic expectations of the congregation or to escape hurts and slights from church members. And many work because it is a source of friends who see them as people rather than as ministers' wives.

Seventy percent of the wives work full time and fifteen percent operate their own businesses out of their homes. Their choices of careers is almost as diverse as their own personalities: business manager for a newspaper, psychiatric social worker, proofreader, copy editor, dietician, column writer, two romance novelists, mainstream women's novelist, children's book writer, opera singer, church organization consultant, miniature crochet furnishings supply, painter, piano teacher, private art lessons, medical librarian, administrative assistant, director of a retirement home, house cleaning, child care, advertising executive, and more. The careers most frequently mentioned were nursing, teaching, and secretarial.

Traditionally, it was in teaching and nursing that a minister's wife could work, if she had to, with the blessings of her husband's congregation. Two respondents, both in their middle fifties, mentioned that "in their day" the congregation didn't look kindly upon a minister's wife who worked. How do congregants look at it today? In the Baptist survey, 72.3 percent of church members stated they don't think their pastor's spouse should have to work outside the home. Luckily for both sides, fifty-eight percent of the wives believe they work because they want to rather than because they have to.

"The era I grew up in didn't approve of mothers working outside the home," wrote Karen who is married to a United Methodist minister working in Austin, Texas. "Especially if she was a minister's wife! Unless, of course, she was a teacher. I was not." Karen is fifty-nine.

Jean Parker has been married to her Episcopal minister husband for thirty-five years. They live in Seattle.

"In our current parish situation, I am the first spouse in

Going (or Going Back) to Work

twenty-six plus years, as the previous priest was a bachelor," wrote Jean. "I'm a kind of 'pet' in some non-negative ways. It was hard for them (the congregation) to understand that I had a good, well-paying job. I don't think many have any concept about what I do. The previous clergy wives did not work outside the home (from 1856–1959) and there are still lots of people around who remember."

Today most wives work from necessity and are developing careers for themselves to make work palatable. Because so many wives work, working ministers' wives also receive acceptance from their husbands' congregations. But not all of them do, and some are criticized for the kind of work they do. Michelle is forty-four, married twenty-four years to a Church of Christ minister in the deep South.

"I have no career as such," said Michelle. "But by being a preacher's wife, I feel I have to be more careful about the type of job I get." Michelle's current job would give her identity away but it does involve cleaning services and might be considered menial work by many. It's not menial to Michelle—she's proud of the work she does.

"It's an honorable job," explained Michelle who's kept it for over five years. "But some feel it's a lowly profession. There were some remarks by parishioners made that my job is beneath the dignity of a minister's wife." Michelle works so that her two children can attend a private Christian school to augment the Christian upbringing so important to her and her husband.

"My husband isn't the type of minister to say he won't come unless they pay him a certain amount," said Michelle. "He's probably the lowest paid minister in this area. I feel some resentment for that. The congregation expects me to dress like a peacock on a parakeet's salary. They want me available to help the minister—go on calls—be a presence. However, working ministers' wives are more acceptable now than twenty-three years ago."

Beth has had the opposite experience.

"We are in an 'upscale' executive suburb," said Beth who works in marketing and research and travels extensively. She and her United Methodist minister husband live in an affluent area of Connecticut. "My career is one that is in keeping with many of our (male) members' careers. They seem to relate at that level and even offered congratulations on my recent promotion."

In 1974, the United Presbyterian Church, U.S.A. developed a bill of rights for ministers' spouses. Number one on that list was: An equal right to seek employment of his or her choice. The other three items listed the freedom to choose church membership, freedom to serve the church without obligation or privileges, and the freedom to be considered for election to boards and committees. The Presbyterian Panel survey, *The Role of the Spouse in the Local Congregation,* never addressed the first item on their own bill of rights. The closest it came was the finding that most members were ambivalent about whether the pastor's spouse "should develop a life based on his or her personal goals and talents even if this precludes participation in the church."

At first glance, this indicates that members don't care if their minister's wife works. But the question was never directly asked. The same study showed that a majority of members want their minister's wife to attend church regularly, to know what's happening in members' lives, and to be a model of Christian deportment in every aspect of her life. The minister's wife who works is less available to members of the congregation as a role model and working also limits her contact with and knowledge of individual members, so it seems more likely that those members would not want their minister's wife to work.

If nursing and teaching are acceptable professions for ministers' wives, are there unacceptable professions? We've already seen that some members think Michelle is performing work beneath her dignity. Have any other wives felt the sting of an unacceptable profession?

One minister's wife whom we interviewed in depth said, "I'm a published fiction writer—contemporary romance, romantic suspense, mainstream." Carla Neggers, whose twenty-seven books have sold well over three million copies, continues, "I have an office in the parsonage and work long but irregular hours.

"Joe and I like to keep our careers separate. What difference does it make what he does? Or vice versa, what I do?" Carla said she never received a negative reaction from any of her husband's congregations because of her sensuous, romantic novels.

"What's amusing is that the surface stuff has caused the most trouble," said Carla. "I never changed my name when I married and this had caused me the most grief." Carla kept her maiden name, Anne Harrell, as her pen name for her mainstream novels.

"My attitude? Damned if you do, damned if you don't—but most people really don't care.

"When my own career took off," said Carla, "it was much easier to tolerate the slings and arrows of being in a clergy family and even to relish the joys just because I had some financial independence (which also gave us as a family more financial independence from the church and more money, generally). Also, I've learned not to ask or in any way try to find out what the 'gossip' about me within the church is—there's always someone willing to tell you, but what good does it accomplish? If there's a serious problem they can take it up with my husband—that's my philosophy. So far no one has!

"In 1981 I wrote my first romance. To my delight, I discovered I adore creating warm, sensuous stories about two people falling in love. I sold that first romance in the fall and haven't stopped writing since." Carla's only negative reactions to being both a women's fiction novelist and a minister's wife come from people outside the church. Reporters and talk show hosts interviewing her on book promotion tours are the ones most apt to try to capitalize on her husband's profession.

"I try not to tell them, generally speaking," said Carla. "Because then *HE* becomes the story. People interview a woman and they always ask: What does your husband do? Does anybody know what John Updike's wife does? No! And nobody cares. The subject of what Joe does comes up. I used to sit there and think, bullshit. Now I'm much more matter of fact about it. I say he's a pastor at the such-and-such United Methodist church.

"It's funny how people who interview you react. You've done all this interesting interview stuff and then they get down to the end of the interview, to the personal statistics, and they ask how many kids do you have and what does your husband do. When I tell them he's a pastor, some of them say okay and then go away. Others go 'Oh wait! Maybe I should change the angle of my story!'

"Interestingly, if a reporter starts out knowing I'm a minister's wife, that's all we talk about. It's something I try to avoid because people have stereotypes of what ministers' wives are. Most people don't go to church anymore so they think ministers' wives are all weird. Ministers' wives' are normal. People are people." Does Carla ever refuse to tell a reporter what her husband does?

"I've done that but they usually figured out I've got something to hide so I don't do that anymore," she said. "I have found the best way to act is just to be very matter of fact about it." One headline about Carla read: "Minister's Wife Writes Racy Novels."

"That was the one that really taught me the lesson," said Carla. "That reporter came with her angle. She knew I was married to a minister. She had her story written before she got

Going (or Going Back) to Work

there. The angle of the piece was who I'm married to and what I write, and how they seem to be at odds with each other."

Reactions from her husband's congregations never were from what she wrote but from the fact that she works at home. In their present church, the phone number for the parsonage is the same for the church. Since the church office is still in the parsonage, phone calls are a problem.

"I'm faced with a triple stereotype," said Carla. "One is the stereotype of being a minister's wife, one is the stereotype of writing romantic fiction and the other is the fact that most people in general don't view writing as work." Phone calls interrupt her erratic, but long, working hours and some parishioners are still upset that she won't take phone messages.

"I had a woman hang up," said Carla. "I couldn't answer her question. I didn't know what she was talking about! I told her I'd have Joe call her back. I was very diplomatic. She said 'Oh, for God's sake' and hung up. I answer the phone, but I'm not the church secretary. I'll take down a name and number. I don't take messages.

"Everybody deals with stereotypes," said Carla. "I don't sit around feeling sorry for myself because I have a couple of stereotypes. I don't see myself as a minister's wife. I'm a writer."

Carla's career, with the advantage of being able to work anywhere there's a desk and a word processor, is highly mobile. When Joe changes pulpits it's relatively easy for her to move her job with his. This isn't always true. With the increase in dual-career ministerial marriages, some ministers move less because their wives have careers that won't move, some wives are left without jobs when their husbands move, and some wives simply stay where they are, adding to the growing number of commuter marriages.

"When my husband moved to Washington, D.C. and his current congregation, I was not ready to leave my job in New York," said Shirley Skirvin. Shirley's husband works in the

Church of the Pilgrims, a Presbyterian congregation. "So I commuted back and forth for a year, staying in New York three days a week and living in Washington four days a week. Close friends in the congregation confided that they only began to relax completely about our marriage relationship when I took a job in this area." Shirley is the Director of Office Administration for Thomas House, a retirement community in downtown Washington.

"I supervise ten people, track all the personnel matters for one hundred fifty employees, handle all the interoffice communication, and edit the monthly in-house newsletter and a marketing newsletter. Having my own work and feeling 'at home' in a milieu that is not the church is extremely important to my psychic well being." Shirley's husband decided to enter the ministry after they were married. Originally trained as a chemist, he really wanted to serve a congregation. Shirley supported his decision but the career switch was not without its price.

"Ministry is a twenty-four hour a day task in many ways," she said. "A minister is always 'on call' and that carries over into his home life, and thus my life. There is seldom an evening that goes by but what I am answering the phone and finding myself in the role of listener, counselor, empathizer. There is a real way in which one must always be 'up' so that the person on the other end of the line feels cared for and taken seriously. That availability and vulnerability are not part of most other wife roles. A person like myself who wants and needs a certain amount of privacy and quiet time can find it extremely difficult to attain.

"*Self* consciousness came with some very hard work on myself and our marriage about the years ago," said Shirley. "I would never return to feeling that life was complete as long as I was only the supportive appendage of someone else. People have undoubtedly been puzzled about my independent style from time to time but they have been careful not to say anything to either Sidney or me.

"I think every minister's wife should be true to herself. If that means she has no particular interest in the church, and she and her husband can negotiate that as part of their marriage contract, so be it. Conversely, the wife who has church interests should have as much freedom as other lay leaders."

There are other professions that require husbands to move frequently. Career military officers, diplomats, and national or multinational corporate executives uproot their families periodically because of their jobs. Their wives, too, must find new work. The difference between those professions and the ministry is money. The diplomat, executive, and military officer earn enough so their wives choose to work rather than need to work.

For Lorraine, the decision to work involved both money and personal fulfillment. The cause of her commuter marriage, in her opinion, rests squarely with the hierarchy in the United Methodist church.

"The thing that had saddened me the most about being a minister's wife is learning about the un-Christian, unfair, and very political nature of the appointment process in the Methodist church," said Lorraine. "As a Methodist layperson . . . I was not aware of the politics at work, both at the local church level and at the cabinet level, which can cause so much pain, ruin careers, devastate families, erode one's faith, and make one very distrustful of 'religious people' who wield power in the church. Ken and I have been victimized by church politics and we have seen other couples devastated by them. One expects a certain amount of 'dirty dealings' in the corporate world, but it is very disillusioning to encounter them in a Christian institution." Lorraine cited two examples. The first occurred in a previous church in a rural town of three thousand people.

"We were there for three years. I taught two of those years, but I quit at the end of the second one because I was having severe conflicts with my principal, whose entire family were members of the church my husband was serving. I quit at the point that my principal's wife threatened my husband with withdrawing all their church participation if I did not 'get off her husband's back.' Lorraine was out of teaching for a year.

"That is why I jumped at the opportunity to apply for my current job at the Texas Educational Agency," she said. The agency is the state's department of education. "Had my husband not been very supportive of my accepting this job, which is about the most prestigious job for someone in theatre education in the state, then being a minister's wife would have severely hampered my career at this juncture. Of course, we have had to sacrifice our being able to live in the same town, because the Bishop and the cabinet members did not appoint Ken to an Austin church even though they had the information that I was in the top two being considered for my position at the time they appointed him to the church of Rockport."

Rockport is one hundred ninety-five miles from Austin. Lorraine and Ken travel back and forth between the two towns, but Lorraine points out that she is in Rockport on weekends when Ken is working. Ken can sometimes be in Austin on weekdays but then she is at work.

"I hate having my life manipulated by, dictated to, and in the control of a bishop and a cabinet who can wreak havoc in my life at their collective whimsy. When I first experienced the appointive process, I told my husband that I felt that we were being treated like pieces on a chess board. I've revised that statement since then. We are treated more like checkers on the board and our unique talents and skills have nothing to do with whether we get crowned or not.

"Ken and I both grew up in military families, but except in wartime, the military system was never as cruel to our families as the Methodist church has been. I think that one of the reasons for this is that the military is made up of people who

Going (or Going Back) to Work

are willing to fight when necessary, and ministers are, generally, nonbelligerent and far too prone to accept the bad things that are done to them as 'God's will' for their lives, or, to expect that some good will come of it in the long run.

"The first time Ken and I bowed our backs and did not accept the cabinet's appointment resulted in a very hard two years for us. The second time we took control of our destinies was when I accepted this job in Austin, and then pleaded for an Austin appointment for Ken. This time has not been as demoralizing and disastrous as the first time, but we have had to sacrifice living together for what will be at least two years and could be longer." The appointment to Rockport meant splitting up their belongings, their pets, and losing Ken's mother. She had lived with her son and daughter-in-law but when the commuter marriage began, Ken's mother moved closer to another son. Lorraine still misses her deeply eighteen months later.

"Because we've been very up-front with our congregation about my work from our first meeting with the leadership of the churches Ken has served, I have not been pressured into assuming the traditional role, nor have I been aware of any particular criticism from church members," said Lorraine. "The congregation in Rockport has been wonderful. At our first meeting with the church leadership there, we told them that I was one of the top two candidates for my job at the Agency. I think the congregation, generally, accepts the conditions that our commuter marriage imposes on Ken; they are sympathetic about our situation, but they want to keep Ken in Rockport, so they are tolerant of his absences. Ken works overtime when in Rockport, to make sure that their needs are taken care of. Generally, I accept Ken's priorities when it comes to the church, but that's been harder to accept in our current situation when it means we may have to go a second week without seeing each other because of church demands.

"Our money is very tight now, because of the amount

of travel we have to do, the doubled expenses of utilities, phone bills, food bills, etc." said Lorraine. "We are buying a house here in Austin, but because Ken is in a parsonage, we have no housing allowance to help with that. Ken's salary package, including the parsonage and utilities, travel allowance, continuing education, etc. is still under $40,000. My salary pulls our joint income to just over $70,000. That sounds like a lot of money, but it doesn't go as far as it should, and it certainly is paltry pay for two people who have six degrees between them and who are expected to dress professionally and to fit in as social peers with the wealthiest members of the congregation. We are fortunate that both of us are working.

"My attitude when we married was that I had taught twenty-two years already, and that no one could take my teaching career away from me, so it was my intention to put Ken's vocation ahead of mine. It might have worked had I not needed to be our main support for those years in San Angelo, but I'm not sure about that. I loved teaching and I love the sense of accomplishment I have in my current job. I especially like working with the caliber of professionals that are my colleagues. I'm not sure there has ever been a time when I would have cheerfully quit working for the rest of my life."

Can being married to a minister hamper a spouse's career? Alice, whom we met in Chapter Seven, said yes.

"I was once told by a good friend that her principal would never hire me because of Dan's being a minister," she said. "With the emphasis on the separation of church and state, I am cautious of my position and rarely make reference to the fact I am a minister's wife. In the early colonial days, a minister's wife may have been given prime consideration for the training of children in the area of education. It is a sad reflection on our present society that a person of this background may be a risk." Alice teaches in a neighboring town and was never asked what her husband did for a living. "I have had no negative reac-

Going (or Going Back) to Work

tion in my career thus far but I do not readily expose myself either."

Karen Meyer Campbell, age thirty-two, married to a Lutheran minister, gave up a full-time job in a law office when her husband transferred to Redding, California.

"In Redding, there are few decent jobs, so I don't work because I can't find work." Several of the wives we questioned mentioned the lack of good jobs at new, sometimes remote, locations where their husbands transferred. One wife noted that her frequent moves have hurt her professionally. She also said that she "mourned" the loss of professional contacts and identity outside the church. For another wife, the distance she travelled to work convinced her to change careers.

"My career was severely hampered by our effort to live a simpler lifestyle and not feather our nest at the expense of the church," wrote Clare Smith of Charlottesville, Virginia. Clare's husband works in the Presbyterian denomination. "My first college teaching position in our current location required one hundred miles round trip on the days I taught. Doing two full-time jobs is okay for superwomen, but I am not one. When my children were out of college I quit to write children's fiction. Great fun."

Marianne Bahmann wrote that she wanted to be an opera singer. She met her husband on shipboard.

"I was on my way to a Fulbright year in Germany. He was returning from an exchange year in the United States. We sat next to each other at the table and fell in love. I am a preacher's kid and knew what was in store. I felt terrible." Marianne likes her life, she hastens to add, but when asked what she would do differently if she knew then what she knows now, she said:

"I would have realized I could pursue my career without endangering his ministry. I would have lobbied harder for living in certain areas where I could more easily perform."

Moving isn't the only disadvantage to the spouse's career in a ministerial marriage. Even professions that can be performed at home have pitfalls. Doris is a "visual artist who paints, does print making and teaches."

"I found myself until recently assuming an unequal portion of home responsibility because of my husband's intense involvement in his work that left me with little time to produce my own work. I find that the compensation to the minister for the hours he or she puts in does not provide for any solution to this dilemma."

Some wives found that being married to a minister helped their careers. Several noted that living in the parsonage took the pressure off them financially and they were free to go back to school, manage home-based business, or work at artistic careers that have long apprenticeship periods such as printing and writing. An essayist told us that being a minister's wife gave her a place to publish what she writes—a religious newspaper—and the confidence to submit her work to non-religious publications. One wife thought that networking among members of her husband's congregation helped her find interesting jobs. She noted that it probably opened as many doors as it closed. A wife who puts her piano training to use for a parttime income wrote:

"I feel it helped. Most folk appreciate having their children take lessons at the parsonage or at school from the 'preacher's wife'."

"I worked eight years in a skilled nursing home as a social worker," wrote Donna. "At times, when I felt it was appropriate to mention that I am a minister's wife to patients or families, it helped me gain immediate trust and rapport. In certain situations I could tell someone I'd be praying for them, or reveal my faith."

Glenda Menger echoes Dolores' view of the advantage of letting co-workers know she is married to a minister. Glenda is thirty-nine years old and works as a certified medical assistant in an internal medicine practice.

"It has provided a bond between my boss and myself because he is a deacon in our church. We share many of our feelings with our patients. Many people come in our office that are in great spiritual need and we share our faith with them. People feel they can confide in me and they know they have a friend."

How do colleagues react when these women reveal that they are married to ministers? Many respondents mentioned that co-workers "clean up their act."

"My co-workers respect our call of service to the Lord," wrote Andrea. "If there had been any unclean jokes being told they stop whenever I come in the room. They know that I do not condemn them even if I do not approve of their lifestyle."

"Co-workers like to tell dirty jokes to see if I will laugh," said Sheryl Doerzbacher. "Or, they try to go out of their way to be goody-goody."

Carol Faus, another minister's wife, wrote that her co-workers "usually refrain from cussing and explain the presence of beer in the 'fridge."

Mary, married to a United Church of Christ minister, wrote:

"I know well the response to the realization that I'm the minister's wife. Actually two responses: nonchurch people are confused and usually back off, apologize for saying 'shit' and generally reorganize their opinions of me and my work. 'Church' people will cozy up sometimes, want to know me better, expect always that I would not say 'shit' and expect that I would be good and upright. I hate both of these pretty much predictable responses and I often rebel and act contrary to the expectations. This is complicated—my need to be seen as 'good' is an issue."

Muriel also noted stereotypical treatment.

"It had a profound effect on relationships with my colleagues," she said about being a minister's wife. "When I entered the teachers' room, certain subjects became taboo, or someone would swear, look at me and say, 'Oh, pardon me.' There were people who were in awe or became stilted when talking with me. It was all most unpleasant for me!"

Donna worked at being herself.

"My co-workers saw me as a friend and co-worker and were just themselves as I was," she said. "Occasionally a few would say "Sorry Dee, but . . ." when they realized they were being less than charitable towards someone or they used a little bad language. If I had felt they really did not feel free to be themselves with me it would have bothered me."

It certainly bothered Diana Kemp of Edmonton, Alberta, Canada. Diana is thirty-five and married to a Presbyterian minister who works in a suburban church with one hundred members.

"My co-workers, upon learning my role, seem to withdraw and seem afraid to carry on a conversation with me," she said. "Christian co-workers seem to draw closer. If I am lucky to be working at a job long enough for people to get to know me before they find out I'm a minister's wife, there doesn't seem to be quite as much stress when they do find out.

"Overall, I feel it's too bad that people have to put labels on people then treat them accordingly. I have the best relationships with people when they meet me for me and get to know me. Then when they find out I'm a minister's wife, they don't treat me any differently, regardless whether they are Christian or not or attend church or not. That is what I really desire in a friendship."

Why do ministers' wives work? For the money, certainly. But also for their own senses of service, their searches for self and their searches for friends. Even with the "goody-goody" reaction of some colleagues, work may provide the only opportunity for the minister's wife to find real friends. Even a congregation full of like-minded Christians who greet her with

Going (or Going Back) to Work

open arms, may be so full of unrealistic expectations that, for her needs, it is actually a lonely, deserted place. Since loneliness can be at its worst when we are surrounded by people, the minister's wife may find herself in the middle of a congregation yet completely alone.

§10

Who Ministers to the Ministers' Wives?

"I have very few friends," wrote Betty. "My husband's career has taught me not to trust people. I know I would never marry a minister again. It's too lonely." Betty is one of only three women who wrote to us without adding her name, address, or phone number. Amazingly, even her postmark was smudged so that even if we wanted to, we couldn't trace her through our files.

"I think that the wife finds it extremely difficult to form close relationships within the church body because she has that image in her mind that she's the minister's wife and somehow she is separated from the rest," said Reverend Norman Levison. Levison is Associate Coordinator of Pastoral Services, as well as a counselor for the general public, at The Institute of Living in Hartford, Connecticut. Together with a social worker, he leads a therapy group that counsels only clergy or people in the ministry.

"It's an extremely difficult position (the minister's wife) to be in today. I think it always has been, but I think the role was more defined in the 1940s and 50s than it is now. There are still certain expectations but I think they come all the way back from their (ministers' wives) own childhood when they were in church. Also from the congregation. As much as they try to break that stereotype they have a very difficult time in doing it.

"I think the wives you've interviewed used the word friends not in a deep sense that I am talking about—that I can share my most intimate thoughts. I don't think the wives can do that." Friendships were one area in which we assumed ministers' wives had no problem. Almost fifty-two percent noted, as an advantage to being in the ministry in fact, that, upon moving to a new pulpit, they had a ready-made, accepting circle of friends and surrogate family to greet them. This acceptance factor was the single most noted advantage to being in the ministry. Yet Marshall Shelley's book, *The Healthy Hectic Home,* showed that seventy-six percent of the wives he polled experienced loneliness in the midst of the very congregations that greeted them so warmly.

Our survey results show that twenty-nine percent of ministers' wives make most of their friends within congregations. Twenty-one percent stated their friends were outside the congregation. Almost half—forty-two percent—said their circle of friends included both. Many wives noted, however, that it is difficult for them to make friends because of their status as the minister's wife. Why?

Sometimes members of the congregation try to be friendly, but others are uninformed or backhanded. In the Presbyterian Panel study, seventy-seven percent of members who responded thought their minister's wife was treated differently some of the time (thirty-nine percent), most of the time (thirty-three percent), or all of the time (five percent). Three-quarters of the congregation believe that their minister's wife is special and deserves special treatment! The ways and the reasons they are treated differently, however, cause serious relationship problems for these women. Because she is viewed as the resident "holy woman" by the congregation, she accrues a power she neither wants nor knows how to handle. Sometimes it is only the members' need to be close to this presumed power that draws congregants to her side.

Julie, married to a Presbyterian U.S.A. minister working in Michigan, resented being dragged into conversations. She sensed there was no sincerity on the parishioners' parts to get the wife involved in the discussion. "They're just fortifying their 'position' with the minister," she said.

"I have friends both within and outside the congregation," wrote Doris, the artist quoted previously. Doris' husband accepted a call to a church in Washington, D.C. two years ago and she is only now adjusting to the move. "In this present setting most of my friends are outside the church. I find this best. I am never sure of the integrity of a friendship with parishioners." Another woman noted that she felt congregants wanted to be her friend just so they could "share their problems more easily" with her husband.

Some parishioners seem nosey, wanting to know more about her husband's personal life than wanting to be her friend.

"Although I am friendly with several women in the congregation, I would not feel comfortable confiding in any of them," said Lisa Chaloner. Lisa lives in New Hampshire and has been a minister's wife for six years. "I think this is because it is too easy to get hurt, should one of them lack the wisdom of keeping quiet. I do not believe any of these women would intentionally hurt me. I might, however, be misquoted. My confidants are my sister and several very good friends I made in college."

Confidentiality backlash isn't always just one way. Parishioners can also suffer from an intimate relationship with the minister's wife. One wife needed someone to talk to about the problems in her marriage. She thought she'd found a true friend in the congregation to discuss intimate matters with. She did, but the confidences she shared cost her friend a dear price.

"Because I have talked of our marital problems with a

very good friend about my troubles, she has a hard time seeing my husband as her minister," said Mary who told us in the last chapter about her experiences with both parishioners and co-workers treating her differently. "She is still a wonderful friend but her church experience has suffered.

"Friends are so very important and my own struggles are intimacy issues," continued Mary. "I have had to work on being open and honest with myself and at least a couple of friends and my husband. I needed my friend and she was, is, a true friend. If I had known that my sharing with her would affect her confidence in my husband as her minister, I would have been hesitant. It confirms my inclination to look for non-church friends. Preferably Jewish people and Catholics!"

Keeping in mind that the Presbyterian Panel study showed that members expect the minister's wife to have more knowledge of their problems than they do, that knowledge is also a barrier to forming friendships with parishioners.

"Sometimes through circumstances and because of my position, I learn things about people who I otherwise would respect and care about that I really would rather not know," said Lisa Chaloner. "And yet I must keep most things confidential so I find I have no objective person to discuss things with."

Even social invitations are suspect because some parishioners feel that rubbing elbows with the minister brings them closer to God or, at least, closer than other members of the congregation. They flaunt the relationship. For some, this need for proximity and power leads them to do things they wouldn't normally do. An extreme, painful, example comes from a young black woman in Texas. Melinda is thirty-five, married to a Methodist pastor. They have moved five times in fourteen years.

"The thing that makes me saddest is that I don't believe these people would be as nice to me if I were not a preacher's wife," she said. "There are social clubs that I have been invited to attend and I am always the only black. It is obvious they would not normally invite blacks, except that their pastor happens to be Black."

These abuses of the roles of the minister and his wife make close relationships almost impossible to make and maintain. Their subtlety gives the illusion that congregants really want to be "friends", yet there is always a distancing between the laity and the minister's wife. They want the minister's wife to be their friend, but they don't work very hard at being a friend to her.

Jennifer Shew is twenty-nine and lives in Ithaca, New York with her Presbyterian minister husband and their two children. She told us of her saddest moments as a minister's wife:

"My saddest is the lack of initiative on the part of individuals to make friends with us, to attempt getting beyond the roles we function in" said Jennifer. "The emptiness of much of my interactions with the people in the church.

"Although in some church situations it does happen that a clergyman and spouse can make close friends with church members, it doesn't often. I was told very clearly by my clergyman spouse mother to assume it won't. In fact, repeatedly, clergy spouses have shared the same.

"People don't treat me like anyone else. They keep their distance and are extra polite or formal. The stereotypes, expectations, assumptions really get in the way of relationships developing. People do not relate to me as my own self.

"It seems easier to make friends with people who relate to me as *me* which happens in my work, or community volunteer work."

"Close relationships are rare," wrote another woman. "Mostly they're at arm's length—in both directions. Betrayal, or the fear of it, keeps you from closeness. Parishioners, on the other hand seem to come only so close and that's it."

Part of this distancing involves the stereotype that clergy people and their relatives, are overly serious. Congregants assume the minister's wife has more important things to do than join in small talk, gab fests, or, a good old fashioned gripe session.

Though she may desperately need that gripe session—even ministers' wives have complaints about their husbands, children and jobs—she is thwarted here, too. She learns to be a little suspicious of congregants who want to befriend her.

Carol Faus of Charlottesville, Virginia is a member of the Church of the Brethren congregation where her husband works. They have been married for six years; she is thirty-two.

"My closest friends are in the congregation, a couple nearly my parents' age," she said. "It is somewhat difficult to have the kind of friends I desire within the congregation. With church people you always have to be careful what you say. Nothing negative about the church, no opinions contrary to church beliefs, etc. Not really allowing yourself to be totally yourself. I do have another friend outside the congregation, in the community, and another in Indiana, a former college roommate now a pastor. All others I would call occasional friends."

Shirley Skirvin, who we first met in Chapter Four, stated that she and her husband are their own "best friends."

"I have several women friends in the congregation, but much as I appreciate and care for them, I am always cautious about sharing any feelings I may have about the church," said Shirley. "I am always fearful of careless remarks and I am also constantly amazed at how personally parishioners will take even the most casual remark."

Many wives mentioned the advice their husbands were given in seminary: Never make friends within the congregation. You'll be accused of playing favorites.

"How many deep friendships can you develop?" said Levinson. "None, not in the church. If you do in the church you play a very dangerous game. Because if you develop too close a relationship with a couple there are always those people who just love to say: 'You know, they spend too much time with Mr. so and so.' It's a jealousy factor because the old image comes back, the father and mother image. They (the minister and his wife) are paying too much attention to the other child."

If these issues aren't enough to inhibit close relationships with the congregation, then the fact that every member considers himself as the minister's boss should effectively limit overtures the wife makes to find close, intimate friends.

"I do appreciate friends in the congregation," said Olivia, "and some are quite good friends, but I also feel that I must pick and choose friends that are quite compatible with me. It is difficult to be friends with someone and then have them set my husband's salary, etc. So I know that I have to be selective in what I share with which friend."

Advice on the friendship issue is sometimes as stilted and stereotyped as other advice directed at the ministerial couple. Some seminaries and church hierarchies do strongly advise against having friends within the congregation to avoid accusations of favoritism. Others are as strident about not making friends outside the congregation to avoid the accusation of snobbery. All strongly advise that the ministerial couple build a network of friends to prevent isolation.

In an article for *Leadership* magazine titled "Turning Points: Eight Ethical Choices," James D. Berkley states that his panel advise ministers to keep friendships within the church at a lower intensity and visibility. Berkley quotes Don Finto as saying: "We have to defend in every way our need to have friendships but go about them in a way that causes as little jealousy as possible." Once again, the ministerial couple comes face to face with the impossible. Such advice may add to their burden and thwart chances for real friendships. Perhaps, like Shirley Skirvin and her husband, minister and wife should be their own best friends and let others go. But this has its own hazards.

In *Divorce in the Parsonage,* Mary La Grand Bouma wrote:

"A good friend of the same sex can be a friend in a way

that a spouse cannot, no matter how good the marriage." Bouma went on to note that if a wife's husband is her only friend that the smallest disagreement can lead to identity problems for the minister's wife. Each spouse relies too heavily on the other to affirm their identity. Any argument can damage self-worth.

Levinson advises care in this situation that neither spouse ends up dumping all their problems on the other. Without an escape valve, such as another friend, tension and stress can build to explosion.

Our author Reverend Sherry Taylor also warns against a loss of objectivity.

"What if the spouse takes his side against everyone else?" said Taylor. "What if you need an objective viewpoint?" The gripes a minister may share with his wife can have a devestating effect on her objectivity. If she is too much on the side of her husband, trying to protect him from another blow from the congregation or one of its members, her advice may deepen a crisis rather than resolve it.

So far it seems we've eliminated almost every avenue a minister's wife can take to find friends. She can't really be herself with parishioners, even her co-workers treat her with kid gloves, and relying on only her husband can lead to disaster in their marriage or his ministry. Where then are the minister and his wife to find friends?

Twenty-nine percent of our respondents did find their friends within the church. Karen's husband is a United Methodist minister now serving a term as a district superintendent of sixty-six churches in Texas. In his thirty-five year ministry he has served in seven local churches.

"Through the years it seems most of my friends are within the congregation," wrote Karen. "When I was employed full-time in my own job, I had a number of friends from work. In many cases, especially in the smaller towns, those friends were also church members.

Who Ministers to the Ministers' Wives?

"It seems easy to have friends within the congregation, as we have so much in common. I feel good about the friendships that we have made over the span of some thirty-five years in the ministry. I also feel good about the few friendships that I have formed from outside the congregation. I could truly 'be myself' with these people and not be concerned whether I would offend some church member who had a definite idea of what a minister's wife should or should not do. However, as I stated, our congregations have been pretty good to accept me for what I am anyway."

Making friends within the congregation, though it enriches those women who find them, has its own dangers. Each congregation possesses its own unique personality based on the average age, income, education and level of commitment of its members. Though their last church may have been forbidding, even devoid of opportunities for making friends, the next church may prove a gold mine. Unfortunately, the reverse is also true.

Diana Kemp is a Presbyterian in Edmonton, Alberta, Canada. She is thirty-five and has eight years experience as a minister's wife. The couple has two boys and moved to their present church six months ago.

"At the present time my friends are from within the congregation," she explained. "In our previous charge, most all of my friends were outside the church. That church consists mostly of older people. I naturally tended to make friends outside. It just happened that way. Where we are now looks like the opposite may happen. The church consists mainly of people my own age. We have more in common."

"From 1976 to 1989, I had very few friends either inside or outside the congregation," wrote Jacquie Reed of Vincennes, Indiana. Her husband works for a "downtown" church in a small town of 22,000 people. The church has a membership of eight hundred twenty-five. "The friends I did have were outside the congregation, because their values and interests were similar to mine. I also, during these years, had more education than most of the people in these congregations and that somewhat influenced friendships although it shouldn't necessarily.

"Since 1989, the year we last moved, I have friends in the church, more than I have ever had. Those people are home, some of them during the day, and their children are the same age as mine. I am, after twelve years of being a mother, enjoying a sense of camaraderie with other mothers that I always observed in other places, but was never a part of. I believe this is partially due to my willingness to make the first effort to get together with other people rather than waiting for others to make the first move and also because I have tried to tell people that I appreciate their friendship. The congregation is wealthy, consequently more women do not work, and they are available for doing things during the day. I am so thankful that I finally was able to experience this joy that I had been desiring over the years."

To move from a loving, open congregation to one more conservative or distanced can cause much heartache. Helen, one wife, wrote that their new church was full of cliques and that it was difficult for her to break into the already established relationships. But moving from a standoffish congregation to a more open one can do much to affirm a ministerial couple.

"In each place I have gone, God has supplied wonderful friends. I do not worry about moving because of this aspect," said Donna who lives in the midwest and has been married to her Presbyterian minister husband for thirty-five years.

"Each friend from former places or new, enriches my life. I have never sought out friends. They have sought me out. Our ties are deep in Christ. But I make a point to not spend extra time with them at church meetings so that probably few people know of my special friendships. I do not want to cause jealousy or dissension and I do not want anyone to think that I have friends to whom I would reveal their confidences." Donna

Who Ministers to the Ministers' Wives?

advises that ministers' wives get professional counseling if they feel it is needed.

"If you are having problems that require a good listener, or professional help—get it!" she said. "Not from a friend with your church if it concerns your husband and of course be sure that the person can be absolutely trusted to keep a confidence.

"This may be easier said than done. I feel I would greatly benefit from talking out some feelings that probably should have been addressed long ago. I would love to go to a clinic for a few sessions with the counselor, but it is not possible due to finances. Sometimes I wonder if there are ministers' wives out there who would just like to let off steam—anger, hurt, loneliness—but because of their husband's position, financial situation, or demands of young children, have no one to talk to. One of the most difficult things about being married to a minister, or someone in a helping profession, is that there is seldom a good time to discuss problems in depth. There are things we should have discussed years ago but the right time, I feel, has never come."

Who ministers to the minister's wife? Parishioners, some ministers and denomination hierarchies as well, assume that the minister ministers to his wife. Because she attends church regularly, is active in the congregation and happens to be married to the minister, people assume her spiritual and emotional needs are met by him. Carolyn Taylor wrote a letter to the editor for the Episcopal Church publication, *The Witness* in which she asked for a clergy wife support system.

"How could I have known that there would be no priestly counselor to aid me in times of crisis, sorrow or discord?" she wrote.

Usually no one ministers to the minister's wife. It is an issue hidden deep in the shadows of the dilemma of where to find and make friends. Because she must be a model of Christian deportment, the pastor's wife cannot confide in members of the congregation. It is the very lack of friends in the congregation and community that contributes to her spiritual dryness. Asking her husband to be her only friend and her minister is akin to asking the doctor to operate on his own wife. While the doctor and his wife both know and accept that he is not her doctor, many ministers and parishioners assume their minister can satisfy his wife's spiritual and emotional needs. The wives, at least, recognize this for the charade it truly is. One woman wrote this simple, poignant sentence on what makes her the saddest in the ministry: Feeling alone in a parish when you have problems and no one to talk with.

In a recent discussion for *Leadership* magazine, "Laymen Talk About Money and the Local Church," panelist Richard L. Brubaker said:

"I've found that once the pastor accepts a position, the lay leadership often stops talking to him about money and other personal concerns." Brubaker noted it was the laity's responsibility to accept the pastor into the church family in a way that promotes frankness and intimacy.

Rather than taking her in and helping her over the rough spots, many parishioners expect the minister's wife to take an active, but not *too* active, role in the church. They want her visible, but not in any position that would endow her with any kind of authority. They effectively lock her out of the closeness with the workings of the congregation that could give her spiritual solace. As we discussed earlier, she cannot appear to play favorites by making special friendships with members of the congregation. By eliminating the one source of friends that may have the closet common bond with her, they isolate her further from the Christian fellowship she craves. And if that is not enough, should she suffer the unthinkable—a death, illness, depression, parental or marital problem—she truly is on her own. Even if she had someone to talk to, she probably would hold back, too afraid of the rumor mongers, or that her confidence would be betrayed, or that she would be the ruination of another person's spiritual experience at church. Visible every-

Who Ministers to the Ministers' Wives?

where, essential nowhere, kept at a distance, and expected to be perfect, a minister's wife who has a either a personal problem or moral dilemma is like a hot potato no one wants to handle.

"I assumed when I arrived that I would be active in the Women's Fellowship, believing that it was a fellowship and that I would find like-minded friends," said Cathy. Cathy was profiled in Chapter Five. "I attended every meeting of the whole group, as well as the circle meetings of the circle I joined. To join one circle was a departure from tradition here, which held that the minister's wife was a member of all circles. I knew I would feel trapped by belonging to all and yet none of them.

"I found a hollow shell of an organization, deeply divided by age and tradition, full of misunderstanding and prejudice, not ready to question its existence and purpose in this day and age. People who claimed to know each other thought nothing of undermining and back-stabbing anyone not present.

"The spirit of the organization is slowly changing, but I have become withdrawn and seldom attend. My attitude has become detached. I had to come to the point of saying, 'It's *their* group,' and, '*they* have to decide if they want it to live or die.' I wanted it to die. I long for anonymity, for friends I choose, for life without the scrutiny of this fishbowl.

"What makes me the saddest is the paralysis I feel in relation to discussing anything personally," continued Cathy. "Any faith issue becomes so cosmic. It is the path of least resistance not to discuss these matters at all. I feel so frustrated at the lack of like-minded individuals who have some sense of what I face that it gives me the screaming meemies!

"I was active in this church out of guilt, inertia, isolation, community expectations, desperation, and despair. I struggled to act the part of the minister's wife according to community expectations but I am sick of acting and want to write my own script. I came here with faith, and I have lost it.

"I would encourage women to find help: Friendships, a

support group, if possible, and getting counseling help if those avenues fail. I owe my hard-won sanity to my work with a therapist who understood my co-dependent issues as well as the pressures of the ministry and would not let me blame others for the shape of my adult life.

"Just as I did not want to have my husband analyze and treat me for psychological concerns I had, I do not want him to be my minister. So in this situation, I have none.

"Another aspect of being 'in the congregation but not of the congregation' is that the pastor's spouse and family do not, themselves, have a pastor. Unless he or she is very fortunate, the pastor experiences the same void," said Mary Weaver of Savannah, Georgia, married for seventeen years to a Presbyterian Church minister. Mary confided that her husband is not technically a member of the congregation but of the presbytery. And she too regrets that she does not feel like an equal member of the congregation because she feels it's appropriate for her to hold a church office.

"Dudley and I discussed this during seminary days and I've always understood that, because we are so closely bound, he cannot possibly deal with me objectively as he usually does in pastoral relationships," continued Mary. "When we have had deaths in our families, though, I have sorely missed the kind of pastoral care that I know my husband dispenses so well. He has, too."

Olivia wrote:

"One of the other disadvantages is not having regular pastoral care. I have to deliberately find a pastor, perhaps a colleague of my husband. It depends on the nature of my concern as to who I get. When I have been hospitalized, I find many pastors call on me, often more than I can tolerate, some quite distantly removed."

Olivia's answer, to deliberately find a pastor, seems on the surface, to be the right one. After all, a doctor's colleague

Who Ministers to the Ministers' Wives?

can operate on the doctor's wife. Why can't a minister's colleague minister to the minister's wife?

First, confiding in his colleague may hurt her husband's standing among his peers. How can any wife go to her husband's peer and openly and honestly discuss their marrital relationship? Just as confidential information that the minister's wife possesses may affect her objectivity in regard to the congregation, so can insider knowledge of the minister's marriage hurt a working, or work-related, relationship. One minister told a wife seeking help that he would have to clear the issue with her husband (the crux of her problem at the time!) before counseling her. Going to one of his colleagues would be like a layman's wife airing their dirty laundry to the worker who sits next to her husband at the office.

What about going to the church hierarchy? Surely the presbytery, conference, and district leaders are aware that the minister's wife has unique pressures to deal with and that they may need help. Although some church leadership bodies are starting to deal with this, most are not very effective. Here again politics enters the situation. If a wife can't confide in her husband's colleague, she certainly isn't comfortable confiding in his boss. Some denominations assign and reassign their ministers through the district leadership. They hold the key to a minister "moving up" to a bigger, better paying, more prestigious, or, better locale situation. Confiding in the hierarchy that promotes, assigns, and moves your husband could prove disastrous. Getting help through them for substance abuse, marital, or emotional problems could sound the death knell for his career.

Some denominations try to form support groups for the wives asking wives of denomination leaders to direct them. This isn't much better than going directly to the boss. In the case of the ministry, where the wife is so closely tied to her husband's work, confiding in a bishop's wife is very much the same as confiding in the bishop. Of course, this isn't true in all cases, but that perception is there for the wives. Until the wives have some assurance that their confidences won't be used against their husbands in the church hierarchy, these groups won't work.

Getting professional help is still a problem for ministers, their wives, and their families. While it is perfectly acceptable for the laity to avail themselves of therapists, psychologists, psychiatrists, and ministers for counseling, the specter of model Christian deportment indicates that, for the minister's wife, her faith alone should be enough to sustain her.

As we've already seen in this chapter, she can't go to members of her husband's congregation for help. Jill, a minister's wife, told us that one time a faction within her husband's congregation wanted him to leave the pulpit. During the infighting that followed, no one checked with her to see how she was handling it, or if she needed any help. Her husband reported other members of the congregation helped him. But she had no one.

She also can't normally seek out and join a different congregation. Her husband's church members want her there, with them, in the public eye with him. The fact that they ignore her needs once she's there doesn't seem to occur to parishioners.

What can she do? She can, like Annie, wait so long that because of her emotional problems and fear of retribution from her husband's members, she is forced, almost kicking and screaming, into a professional program to get help. Before the problem get that severe, we suggest that she could surround herself with a network of other ministers' wives. This would seem to be the one group of people she could most closely relate to, vent some resentment and get some support. Unfortunately, even this source has its pitfalls.

In his conclusions to *Married to the Minister,* Roy Oswald makes the distinction between two philosophies among

Who Ministers to the Ministers' Wives?

ministers' wives. He sees wives who feel a call to the ministry that is as strong as their husband's, who want to take an active part in the congregation and fulfill the role of a two-fer ministry. Then, he notes, there are wives who want to be connected to their families, jobs, and individuality who seek no role within the church. Because clergy wives do not always share the same views of their role, a support group that combines the two philosophies may serve neither.

"When those who feel constrained by the role begin to voice some of their difficulties, those who feel called jump all over them and tell them they shouldn't feel that—it's an honor to serve as a clergy wife!" Oswald wrote in "Part II: Why Clergy Wives Burn Out" in the March–April 1984 edition of the Alban Institute's *Action Information*.

This was true at a ministers' wives retreat attended by Liz Greenbacker, where the two philosophies clashed over church attendance, use of the parsonage for committee meetings and the number of hours their husbands were required to work.

"Someone in church systems needs to take the initiative to see that like-minded spouses are able to meet for support and sharing," said Oswald. ". . . Denominational officials need to be more intentional about pastoral care of clergy families needs to come from the Judicatory (hierarchy)."

Some judicatories are doing just that. Reverend Norman Levinson at The Institute for Living noted an increase in the number of referrals of clergy from denomination leadership.

And the congregations are not as bleak as they appear. Many wives noted that in times of crisis, it was members of the parish that came to their aid.

"When our daughter died at eighteen months, the congregation functioned as a surrogate family," said Anne Ader, a minister's wife in Austin, Texas. "They were a blessing."

"My mother was with us for some years," wrote Betty Sweet, whose husband is a United Methodist minister living in

Rhode Island. "When she became fatally ill the church was supportive as they have been during numerous crises—son's seizures, surgery for the children and for us. It was through the church that we found sitters for mother and aides for her during the last months.

"The church is where you can and do disclose the hurts and pains and where you celebrate the joys and highs," said Betty.

In the Maces' study prepared for their book *What's Happening to Clergy Marriages?*, ministerial couples ranked "no in-depth sharing with other church couples" fifth on their list of disadvantages in the ministry. But they ranked third on their list of advantages the "nurturing support of the congregation", and ninth the "ready-made community of friends" they found there.

The trust to make friends and confidants, to find adequate spiritual and emotional counseling, is an issue fraught with contradictions. As unclear as the issue of making friends is to ministers' wives, no such vacillation exists when they talk about the issues confronting their children.

11

And Baby Makes Three. Or Four. Or Five . . .

"Boy, you better not attack my man or my kids!" said Jo Moore when asked what made her the angriest about being in the ministry. If ministers' wives temper their behavior, whether by choice or feeling forced to, acting a little nicer, more tolerant, or more diplomatic that the rest of us, most feel no obligation to allow the fallout from their husbands' occupation to affect their children.

Eighty-seven percent of our respondents have children. The number of children ranges from one to seven. One woman said they also took care of eleven foster children and another cared for twelve.

"I think the high expectations are hard on the kids," wrote Barbara who talked about the arm's length distancing of laity in the last chapter. "They didn't ask to be born into a minister's family. When one does go astray, somehow it's worse, like a black smudge on white rather than on grey."

That ministerial families have the same problems with their infants, adolescents, and young adult children as everyone else, should come as no surprise, but to some members of the laity, it does. Like the minister's wife, the minister's children cope with a long list of expectations and stereotypes.

"Pastor's kids can't win," wrote Marshall Shelley in *The Healthy Hectic Home*. "They get less credit for their virtues and more attention for their vices. Whatever they do right it's 'because of the way you were raised.' If they do something wrong the response is, 'You, of all people, should know better.'"

The ministry is replete with stories of preachers' kids' supposed bad behavior. It is another myth within the laity that ministers' children are usually the worst behaved. The assumption is that preachers' kids act up in rebellion to their father's goody-two-shoes profession. If they do act up, and most don't, it's more a reaction to the fishbowl existence they live in than opposition to their father's work.

All children, as they stretch and mold themselves into unique human beings, lapse into unacceptable behavior from time to time. Because the laity sets up the ministerial family as a role model to follow, they don't allow the same latitude to the preacher's kids as they do to their own. What's tolerated as normal, active behavior in anyone else's child is condemned for the minister's children. It's hard for anyone to maintain perfect behavior when they're illuminated by a perpetual spotlight. For children, it's impossible.

"The biggest problems were not physical but more rebelliousness," wrote Jean Parker of Seattle, Washington. Jean has a thirty-five year perspective of marriage and parenting within her husband's ministry in the Episcopal church. "We sought and received counseling for them and us to help us through the situations. We have excellent relationships with all of our children but there were days, weeks, and months when I wondered if we would make it.

"My philosophy on raising pastors' kids was the less

And Baby Makes Three. Or Four. Or Five...

obnoxious they were, the greater acceptance they would find within a congregation. So, they were brought up in a disciplined atmosphere. My model for my mother and wife role was that of the pastor's wife of my church (Lutheran) when I was growing up. She was a sweet and loving person with children who were nice to be around. She seemed a very gracious person. I also believe that a good sense of humor is an absolute necessity for survival as a clergyman or clergy wife. I have a somewhat warped one, I think. But we had lots of fun laughing at ourselves through the years. It has served us well."

Some wives aren't laughing, however. The expectation of better than good behavior causes more concern in their already complicated lives. Child-rearing is another area where church members expect them to role-model for them, and many women feel this expectation quite heavily.

"We have two boys ages two and a half and six years," said Diana Kemp of Canada who we also met in the last chapter. "We are pretty new at this. I haven't really found it too much of a problem. I'm really conscious of their behavior. I'm determined that no one is going to say that they are rotten brats.

"Only once at a previous church, while I was at work, my husband had the youngest with him in the pulpit. He was about one year old and he fell asleep on my husband's shoulder. At the next session meeting, he was told that 'people didn't like that.' Imagine being so petty as criticizing my husband over something so trivial. However, on the way out of church, he had received comments from many that it was really cute."

"This was a church situation just a few weeks ago," wrote Nancy. Nancy's husband is pastor of a United Church of Christ congregation in the northeast. The church has fifteen hundred members. "I got a call from son John's Sunday school teacher stating that he was so disruptive in class that no one could learn and she just couldn't handle him and wanted my help." John is one of their three children. "We'd been having our 'trials' at home and I sympathized. The teacher went on to describe what had happened the previous Sunday. At which point I said: 'That's very interesting. We weren't in church on that day.' The conclusion—that the teacher had identified another child as John. The situation has been taken care of, but I wonder if it would have happened to another child whose name, at least, didn't have such a high profile."

Several wives said that they would have raised their children the same way even if their husbands had not been ministers. Marylyn and George True have two children. George works in the United Church of Christ denomination at a church in Connecticut. Marylyn is a teacher.

"The traditional view of a minister's family life has been one of an ideal, orderly, perfect relationship," said Marylyn. "We are careful to balance our professional and home lives. We have need to take our children to many church functions and we do not want them to grow up hating church. We don't think that they should be expected to do more or be more special than any other children in the congregation. We are all just human beings. If George were not a minister, we would be raising our children in the same way we are now. We have certain standards by which we live and hope that we can be loving and trusted parents."

If their problems ended with the behavior issue, ministers' children would consider themselves lucky. But, just as with their mothers, the expectations are diverse, complex, and interrelated. Ministers' kids are also expected to have perfect church attendance. They're expected to set a good example for the members' children by always being on time for services, choirs, youth groups, Sunday school. They, too, must possess superior biblical and spiritual knowledge.

"We have raised our children according to standards we believe to be scriptural, not according to what others might require or expect," wrote Sharon Yeats of Topeka, Kansas. She and her husband, a Southern Baptist minister, have three sons. "Until our sons reached teen years, I'm not sure they even real-

And Baby Makes Three. Or Four. Or Five. . .

ize that they were a preacher's kids. Problems began when our oldest son became a teenager. If he excelled in anything, Bible memory, knowledge of God's word, leadership skills, he felt it was attributed to the fact that he was the preacher's son and not because he had studied himself."

If the parsonage is used for church committees and fellowship group meetings their privacy can be invaded. Home isn't home, but a committee room. They live in the same spotlight with their minister parent and are subject to the most conservative attitudes of the community. Ministers' children, like their parents, are supposed to be overly serious, too.

"We have a daughter age eleven and a son age eight," said Cathy who suffers from the lack of a personal minister in her life. "Life in the fishbowl is something we can all agree we dislike. We all are held to an unrealistic standard about our language, our activities, and our convictions. Because this is a conservative area, and the Wesleyan and Baptist churches are strong here, some people have assumed that our kids are not allowed to dance or play secular music!"

More often than they like, ministers' children feel they compete with parishioners for their father's time, patience, and emotional support. Reverend Norman Levinson, at The Institute for Living, remembers his daughter telling him: "You were always the empty chair at the dinner table."

"To this day he had guilt feelings that he didn't spend as much time with the children as he would have liked," wrote Betty Jean Souers of her husband. He works in a United Church of Christ church in Jacksonville, Florida, with five hundred fifty members. They have two children.

"They are both grown with homes of their own. We tried to keep our household as normal as possible when they were growing up and we, as parents, made a concerted effort not to put undue pressure on them just because they were pastor's kids. There were many nights he wasn't home. But he was always there for the important events in a child's life, sports events, recitals, plays, graduations, honor awards, etc."

Rosemary Todd, of Cheyenne, Wyoming, is married to an Episcopal minister. Married only fifteen years, Rosemary and her husband each had three children from previous marriages. She addressed the patience issue:

"I think he had enough available time, but just didn't relate well to problem teens," she said. "Perhaps it is too difficult for a man who deals daily with problems in the family or in relationships to deal with problems at home. At times there were conflicts with church activities and children's activities that made it impossible for him to be the father he would like to have been."

Some parishioners expect the minister's children to be as knowledgeable about members as are their parents. Marshall Shelley reported one minister's son was actually grilled by a parishioner about the counseling sessions the boy's father had with another parishioner. The child was understandably confused. His father reassured him that he'd handled it well. He also defended his son by pointing out to the parishioner that member concerns were the pastor's job—not the responsibility of the pastor's son. The incident was never repeated.

Members' children sometimes mirror their parents' expectations and special treatment when dealing with the minister's children. Some treat ministers' kids with the same arm's-length distancing that ministers' wives experience.

"My children are shy—probably a genetic character trait!" wrote Jeanette Paulson who, in the last chapter, felt there was a wall between herself and others. "They have a hard time getting acquainted in a new place. They no doubt feel some of the same things I do about being thought special or different. There's been no overt rebellion . . . yet." Jeanette's tone was decidedly humorous, yet with its own grain of truth.

On top of it all, the minister's child sometimes must bear the anguish of hearing criticism of his own father as

And Baby Makes Three. Or Four. Or Five. . .

though, somehow, someway, the child was either responsible or could effect some change. That's a heavy burden to lay on any child. For the child of a minister, who may live with the undercurrent of tension that what he does affects his father's livelihood, it's too cruel a burden to bear. Betty Sweet listed as one of her saddest moments: "Times when our children were subjected to pressure or sarcasm because of what their dad had done or said."

"Probably the thing that makes me the angriest is hear criticism of my husband or children," said Karen. "Some congregations are prone to blame the minister for all problems in the church. It angers me to see my loved ones hurt by people's thoughtless words and actions."

Evelyn Roberts, wife of evangelist Oral Roberts, knows the sting of public criticism, perhaps more so than other wives because of her husband's highly visible ministry.

"We have four children. They did not like people to throw pot shots at their dad," she said. Evelyn said that she felt angriest being a minister's wife when people ridiculed her husband. She also listed the fish bowl existence as a disadvantage to the ministry.

"Being in the public eye, living in a fishbowl and having to put up with media stories either exaggerated or not true," she said. "Having to explain to people that newspapers don't always print the truth. It's so sad when a minister obeys God's calling and people misunderstand.

"The children's problems were mostly because their dad traveled so much and they resented his being away. I have resented doing things for my family that I felt were my husband's place to do, but I learned something that has helped me so very much. I've learned to count everything I do for someone as a seed of my faith. Seeds grow and multiply and produce fruit."

It might be easier on ministers' children if the high expectations of them were confined to the church membership.

Unfortunately, they're not. Admitting your father is a minister can also cause problems in the secular world.

"The children loved it when their father went to work in our national office," wrote Muriel. "When their friends asked, 'What does your father do?' they would say 'He's an executive!' When he was working in a parish their school teachers expected them to behave perfectly as did the congregation. This is quite a burden for children to bear!"

Expectations outside the church, in the secular world, are slightly different from expectations within the church. All the pressures of peer acceptance and rejection come into play with ministers' children as they do will all children. Here, though, the minister's low salary can affect his children's acceptance with secular friends.

"The other side, which we see vividly in our current situation, is that because we as a family have priorities which reflect our beliefs, our children are not of the current trends and tend to be looked down upon by their peers for a variety of reasons." said Nancy. "For not being superconsumers, for not having jobs of disposal income, for not having Nintendo, for buying clothes on sale, etc. This give rise to good discussion at home about how we choose to live our lives and use our resources, but causes some pretty unkind situations among their peers."

"And there was always a bunch of little spies at public school who went to your church," said Joseph Stowell III, the son of a minister and now a minister himself. Stowell reminisced for a *Leadership* magazine panel article on "The Pastor as Parent."

" 'You know what the pastor's son did at school today, Mom?' " he quoted. "And then the mom would tell the deacon's wife and so on. You never escaped the tension."

"I tried to inculcate in our children that we were a normal family especially committed to love others for Jesus' sake with a desire to let the beauty of Jesus be seen in us," wrote

And Baby Makes Three. Or Four. Or Five. . .

Marjorie Udall. Marjorie's husband, John, is retired from the United Church of Christ denomination. "I became aware, however, that others set us apart as different when our children shared with us occasionally that they got taunted at school."

One of the most distressing stories we found was included in Shelley's book. It ties into the difficulties ministers' wives have making and keeping friends inside or outside the congregation. Only, in this case, the stress was laid on the child.

Shandra is the eight-year-old daughter of a minister in a rural church in Kansas, Shelley wrote. It seems Shandra had a best friend at school. Another girl, whose parents attended Shandra's father's church, felt ignored by the minister's daughter. The pastor explained that Shandra wasn't going out of her way to exclude the member's daughter, she just preferred her best friend. The other girl's parents complained to the pastor that his daughter was ignoring theirs.

An adequate reply at this point would be a laugh of derision, or, at the least, an explanation to these parishioners that Shandra was free to associate with, and make friends with, whomever she pleased. Shandra's father didn't do either.

This pastor had to talk with his daughter and explained to her the importance of making everyone in Sunday school feel welcome.

"She's conscious," said the pastor speaking of Shandra, "that part of our role in the church is to help befriend everyone."

"This guy should have his parent's license revoked," said Reverend Sherry Taylor. "That's a terrible way to treat a kid—and so unnecessary. She's eight years old and can have friends. She's not the pastor. Who encourages these ridiculous expectations?"

Well, books like Marshall Shelley's *Living With Great Expectation* which does not take this pastor to task for the injustice he's perpetrated on his daughter, unfortunately perpetuate the myths of perfection. Nowhere in the chapter, or elsewhere in the book, does Shelley point to and denounce the burden this pastor placed on his own child.

This pastor's overzealousness is apparent in his choice of the words "our role" rather than "my role". It doesn't seem likely that eight-year-old children are now being ordained.

In one fell swoop, Shandra's father took away her freedom to make and develop close friendships and added to her life the responsibilities of the profession he chose for himself.

There were other consequences to ministers' wives because they chose to have children. Theresa raised an issue that ties in to the subject of the last chapter: Who ministers to the minister's wife? In this case, not only did she not have a minister, but she almost couldn't attend Sunday services.

"When we first came here, child care was sporadic," said Carol Faus. "If no one was in the nursery, I was expected to volunteer to stay or take my kids into church with me. After this happened a couple of times, I wrote a letter to the chair of the responsible committee and told them, basically, if they didn't start providing child care for me and the other young mothers so that we could participate in the life of the church, then I would stop attending any service when it wasn't provided. They began providing it, even though they never failed to point out it was usually just for my kids." All that bother just so she could do what they expected her to do anyway—attend church!

The husband of one of our authors, Reverend Sherry Taylor, is also a United church of Christ minister. One Sunday, while Sherry was away, Harry got their three children ready, took them to church, and took his place in the pulpit. The next Sunday, a parishioner mentioned to Sherry how hard it was for Harry to have to get the kids ready *and* preach.

"I did that every Sunday!" our author exclaimed.

Just as one woman listed "high visibility" as both an advantage and a disadvantage to being in the ministry, some of

And Baby Makes Three. Or Four. Or Five. . .

the disadvantages of being a preacher's kid can also be advantages.

Jacquie and Tim Reed have two daughters aged twelve and almost six.

"I do not think they have ever experienced difficulty because of being 'preacher' kids," said Jacquie. "I cannot recall anyone making any comments to them of this nature. They are well-behaved girls, most of the time; they are friendly and respond appropriately to adults." Jacquie saw two advantages for her daughters growing up in a ministerial family.

"We have never lived close to family," Jacquie explained. "But each place we have lived, people in the congregation have given them extra attention and taken an interest in them that has helped fill this gap. They have been remembered very thoughtfully with gifts, cards, and other expressions of care and love. Because of this interaction with large groups of people from the time they were young, I believe these times of interaction have helped them mature.

"Many times, if I am unable or do not want to attend an event with my husband, our older daughter will go with him. She enjoys these times with her dad as well as with other persons.

"Second, these children have also been exposed to many well-known people as they have dined in our home. These times of conversation have enhanced their development. People also have offered us tickets to events, which we would not have been able to afford. Consequently, attendance at these functions has helped in their maturation." Jacquie is noticing that their eldest daughter is more aware of what her father does for a living.

"She is becoming conscious of her father being the pastor." said Jacquie. "For example, he recently substituted in her Sunday school class. Later that day I asked her if her dad had done a good job. She said no. I then said to her: 'If your father was not the minister, would you say he did a good job?' She said yes. I guess that is a backhanded compliment for sure. Of course, some of her embarrassment regarding her father being the teacher could be because of her age. Most kids her level would be self-conscious if their parent taught."

Cathy mentioned that visibility has its positive side. Parishioners may be on constant watch to see a minister's child make a mistake, but they also watch, with pride, their accomplishments.

"The only possible benefit I can see to this life in the fishbowl may have as much to do with just being a big fish in a small pond. Whenever our daughter does something well, such as performing piano in church, she gets a lot of positive regard. She claims she hates the comments, but she is poised and confident."

Karen didn't have a problem with her children knowing confidential information about the congregation. Karen has a daughter and a son.

"I don't think that living in a parsonage (most often next door to the church) has had a negative effect on either child. They grew up knowing that any conversations they overheard in the living room or on the telephone were strictly confidential and not to be repeated anywhere outside the home. Both children were active in our congregations and, I am happy to report, are still active in their churches. Maybe we were just lucky, but I don't believe our churches put us in that fishbowl environment."

"The kids feel very comfortable in church," said Mary who has four children ranging in age from six to fourteen. "They know exactly what their father does for work. Their friends know and like their dad. They can call him at work, usually. They see and feel the great respect and admiration people have for him and his work. Most kids don't have that advantage."

Many wives mentioned that although their husbands worked long hours, the time could be flexible. It was easier for

And Baby Makes Three. Or Four. Or Five...

their minister husbands to arrange for time off during the day to attend important school functions, care for sick children, and handle emergencies than it was for most of the laity.

Another advantage for parsonage children is the diversity of the life their parents lead.

"Nothing is static, everything is rarely predictable, which is growth-producing," wrote Barbara Cleveland. At age thirty-eight, Barbara has been married to her Presbyterian minister husband for thirteen years. The couple has two children. Barbara stated that she and her husband have always sought out unusual situations. "Diverse people, race, age, sexual orientation, ethnicity, for all of us to know. I enjoy this opportunity for my kids especially."

What happens to kids raised in the parsonage? Are they turned off church? Or do they embrace it all the harder? Sylvia is a thirty-year veteran of ministry marriage. Her son is twenty-eight and her daughter is twenty-three.

"One little story about our children," wrote Sylvia. "On a hot summer Sunday some years ago when our children were the only small fry in the congregation, our son asked how come he had to be there. I replied because your father is the minister and you have no choice. As our children grew, attitudes developed. Our restless son has grown into a staid, dedicated, deeply religious young man, heavily involved in his church as organist, director of music, and member of several committees. Our tranquil daughter who did not complain, attends church now only when she is engaged as the vocal soloist and has no use for the organized church."

"The double standard for a preacher's family has created some problems," said Michelle. "My children have been totally turned off being a preacher or a preacher's wife because of the way we have had to endure certain problems in the ministry. Many times our family needs have had to be put on the back burner in order for the members' needs to come first."

The myth among the general public is that ministers'

daughters marry ministers and ministers' sons become ministers. Certainly this does happen and examples abound particularly in the televangelist's world. Pat Robertson's son, Tim, followed in his dad's footsteps, preaching for the '700 Club.' Richard Roberts, son of Oral Roberts, has his own television ministry and appears often with his father. Robert H. Schuller, Billy Graham, Jimmy Swaggart, and Jerry Falwell all have sons who chose some aspect of the ministry either within their fathers' empires or in ministries of their own. Prevailing wisdom implies that the children of ministers are more apt to marry ministers than other children. We found no data to prove or disprove this theory but suspect that, televangelists aside, preacher's kids aren't any more likely to got into their father's line of work than any other child raised in a "family" business.

Now, our sample minister's wife has children, a life lived in the fish bowl, and a husband whose bosses have high expectations, not just of him, but of the whole family. The hours, energy, and emotion he devotes to meeting those expectations can cause the number one complaint among ministers' wives.

Though surrounded by people who may be her friends but who also may be just buttering her up to get in good with her husband; by children who feel the same hurts, abuses, and denials as she does; and by a husband who works long erratic hours, she spends too much time alone. She ministers to her husband by taking care of the household needs so he is free to do his good work.

She's not just alone. She's lonely. And sometimes that loneliness leads to an emotional state of mind that borders on mental illness.

§12§

Who Created This Hell?: him, her, or Him?

"I'd never marry a minister again. It's too lonely," Betty, our depressed minister's wife, told us. So far, we've only looked at pieces of the private life of the minister's wife: she's the role model of Christian deportment for the congregation; she's expected to attend her husband's church and therefore may have no pastor of her own; it's difficult to find close confidants; she's beset with financial worries; and now she has children to take care of—sometimes alone.

Fifty-five percent of our survey respondents were asked if their husbands shared in child-raising duties. Of those, forty-nine percent said that child-raising duties were left mostly to themselves.

"I have, over the years, been working constantly with trying to keep family life on a healthy level while my husband is consumed with church work," wrote Doris. "Sometimes it has created contention. Sometimes I have been very angry. Often I have been overwhelmed with responsibility of family."

Forty-two percent of our respondents said that their husbands shared in child-raising duties.

"My husband is extremely responsive to my needs," said Jody Maas of Denver. Jody is an Independent Lutheran and the couple has three children. "When I need some time away from the children and when he's home, he will often just take over, 'shooing' me away, allowing me to regain my composure." As helpful and sensitive as Jody's husband is, getting time to help her is still a problem.

"He doesn't have a lot of time, as he has two congregations in the Denver metro area, a full-time pastor at each. It's rather difficult due to availability of a sitter and his schedule. Evenings are when he does most of his meetings and calls. Daytime is studying, running here and there, more calls. Sometimes I go with him so that we at least can talk enroute. But we do get, and have gotten, some wonderful memories to savor."

Children are the last piece of the puzzle of life for a woman married to a minister. What are the sum of the parts? Layered together, the issues we've dealt with can add up to isolation and loneliness. Almost a quarter of our respondents mentioned their loneliness. Our survey was conducted over three years, from 1987 to 1990. Another study, done in 1978 by the Task Force on Women of the Synod of the Trinity of the United Presbyterian Church showed thirty-three percent of their respondents selected isolation and the lack of friendship as a major frustration of their husband's ministries. The nine percent drop from the 1978 study to ours hints that there's been improvement in this area for ministers' wives. In our survey, although loneliness wasn't always specifically mentioned, sixty-seven percent did say that lack of time together as a family was a problem they dealt with often. In the Presbyterian Task Force on Women study, seventy-six percent noted little family time as a major frustration. It was the number one an-

Who Created This Hell?: him, her, or Him?

swer. In the Maces' research for *What's Happening to Clergy Marriages?*, fifty-five percent of the wives polled said time pressures due to their husband's heavy schedule was a disadvantage to the clergy marriage. It was second only to feeling that their marriage had to be a model of perfection.

The results of our recent statistics, compiled ten years after both the other surveys, fall between theirs, so we assume that time pressures for the ministerial family are as problematic now as they ever were. In fact, half of the thirty-two percent who said time was not a problem for them mentioned that their children were grown and gone, or that their husbands were retired. Even the women who said their husbands shared child-raising duties mentioned lack of available time because of their husbands' jobs.

"Yes we shared," said Shirley Keltto. "When they were small, he always was involved in putting them to bed and reading to them regularly at bedtime and subsequently making a weekly trip to the library to check out more books. Even though he was gone a lot and busy, he was very much aware of their schedules, activities and needs. I sensed we were together in all of this.

"He would regret that he didn't have more time," Shirley continued. "A deliberate attempt was made for the one day off a week. We always took our four-week vacations as a family until they were sixteen and held down jobs."

Many wives mentioned resentment over the lack of time they have to spend as a family. And being famous and successful is no hedge against the problem. Even Evelyn Roberts, married fifty-one years to evangelist/healer Oral Roberts, expressed resentment about some of her duties as an almost single parent.

"My husband never spent as much time with the family as he would have liked to," said Evelyn. "I felt it was not enough but he explained to the children that God had called him to have crusades and he had no choice but to go.

"I handled most of the day-to-day affairs because I was at home with the children a great part of the time. My husband took care of big discipline problems when he was home. It worked out okay."

We asked if the minister had enough time to spend with his family, and sixty-seven percent of our respondents said no. They said it in various tones ranging from outright resentment to passive acceptance. Betty stated that her husband spent about ten hours a week with the family and that she resented it. Lyn Kratz is married to a United Church of Christ minister and has three elementary school-aged children. She felt that her life was different from women married to men in other occupations because of time.

"One big way is the hours David works. They are longer than the traditional eight to five (but also have flexibility). I used to resent that, always fight for more time. Those feelings and fights have all but faded. I learned early on that waiting for David was a set up. I needed to turn to myself. In many ways the schedule has enabled/forced (?) a more independent, capable me."

"I handle most of the child-rearing duties," said Andrea. "Sometimes this bothers me especially now that I'm going to school full time and working part time. It's still my job to worry about getting the girls to school and baby sitter; to any after school activities or functions. Not much extra time is in our busy schedules but we block out one evening each week, usually Friday night, as family night and nothing comes before that unless an emergency arises."

Some phrases were common among thirty-two percent of the women who answered our survey; they felt they never had enough family time: time with children 'when he was home,' or 'when he could.' Whether you call it loneliness or the pressure of too little time, home alone with children is still home alone without the benefit of adult company. Although three-quarters of the wives who answered our survey didn't specifi-

Who Created This Hell?: him, her, or Him?

cally use the word lonely, we suspect that's still what it amounts to.

Who created loneliness in the life of the minister's wife? Did she do it to herself? In part, she did. Why didn't Evelyn insist that Oral spend more time with their children? Why didn't Andrea ask her husband to do some of the chauffeuring? Although it had a positive effect, why didn't Lyn keep fighting for more time together as a family?

Part of the answer to these questions is the reason their spouses chose the work that they do. Many ministers refer to their work as a calling; something stronger than just choosing a profession. A call to serve God is potent and powerful. If both minister and spouse feel it, then the wife may accept being alone while her husband serves the church as part of her own call from God. In the Presbyterian Task Force On Women study, forty-four percent of clergy wives polled said that their role as the minister's wife was to be supportive.

"Supportive had many interpretations," the Task Force wrote. "Support of husband, family, church, persons in the congregations; support by providing a calm, well-ordered home, by taking major responsibility for the children; by participating in the church program, by remaining in the background; by taking leadership roles and not taking leadership roles." Our survey showed similar results. In our survey answers, many women noted the lack of time but also said that they didn't mind since their husbands were doing God's work. However, our conclusion based on the larger number of women reporting is that the lack of family time in ministerial marriages is a major problem. If both partners respond to a call from God and the wife decides that loneliness is her cross to bear, this often is a long-term irritant causing psychological wounds whose repercussions take many forms. Not a single spouse mentioned that their husband worked a forty-hour week. Most gave us a range of fifty to eighty hours of work per week. Many noted that these hours were evenings. From their own wives' answers, ministers are out at least three nights a week and some wives mentioned seven nights. Did God really expect his disciples to neglect their families in His service?

It seems unfair to blame God for the lack of time a minister can spend with his family. It is fair, however, to blame, in part, the congregation and the individual members within it for the demands they make in God's name. It seems too many congregants have taken the pastor-as-servant philosophy to heart. Gene, a minister's wife, told us her husband said she would always come first. She also told us it didn't work out that way. Catherine wrote that what made her the most angry was that church schedules needed to come first.

"I feel resentful of the amount of time the church demands," said Beth. We met Beth in Chapter Nine. She is an executive in a marketing and research company. "We have little family time. This is despite the fact that he is supposed to be part time.

"We are both chronically short of sleep, so quality of time can be pretty ragged. Saturday, once our R & R day, now starts with an 8 a.m. committee meeting. He counsels Monday through Thursday nights and Saturday is an early morning followed by 8 a.m. Sunday. So Saturday evenings are not party night. Friday is the end of my work week and I try to get home by 5 or 5:30. Sunday night from five to nine is youth group activity and church. If we go out for dinner, etc., Friday is it."

"I believe the greatest disadvantage in being a minister's wife is that you can seldom schedule anything for your own family or yourself that doesn't seem to get torpedoed by church activities or needs in the church family that appear to be greater at the moment than the minister's family's needs," said Karen. "I'm sure a doctor's wife or a lawyer's wife could make the same statement (or probably just about any layperson's wife, too!), but somehow in the church it seems that the minister belongs more to the congregation than in a lot of other professions. It's more difficult for the minister to say no than for

Who Created This Hell?: him, her, or Him?

a lot of other people. I guess it's like saying no to God and that makes a big impact."

Ministers' wives are constantly compared with the wives of other professionals who have high time commitments to their work—doctors in particular. There are parallels. Doctors work long hours, have high emotional involvement and plenty of stress. They have a high investment in education. They are "on call" nights and weekends. But they are not on call every night or every weekend. Because eighty percent of all churches are small, one minister is responsible for filling the pulpit. The sole pastor rarely has staff to assist him and in too many cases doesn't have a secretary unless his wife works for free. Unlike the doctor, he has no pool of other pastors to cover for him at odd hours of the night, weekends, holidays or vacations. If you call your doctor on his day off, though you may insist on speaking to him, you'll get referred to another doctor. Everyone knows that if you call your minister on his day off, you'll get your minister. The doctor's wife, as the wives of other professionals in high-time commitment jobs, spends a great deal of time alone, too. Unlike the other professionals' families, the minister's family has little discretionary income to offset the time demands. Money rarely makes up for losing time with loved ones, but it can make the waiting more comfortable.

Even if he does take his day off, and it usually is only one day off, mid-week at that, he'll still be interrupted with phone calls. Parishioners know he's at home if he's not in the office or if it's after office hours, so they call him there. Frequently. Many wives said that they went out of town on his day off just to avoid the phone calls and drop-in visits that brought church business into their lives even then. Many wives also mentioned that they couldn't afford much in the line of entertainment because of his low salary.

Because his day off usually is a week day, a minister's time off rarely matches up with his wife and children who are off on weekends. If he has school-age children, part of that day off is taken up by school hours. The two days his wife is off from work and his children are home from school, both ready to relax and recreate, he's either preparing for Sunday service or preaching it.

Some denominations recommend that their member churches give the minister one Sunday off a quarter that is not vacation or continuing education time. But that's all it is, a recommendation. Most churches negotiate a salary, hours, holiday, vacation, and education package one on one with the minister. If he's not good at negotiating, he can end up with a work schedule that shortchanges his family and himself.

Fortunately, there's always vacation. According to the Ministers and Missionaries Benefit Board of the American Baptist Churches study, sixty-seven percent of all ministers get four weeks vacation. Almost twelve percent get three weeks; eight percent get two weeks or less; ten and a half percent get over four weeks. In the same survey, almost thirty-two percent of the pastors said they did not use all their vacation time. Fifty-six percent said they did. Twelve percent didn't even answer the question.

Don't forget Christmas and Easter, the two most important Christian holidays. They usually require an even heavier workload for the minister as he prepares special sermons and extra worship services while increasing his counseling schedule because more members suffer depression at those times then any other time throughout the year.

"There's not one other occupation anywhere that interprets 'full-time commitment' to mean: available on demand and at anytime," wrote James Allen Sparks about the ministry in an April 1987 article for the *Clergy Journal.* Sparks is associate professor of Mental Health at the University of Wisconsin-Extension.

"It is very difficult for us to have a family life while we are home," wrote Lisa Chaloner. "My husband gets non-stop calls and has people after him all the time. He is out three or

Who Created This Hell?: him, her, or Him?

four evenings a week and goes into work from 7:30 a.m. to 5:00 p.m. most days except Saturday and Sunday when he only goes in to work in the morning. I don't know any other jobs that are so demanding, except perhaps a doctor. Also, many of the issues we deal with regarding church people are so emotional—deaths, illness, divorces, people in desperate need. We find that we have to leave town to escape it all."

Our survey results also show that there is no other profession where the wife feels she is such an integral part of her husband's ability to perform his job. She takes the home load off his shoulders, enabling him to devote himself to his work. No wife with whom we spoke lays the blame for a twenty-four hour, seven-day-a-week commitment only at the feet of the congregation. Some say the minister, too, is at fault. Because the congregation pays him, he may feel he's the only person who can minister to their needs. Sparks proposes forming a ministry pool in the community so that ministers can take turns being on call just as doctors do. There'd be little resentment over odd hour phone calls this weekend, if the minister knew that next weekend another minister would be taking those calls. Sleep, quantity and quality time with his family, and vacations would be uninterrupted. Sparks notes that this would require planning, self-discipline, and educating the congregation.

Would it work? It is difficult to know since the stereotypes of ministers always on call are difficult to defeat. Moreover, as long as their wives see their call to the ministry to be supermoms, superwives, superwomen; and as long as ministers feel that their long hours are "doing God's work," it seems unlikely. It isn't only the congregation's expectations that compel a minister and his wife to suffer gladly the long hours, interrupted free time, and cancelled family events and vacations.

Workaholism runs as rampant in the ministry as it does in other professions. For too many ministers, the pull to work isn't *Him*. It's him. The minister casts himself in the role of pastor as servant.

Private Lives of Ministers' Wives

When we asked ministers' wives, "is your husband a workaholic?," forty-six percent of the women answered yes. Thirty percent said no and sixteen percent didn't answer. We also wanted to know why they were workaholics. Was it congregational demands? Was it his own personality? Was it a combination of two? Sixty-two percent of our respondents indicated that their husbands' personalities and perceptions of the ministry made them workaholics. Thirty-five percent thought it was both the congregation and their husband who created the strong pull to work too long and too hard. Only one woman laid the blame solely on the congregation.

"It is his perception of his ministry and the size of the church and the terrible amount of need in the congregation," said Donna. "He has no free time. He is an excellent administrator because he dislikes it and simplifies, delegates, etc. He loves people and his time is absorbed with the sick and hurting. As a young man he once went to his minister wanting to talk over some serious things, and was given twenty minutes. He vowed he would always be available and he is.

"You have to understand that we are of a generation in which if you were called to church work, you expected to work all the time." Donna is sixty-one. "It has only been in recent years that the realization came to seminary professors, church leaders, and was passed on to new ministers that the family must come first, that a person is first a husband and father, then a minister.

"He is not a workaholic in the true sense of the work— but along with everything else he fits in more studying than I'm sure many ministers do. I did the child-raising, although when my husband was home, he was certainly involved in it. In the years I worked, he did most of the transporting to things since his time was somewhat more flexible and he was nearer to the schools. Since he was gone night and day except for meals at night, he was not always in tune with what was going on.

"Lest you be misled by all this, he is a good father, very

Who Created This Hell?: him, her, or Him?

proud of his children and grandchildren and never missed events in which they performed and rarely missed parent-teacher conferences.

"He gets tired," continued Donna, "but never burns out, because of dependence on God, and an ability to not worry much about things about which he can do nothing. He does pray about them."

How does this devotion to duty happen? One reason is that people don't see the ministry as a profession. They don't quite see it as a job either. It's that "call" aspect of it that seems to require more of a minister than anyone else. We believe our ministers are called, by God, to teach us, heal us, and set us an example of the holy life. The fact that, in the eyes of some congregations, it seems few of them succeed at this, leads the next minister to ever greater efforts. For his own part, the minister himself may have brought his own inadequacies with him into the ministry. In an article in the January 1989 issue of *Atlantic Monthly,* Thomas Maeder states that studies of clergy at least suggest that this profession includes a host of problems involving interpersonal relationships.

". . . they may be driven into a veritable frenzy of wholesale helping," wrote Maeder. He attributes this helping frenzy to the minister's need, conscious or unconscious, to fill a void within himself.

"He is often emotionally drained and has little left to give at home," wrote Mary. "This was worse before we had a very big marital crisis and we had to work on the roots of the problems. His minister role fed his need to be needed and this became unmanageable. My anger made me feel guilt, of course he was only doing his job. This has proven to be bullshit. And my response to his emotional absence just compounded the problem. We have, since our crisis, been working on all this and things are better."

The high visibility of the ministry can also feed the ego while it hurts it. As they are performers in a way, there's something about Sunday morning, with all those people sitting in the pews waiting to be spiritually fed, that can get a minister through the rest of the week. Criticism and pats on the back are immediate on Sunday morning. If the audience cheers, it can be like winning an Oscar.

"My husband tends to be domineering and demands a great deal of attention, which I feel is one of the reasons that he chose to enter the ministry," wrote one woman who requested complete anonymity. "I have discovered that he is not alone out there. The pulpit is the stage where one performs weekly. The feedback is immediate and the affirmation is rewarding, especially if one is insecure."

Then, there's the numbers crunch. Laity and pastor alike can be obsessed with numbers as his primary performance evaluation. The more weddings, baptisms, burials, new members; the more visits to shut-ins, the sick and those in crisis; and the higher the Sunday offering, the more money he raises for the current church renovation project; the more both feel like the job is getting done properly. But the pursuit of numbers also leads to workaholism.

". . . the ministry in the U.S.A. is a highly competitive system, squarely based on the American success syndrome . . ." wrote David and Vera Mace. "The rewards come in terms of recognition, status, and salary. The credits are awarded for skill, popularity, and hard work. The evidences of worth consist mainly in increasing congregational membership, raising money, putting up buildings and achieving favorable publicity by whatever means."

"It's a combination of both (the congregation and him)," Diana Kemp responded to our survey this way: "In order for him to feel that he is doing what he needs to do and by encouraging people to come to church, I think he feels he needs to visit. He has to work around people's schedules, not his own. Therefore he may be out three to six nights per week . . . I think he used to be a workaholic only because he felt he had to

Who Created This Hell?: him, her, or Him?

meet the expectations of the congregation. Anything he did didn't seem good enough for them. One lady told him that he should consider the church first and what I wanted to do was okay as long as it didn't interfere with his work. He has since drawn his own boundaries and let the church know where he stands before he starts at a new church.

"Whenever I get discouraged, angry, frustrated, lonely, I stop and think of the puzzle pieces of my life," Diana continued. "I then realize that it takes a very special person to be married to a minister. I feel very strongly that it is indeed a Calling from God. So, then as a person of God, we must obtain our strength from Him who has given us this special job in life to do."

Money is also a source of workaholism. Not the minister's money, he doesn't get any extra for working overtime, something he does share with other professionals. It's the church's money. As we saw in Chapter Six, many ministers fall prey to the "poor" church argument; churches that claim the inability to raise a single penny more to either increase his salary or hire him help. Since ministers also feel a call to a specific church as well as their call to the ministry, he also feels called to do more than his share to save his church any extra expense. Several wives mentioned that their husbands didn't ask for more money because the church couldn't afford it. Tom felt so called to serve a particular church, he accepted the position as minister at no pay.

Sometimes special problems within a church seem to pull a pastor into extra work.

"Since 1/1/91 he hasn't had a day off," wrote Nancy. Her survey was dated 2/9/91. She and her minister husband have been at their present church for two years. "My husband followed a minister who had been dismissed, having been involved intimately with a number of women in the church, abuse of the power of the office. As a result we are in a situation in need of great healing and rebuilding of trust. This was followed closely after our arrival with the disclosure that the former male organist was a pedophile and had been involved with boys of this congregation which went from intense investigation the police, to trial, and jail time. Here was a split situation with ministering to the families of the victims as well as being pastoral with many families who had looked upon the young brilliant organist as their son. This is a prelude to saying my activities here have been very attentive to making time to listen and help as I could to promote the rebirth of trust. This has been such a drain on my husband that support of him has been a priority.

"But my husband is here for meals and is really available to the kids when he's able," continued Nancy. "It would be great if he had more time with us, but I don't see my getting upset about it as improving the situation any. This is the way it is for now. We can make the most of the time we have and that beats using energy to be dissatisfied. The kids have said—I wish Dad was home more and didn't have a job that kept him out nights and weekends. We try to talk about the good points of the job and give it some perspective. But there's no denying it's not the greatest situation. I always pray for snowstorms that cancel everything—that's a gift."

An article in the *Clergy Journal* by Eldred Johnson listed twenty-six different roles a minister could take within his ministry ranging from evangelist to moral reformer, from administrator to preacher. It's no wonder with such a range of possibilities that the minister may feel he has to choose between his calling and his wife and family. And choose they do. James D. Berkley is associate editor of *Leadership* magazine and he found that the range of commitment to the ministry went from putting the family first, to a blend of family and ministry, to the flat statement that the church comes first. Melinda feels her husband is in the latter group.

We met Melinda in Chapter Nine when she told us she felt invitations to social events were extended only because she was married to the minister. As a black, Melinda felt they would not have invited her otherwise. Melinda feels the isolation and loneliness of the ministry on many counts. Her husband's absences add to the loneliness.

"His personal demands are the church," she said. "The congregation knows he is always there and they take advantage of this. He has spoiled them. He doesn't see it as a bother. He is a workaholic. He doesn't take a day off. He never uses his vacation time. The church is his first love and for him the church is the world. He loves what he is doing and he never sees it as a bother or a burden."

Melinda included a poignant, angry, painful essay. Here, in her own words, is the anguish she feels over her extreme situation.

"Being married to a preacher, for me, is like being the wife of a man who is having an affair. The church is often referred to in the feminine gender. So for me the church is the 'other woman.' I'm like the wife who knows her husband is being unfaithful but doesn't do anything about it. I guess it's because I know my husband loves me but the 'other women' will always be there. Though I know what's going on, I love him too much to let him go. I'm also afraid to make him choose between us because in my heart I know he will choose 'her,' the church. 'She' will be the one that he works late with. 'She' will be the one that gets his energy and his enthusiasm. 'She' will be the one that he will always find excuses to go to. 'She' will always be first for him but I am his respectability. I am the constant in his life. I am the American Dream—home, wife, and kids. But 'she' is the excitement and joy of his life. After he has tended 'her' needs, I get what's left over. But 'she' requires so much.

"Sure I have the respectability, the title of pastor's wife but 'she' has him. I get the bulk of his pay check but 'she' gets a tremendous part of his check also in tithes and offerings. 'She' has him and when he tires of 'her' for whatever reasons or when 'she' tires of him, he moves on to a better 'mistress,' one more exciting and more challenging." Melinda's husband has worked at five different churches in their thirteen years of marriage.

"He flaunts this 'other woman' all over town but since 'she' is so well liked by everyone and since 'she' has such a good reputation and he is an upstanding minister, no one would ever suspect or accuse them of having an affair. It's just seen as a business relationship or 'the Lord's work.' But I know better because I know what he gives 'her.' I know where 'she' is in his life. I'm the one that takes the back seat to 'her' daily. Do I complain? Darn right I do!" Melinda originally wrote 'damn' here, but covered it with the word 'darn.'

"I complain and I nag but it doesn't do a bit of good. How can I compete with 'the church?'

"He sees no reason to give 'her' up and can you blame him? 'She' brings him social prestige. I can't do that. 'She' makes him look good everywhere they go. I can't do that on his salary. They can do anything and to anywhere under the guise of work or a meeting. He can publicly proclaim his love for 'her' and no one is offended. They can meet anywhere, anytime, and it's acceptable to the community.

" 'She' has a good thing. 'She' has my husband."

Even though Melinda's essay seems particularly harsh on both her husband and the church there's nothing in it that wasn't echoed, less vehemently perhaps, in each of our survey responses. Some bitterness, some resentment, anger, and frustration exists in many, if not most, of the women in the parsonage, and it is directly related to their husband's relationship to the church. Would Melinda do it again?

"I would have married my husband anyway because I love him," she wrote. "I just wish I could find a way now to be married to the man and not to the preacher."

Melinda's words reveal the issue of our next chapter. If there's little time for the minister to be a father and family man, is there time for him to be a husband? What most wives give up, in the name of supporting their husbands, is the intimate

Who Created This Hell?: him, her, or Him?

time their marriage needs to survive. She doesn't shortchange him, and she tries not to let him shortchange the kids. Her devotion to her own call from God often means abandoning her own time and needs as a wife.

13

Cleaving

"Ha! Ha! Does the comment when I climbed into bed recently: 'Hi! Who are you?' sum it up?" said Dianna Higgs, another minister's wife who shared with us. In her survey answers, Dianna always addressed the important issues in her life with humor, not sarcasm. "It's becoming very difficult to find time set aside just for us! We go out to dinner or breakfast once a week. Time is very precious and we get very little of it. Just sitting close and watching a baseball or football game is nice." Dianna is forty-three, has two children and lives in Las Vegas.

Sixty percent of our respondents said that finding time alone with their husbands was difficult. Fifteen percent left that question blank (it was the most unanswered question), and twenty-five percent said that finding time alone was easy.

In the previous chapter, we covered the reasons for this dearth of available time to the ministerial family. Congregational expectations, added to the attitude for both the minister and spouse, can lead to workaholism and use up all their waking time. In keeping with her maternal instinct, her own call to the ministry, and its pressure to support her husband in his calling, she places her family's concerns before her marriage or her own needs.

But married life isn't only sharing children. The family includes children, certainly, but a marriage includes only husband and wife. In our survey, sixty-three percent of the respondents said that alone time with their husbands was squeezed in between the demands of his job, her job, and their children.

"It is moderately difficult for me to get 'alone' time with my husband," said Cathy. "We do have some time together most evenings, but it is at a premium because of interruptions from the phone, our children's advancing bedtimes, general weariness, or exhaustion. Neither of us is very good at giving ourselves time to do what we want. Our time as a couple usually suffers. We rarely go out, much to my exasperation, but this is partly due to the obstacles presented by our isolated living here, having a daughter with a chronic disease (diabetes); she still needs help and support to manage, as well as my husband's busy schedule." Cathy lives in a rural area of Michigan. Her husband is a United Church of Christ minister working for a church with approximately one hundred-fifty members.

"This past weekend we carved out time to go to a retirement party for my parents, who live three and a half hours away. We all enjoyed the time away, but it was short. The kids, my husband and I all shared a suitcase and slept in the same room. We would like to have stayed longer, but had to get back at a reasonable time Saturday night to prepare for Sunday's worship.

"Once in a long while, my husband and I go out to a meal or a movie alone," said Cathy. "The last time we tried, after finally finding a movie we wanted to see that had a Monday matinee, we ended up quite by accident at the wrong end of the city we went to, having gotten mixed up about which theatre it was. We could not get to the movie on time, so we ended up dropping by a nice restaurant for dessert. However, there was a long wait to be seated, which did not seem worth the bother, so we bought a couple of pastries to eat in the car! Some date!

"I cannot honestly say things are this way because of the congregation," explained Cathy. "His *hobbies* are spiritual growth and that sort of thing, so he does not have a clearly defined sense of when he is not doing the work of the church. I wouldn't call him a workaholic. I wouldn't let him off the hook, either, though. Maybe he is a churchaholic. Growthaholic. Meaningaholic."

It isn't just the time he's away that affects the quality of time a minister has with his spouse. The counseling aspect of his job can leave him drained at the end of the day. In a Forum article for *Leadership* magazine (Spring Quarter 1987), Reverend Paul Koehneke stated that out of a work week of eighty to ninety hours, he spent fifteen hours counseling. In the same article, Reverend Frank Tillapaugh stated that in principle, counseling would be sixth on his list of priorities in his job. As a practical matter however, in hours spent, he estimated that it would rank as first, second, or third among his duties. Ministers counsel on as many issues as professional therapists, running the gamut from impending death and actual death to financial crises, marital problems, family problems, low self-esteem; and, because they are ministers, theology, spirituality, and their members' attempts to live up to the examples of the Bible. Although a *McCall's* magazine reader survey showed that most people will turn first to their spouse, second to a friend, and third to their minister for help with a problem, ministers report they are doing more counseling than ever. One reason is because, unlike the professional therapist, the minister's time is free to the counselee. Long hours, high expectations from both the congregation and the minister, and a high percentage of counseling, leaves the minister drained.

"But too often at home, the kids hear, 'Daddy's had a rough day'," wrote Marshall Shelley in the *Healthy Hectic Home*. " 'Let's be quiet.' They vanish to another part of the house," continued Shelley. ". . . They've learned this is not the time to demand Dad's time and energy." Anne Ader, a minister's wife who we interviewed, accepted this part of her life.

"I used to wish for more conversation, but he is not the chit-chat type, so I accepted him for what he is," she told us. "Once I started work, I realized that by the end of the day I was drained, so understood that he was also."

It isn't only the minister who is drained at the end of the day. If both minister and spouse are deeply involved in the church, they can bring all the issues, debates, problems, and crises home, further depleting their store of marriage time.

Harriet is sixty-two years old and married to a United Church of Christ minister, who works at an urban church in Iowa with a membership of three thousand people. The couple has grown children and Harriet said that though she handled most child-rearing duties, he shared when time allowed. Harriet noted that their time together has to be "scheduled on the calendar as a commitment." Bringing church work into the home was an issue she and her husband dealt with early in their marriage.

"We had two children and I was beginning to do more in the church," said Harriet. "I loved the church and had talents to give. This got to be too much. When my husband came home exhausted he found me all wound up waiting to talk about 'church work.' There was never a break. Finally we talked about it in the open and I gradually cut down on my activities and began to develop in other areas. I had a third child on the way. I took over our family finances, went back to some art work, and by that time had a wonderful close friend who shared in ideas and mutual child care. The church work I did was with love and caring. But ever since that time, I have not gotten involved in being an officer or chair of a group in the church. Issues in the church do not become family issues. I found that I can do my share in many ways in the church without taking a leadership role. I think my husband feels more free to share and talk about problems when he knows I don't have a personal stake in the outcome."

Nancy, who shared with us, in the last chapter, the difficulty of her husband's job because of scandals that preceded him, accepts the lack of time and energy as a stage in their married life.

"I look at it as a particular time in our life and believe that as the stages progress there will be time for different things," said Nancy. "The job makes it difficult to get a weekend away—but having kids does too—at their ages. It was by choice that we began and are nurturing a family. I believe there will be time for us as time goes by, but that now we have a commitment to meet the needs at these ages. Our special treats now include take-out dinners after the kids are in bed. And it's amazing how some time together can make up for a lot of time apart."

Thirty-five percent of our respondents thought the time they spent with their spouse was quality time. For the wives that didn't work outside the home, the ministry's flexible hours were an advantage. Many mentioned lunches out, afternoon movie matinees, long walks, and long talks. Even women who held full-time jobs said that their time together was quality time.

But of this group, almost half stated that the time they spent together was doing something related to his job. One woman added in her volunteer work.

"He takes his day off now," said Rose. Her husband entered the ministry when their youngest child was nine. "We do a lot of things together. I stand at the door with him and shake hands after church. I go to the hospital or homes (calling) with him as much as possible. He goes with me to some of the Hospice meetings, to some of my patients' funerals, etc. I think it is great to help each other. He seems to appreciate it too. You have to cope the best way you can for all—not only for yourself."

"Our time is quality even when it is between commitments," Pearl told us. Pearl is sixty-eight and has been married forty-six years to her American Baptist minister husband. "It is easy (to find time) because we think alike. The minister should not be singled out as the only profession having a crowded schedule. My husband and I keep close tabs on each other's schedules and make adjustments as needed. We meet for meals and various functions and are in church together always."

"Quality time is not late at night when either he or I are exhausted," wrote Olivia. She is forty-seven and has three children. Usually this is quality time: "About once or twice a month my husband and I have lunch together at noon alone and that works out well. We have also attended day-long meetings together and that has been helpful because we can discuss the events together and also with the people we have met. When he has a person in the hospital, I will occasionally ride to those places with him (twenty to thirty minutes of driving time each way) so that we can talk during the driving time. Since the children are all in school, we often attend school functions as a family so that gives us some common reference and some time together. Again, this is a struggle and we continually work at spending time together."

Several women mentioned attending conferences with their husbands. While he attends meetings, she rests, takes in the sights or attends the meetings with him. Evelyn Roberts noted that her husband's crusades actually made time for them to be together.

"This was never a problem for me because I often spent time with Oral during crusades, away from home," she said. "Part of the day he was available to talk to me. Now that our children are gone we have a lot of time together."

Almost half said they had one evening a week alone with their husbands. One woman noted that they always take

Cleaving

Friday nights off—unless someone dies. Death is the only church duty they allow to interfere with their time together.

Thirty-five percent said they only got a couple of days a year alone; maybe a weekend twice a year. Two women wrote that they go out with their husbands only twice a month and one noted that they went out alone only once a month. Another woman said the only time they got together was once every two months. Lack of money for tickets, meals, and babysitters was mentioned by twenty-five percent of the respondents. And these are the women who felt it was quality time!

"At times (during seminary for example) our time was squeezed in," said Cindy Chenewerk of Salem, Oregon. Cindy has two children and provides child care services in her home. Her husband is a Southern Baptist minister. They have been married for fourteen years. "So I always went visiting with him and he came to the grocery store with me. I have also 'kidnapped' my husband for dates during the middle of the day. Or told people we were going out, then stayed at home for some quiet time."

"I'm sure this question applies to people who are burdened with young growing families and big busy churches," said Margaret who lives in a town of five thousand people in rural Texas. Margaret's husband is a United Methodist minister. "Our children are gone and our church is relatively undemanding. However, when we were in a busier lifestyle, we always ate breakfast together, the kids, too, and dinner. We always have risen and gone to bed at the same time. We are eager to talk and share our experiences and thoughts. We enjoy movies together, reading and discussing books, news, politics. We enjoy travel, family get-togethers, cooking and eating good food. One of the benefits of a small town existence is the opportunity to be together a lot!"

Some wives, however, are not satisfied with squeezed-in time between commitments. Just because the few hours they find themselves together during a week are good, doesn't mean they're enough. As with other professions, ministers' wives find that a certain quantity of time is required for real quality in their marriages.

"I feel most of the time spent together is squeezed in," said Diana Kemp. "We have tried, and done so, to schedule an event or evening out for ourselves or with other couples. A group from the church is going to hear the Messiah. At least it's better than no time at all. Babysitting does get expensive. We have women who have offered to sit for us free and we take them up on it occasionally. For birthdays we like to go out for dinner—a wine and dine, candlelight type dinner. This is generally good quality time. We have on occasion done this and stayed overnight in a hotel, out of town, with the help of my mother-in-law who stays with the kids.

"We have planned a date at home for next week (first time trying it) after the kids are in bed. We will have an intimate fondue by candlelight in our dining room. Usually once the kids are in bed they are there for the night."

"Fortunately we have, through some very painful crises in our marriage, learned that we must talk, and be open and honest and take that time we need before either of our jobs," said Mary. Both Mary and her husband arrange their work schedules and she noted that they have time to 'jump back to bed at 8:30 a.m.!'

"Through counseling and rebuilding a damaged relationship over the past two years, we have developed some very strong habits," continued Mary. "Regular out-to-lunch conversation, mid-morning getaways, yearly us-only mini-vacations, and spending a couple of extra hours in bed. All that has helped our marriage. Other jobs would not have allowed us flexible daytime choices."

Another couple arranged their days off from work to coincide. They have no children at home.

"I have Fridays off and so does he," said Marlene Northrup, a minister's wife from Arizona. She and her husband married ten year ago. "We know that we're spending the day together, plus Saturday too. It's quality time. We are big movie buffs and enjoy eating out a lot. We also love to browse at new malls that have opened or take day trips away. We really enjoy being with each other and doing things together."

"We schedule in our 'intimate time,' " wrote Marianne Bahmann of New York City. "It is easier for us than people in other occupations, especially regarding sex, because he can be home at odd hours."

What about sex? Do most ministerial couples find it as easy, or easier, to fit into their lives than couples in other professions? Here timing as well as time is a factor.

"We try not to have sex at hours when someone might call him," said Karen Campbell. We met Karen in Chapter Nine where she explained the difficulties of finding a job because of her husband's transfer to a small town. "With both of us at home, we have enough time together, but sometimes sex has to wait so no one will interrupt it till we're too tired. At present we get quality time during the day. It may not be as easy to get when I go back to work, since most meetings are at night. We've had times where one or both of us has been in meetings every night for over a week. Then we got by on telephone calls at lunch hour."

Only about six women give specific advice. One advised making love in the afternoon while the kids were at school and another said to "jump back into bed after breakfast."

"Often our time is squeezed in but how else when he's on call twenty-four hours a day?" said Gloria. "He takes Monday off, (Why do pastors seem to think they're only entitled to one day off when most other people get two?) My husband sometimes thinks of just us going to a play but living in a rural area, everything is forty-five minutes away. We make time to talk more than go out.

"I don't really try (for intimate time) anymore. Perhaps I am jaded but it's just easier to get my cuddling from my kids.

No strings attached, no complications, no hassles. We see this as a problem and so are anticipating a marriage encounter weekend in April to help rekindle the spark or at least sort out our feelings. Actually we feel okay but the rest of the world seems to think differently.

"From my experiences as a family planning educator and counselor, I don't think 'our problem' is at all unusual. At least not from what women in their later twenties and thirties were telling me." Gloria is thirty-eight. "Sexual intercourse is a highly overrated recreational activity in our society. Any woman who has given birth or even been pregnant and who is honest and knows her own self well enough can probably concur that she no longer takes intercourse as glibly as before pregnancy. For me, pregnancy and giving birth changed me forever so that I don't take sexual activity lightly at all anymore. Moreover, as I look around at my peers and older couples, I surmise we're all pretty much in the same boat. We just don't like to admit it. As long as my husband and I continue to agree on the deeper issues of faith and values, being best friends and confidants I think our marriage will survive and even thrive in the future. I've read of many couples who are celibate for years. If it's mutual, it can be cool. Besides we still hold hands. It's less of a 'danger,' our children like it and 'let us,' and we'll not be 'oopsing' another bambino into our world."

"The church is not a drain there as much as the four kids," wrote Mary, a young mother from Florida about sex and alone time. "By the time we get them to bed there isn't much time left for us or I find that I'm exhausted. Our time alone together is quality time since there isn't too much time for it. We make good use of it when it comes. My husband and I communicate very well both verbally and physically."

As noted, an adequate sex life, or the lack of it, cannot be blamed solely on the minister's job. In fact, none of the complaints about lack of time can really be solely traced to the minister's job. Most can be traced directly to peoples' expecta-

Cleaving

tions: The unreal expectations of parishioners, the unrealistic expectations of the minister for himself, and the real pressures the minister's wife puts on herself to aid him in his call. But intimacy is a key element in the marriage relationship. As long as intimacy continues as guarded, shielded, or squeezed in, the marriage is susceptible to problems. Several women mentioned that they and their husbands sought counseling for marital problems. For Gloria and her husband, abstinence may prevent 'oopsing another bambino into the world' but it may also 'oops' her marriage out. As many other couples can confirm, problems in a marriage, if not dealt with, lead to more problems. One of these is infidelity.

    First, let's not make extra-marital affairs the only scapegoat for a bad marriage. Sometimes infidelity and a bad marriage are so interlinked it's impossible to separate them. Let's also not solely blame a bad marriage for infidelity. Much of the current literature on clergy extra-marital affairs seems to do just that and it's usually more than hinted that it's the wife's fault. If Gloria and her husband's celibacy within marriage is mutual, more power to them. If it isn't, then the statistics on clergy affairs should give them pause. It has long been known that sometimes sex is power. And ministers have access to a certain kind of power that makes them vulnerable to abusing it.

    Of the pastors surveyed by Marshall Shelley for *The Healthy Hectic Home*, fifty-three percent selected "building a better relationship with my spouse" as a challenge in their lives. Forty-five percent of their spouses selected it, too. In the Presbyterian Panel study, fifty-eight percent of the pastors said their period of greatest marital stress was the first ten years of their marriage. Only forty-eight percent of the members said their greatest marital stress was in the first ten years. In each group, after the first ten years, the percentages for ministers and members noting the greatest period of stress drops dramatically. After the ten-year mark, there is only one percentage point difference between the two groups. Eighteen percent of pastors chose the second ten years of marriage as the most stressful, while seventeen percent of members chose it. Ten percent of pastors and eleven percent of members said the period after twenty years of marriage was the most stressful.

In a Special Report for *Leadership* magazine titled, "How Common is Pastoral Indiscretion?" (Winter Quarter 1988), a reader survey revealed that twenty-three percent of the pastors responding said that since they had been in local church ministry, they had done something with someone other than their spouse that they felt was sexually inappropriate. Twelve percent said that inappropriate behavior was sexual intercourse. Eighteen percent said they engaged in sexual contact such as passionate kissing, or fondling/mutual masturbation.

In the same issue of *Leadership* magazine, in the article *Private Sins of Public Ministry,* Louis McBurney, psychiatrist and founder of Marble Retreat, a counseling center for clergy, said that only about five percent of their case load involved infidelity by the minister's spouse.

Leadership magazine asked their non-clergy readers the same questions. Forty-five percent of the laity readers, almost double that of pastors, said they had done something sexually inappropriate. Twenty-three percent admitted to sexual intercourse and twenty-eight percent said it involved other areas of sexual contact. Before we breathe a sigh of relief that the infidelity among our clergy is only half what it is in the general population, we have to look at who the "someone other than my spouse" actually is.

According to the same *Leadership* poll, the pastors who admitted to extra-marital sexual contact said it was with a ministerial staff member (five percent); other church staff member (eight percent); someone outside the congregation (thirty-one percent); someone in the congregation (thirty percent); or a counselee (seventeen percent). It is the last two figures that bring us to the convergence of ethics, sexual harassment, and the ministry. The figures show that forty-eight percent of the pastors who admitted infidelity engaged in sexual contact with a person under his spiritual or consoling care. If these pastors used their position, or capitalized on the member's or counselee's awe and respect for them, to get sexual favors, this constitutes abuse of the power he accrues both from being in the pulpit and the pedestal they placed him on.

The pastors who responded affirmatively to the *Leadership* survey said that physical and emotional attraction (seventy-eight percent) was the primary reason for the infidelity. Forty-one percent also blamed marital dissatisfaction.

For thirty-one percent of the pastors who engaged in extra-marital sexual contacts, there were no consequences. Only four percent reported that their churches found out. Sixteen percent said it led to other marital difficulties and six percent said they lost their jobs.

One account of a minister's adultery, written by his wife, also appeared in the Winter Quarter 1980 issue of *Leadership* magazine. The article sheds light not only affairs among clergy, but also the abuse of the power of the pulpit.

Heather's husband Jim admitted to infidelity on the day after Christmas and only after spending three hours with another pastor and his district superintendent discussing charges of sexual misconduct signed by a member of his former congregation. On that day, he admitted to only one affair. The four met: the minister, Heather, the other pastor, and the district superintendent. Heather said she was willing to stay with her husband.

"Though still in shock, I knew I loved him," she wrote. "And besides, where else would I go?"

All four agreed that the couple should spend two weeks at a retreat and counseling center. The district superintendent told them to request a leave but not to tell the church board why they needed the time away. The district superintendent also stated that Jim must leave the pulpit and the ministry.

Heather was understandably shaken. In the three days before they left for the retreat she confronted several emotions.

"I'm married to a man I don't know," she wrote. "I'm not a pastor's wife anymore." Heather wandered around the parsonage, trying to imagine packing up and leaving. That deepened her depression. Then she blamed herself.

"I could see where I had fallen short of meeting his needs to be close," she said. "The Lord brought to my mind many times I had been prompted to reach out to him, to make advances, to go and sit by him, even to sit on his lap. Usually, however, I would give in to continuing the busywork at hand. I was determined to heed those promptings in the future." Heather noted they hadn't taken their vacations for three years but she didn't explain why.

Then they left, by car, for the retreat center. Along the way Jim admitted to more affairs. Most with close friends of Heather, most within their former church's membership. Angered, Heather threw her rings at him. Then, retreating to her religious training, she swallowed her rage.

"God's word instructs us to forgive one another," she wrote. "Since not to forgive is also sin, I had no choice but to forgive. And so I did, not just my husband but all participants. Noble? No! There is simply no choice."

The affairs started fourteen years earlier. Heather said her husband had been "confronted" by a woman in the church who seduced him. Then years passed without an affair. Then:

". . . one of the women who later signed a statement against Jim chased him until she caught him," wrote Heather. "I knew she was chasing, but I assumed he was running." Several short-term affairs followed and then the women signed statements against Jim with the denomination hierarchy.

When they returned from the retreat, Jim announced from the pulpit of his former church his moral failures. Then, the current pastor asked people to come to the altar and pray for their past sins.

Cleaving

He also selected altar workers to assist. One of these was the woman Jim had an affair with fourteen years earlier.

"My mind was screaming," wrote Heather. "I passed my hands over my mouth to keep from saying anything."

Heather gave us reasons why she feels ministers stray: Insufficient income, undefined success in ministry, high expectations, loneliness.

"In order not to spend all her time jealous, curious, or angry, a pastor's wife has to give her husband to his work—almost to the point of not caring," Heather said. Heather made a list of things to do to prevent this same situation from occurring in other marriages. Some positive points on her list are: making time, learning about intimacy, explaining, and talking.

"Sit still long enough for him to catch you," she advised. "Enter into sex with abandon." Heather's list for husbands is not only shorter, but leaves off any advice to him about his responsibilities regarding their sex life. In fact, the closest she gets is advising him to write loving things to his wife. Heather notes that most of the support during this troubled time given only to her husband.

"Many, many letters to both of us encouraged me to forgive him, and assure him that good has come from his past ministry. Many times the help I get is in the form of 'Have you lost any weight? How are you treating him now?'"

"How did you let yourself get so isolated?" asked Reverend Sherry Taylor, one of our authors. "This is one of those 'blame the church, the ministry, the other women, myself, Satan—anybody but him.' So he isn't really responsible which seems to me to be one of his problems in the first place. He's not taking responsibility for anything, his role as pastor or husband.

"This man has serious problems and shouldn't be in the ministry," further advised Sherry. "This man victimized women everywhere he went and the wife sees him as the victim. She apparently needs to stay with him so much that she blames everybody but him—including herself. Her blame is only because she tolerated his abuse. And apparently she'll keep on doing it."

In truth, this pastor abused not only his marriage but the power of the pulpit as well. It is a myth that the laity see their pastor as human. Too many see him more as God himself, placing the minister on a pedestal, absorbing his teaching, and obeying his commands.

"Many pastors haven't been trained to understand how often a parishioner can be attracted to the role of the pastor—the power, the holiness it represents," said Arch Hart, Dean of the School of Psychology at Fuller Theological Seminary in the article "Private Sins of Public Ministry" in this same issue of *Leadership*. "There's often tremendous idealization, which affects everything including sexual attitudes. If the pastor allows it, it must be okay."

For the Jim Bakkers still among the ministry, the power of the pulpit works to their advantage. Vulnerable women among the parish are susceptible to the sex-power plays of sick or unscrupulous ministers. One pastor described his sexual contacts as "authority rape."

And the power of the pulpit acts to preserve the integrity of the ministry as a whole by covering up the lack of integrity of some unfaithful ministers. In the book *Is Nothing Sacred? When Sex Invades the Pastoral Relationship* (Harper & Row 1989), Marie M. Fortune explores a case of sexual abuse and harassment involving a single pastor. Fortune is Executive Director of the Center for the Prevention of Sexual and Domestic Violence in Seattle.

This book, which we strongly recommend, detailed the accounts of several women in his parish whom he seduced. These women filed statements with the church and the denomination hierarchy.

For the most part, they were not believed.

"Many women don't speak out about sexual abuse by

pastors because, along with enduring terrible damage to their own self-esteem and relentless public shredding of their reputations, they will suffer the loss of personal and community relationships—what may amount to devastating social and spiritual exile," wrote Ann Janine in *"Blaming Women for the Sexually Abusive Male Pastor" (The Christian Century,* October 8, 1985). "The time-honored response to such situations is to blame women, the "other woman" or the pastor's wife—for the sexual transgressions of a male minister."

The pastor profiled in *Is Nothing Sacred?* was transferred to another church. Fortune was called in to minister to the wronged women. *Is Nothing Sacred?* was the result of that ministry and it highlights and explains the reasons why Elmer Gantry-type ministers can abuse and not lose. It was the women this pastor stalked who paid the price, losing their church, their pastor, and their friends with no legal recompense or feeling that justice was done. Unlike the very public scandals of Jim Bakker, Jimmy Swaggart, Marvin Gorman, and Gordon MacDonald, many unfaithful ministers stay in the ministry. They are required to get counseling, but they are transferred to other parishes. The minister in *Is Nothing Sacred?* moved on to a larger, wealthier parish. Part of his negotiation stipulated that the record of his abusive acts would not be placed in his personnel files. Therefore, any church calling him in the future would not know about the charges. And it was all done in the name of preserving the integrity of the ministry. Thankfully, it is rare, but that does not ease the pain of the women already hurt.

As already noted, most clergy affairs start with a mutual attraction, and some are fueled by bad marriages, or, at least, the perception of bad marriages. In ministerial marriages, as in all marriages, communication is the key.

". . . relatively few of them plan to have an affair," wrote G. Lloyd Rediger, Director of the Offices of Pastoral Services, Wisconsin Conferences of Churches in an article in the

October 1986 issue of *The Clergy Journal.* He speaks of the early 1970s when clergy weren't counseled about having affairs, versus today, when counseling is often done.

In *The Problem Clergymen Don't Talk About* (The Westminster Press, 1976) Charles L. Rassieur advised couples to affirm each other and their commitment to their marriage.

"For some pastors and their wives that frankly may be very difficult for them to say," he wrote. According to Rassieur, pain and anger are emotions many deal with silently for years and then have little strength left to really work on the marriage, Rassieur could have been describing Agnes.

Agnes is sixty-three years old, married almost forty-one years to an Evangelical Lutheran Church of America minister who has worked at the same church for the past thirty-five years.

Agnes knew her husband-to-be was headed for the ministry and felt inadequate to fulfill the role of the minister's wife. He told her he wanted a wife, not a Sunday school teacher. She did both, teaching Sunday school for twenty-two years.

"I have been the church secretary all my life, going on forty-one years," she wrote. Agnes, who wants to remain anonymous, says "I work with the women in all projects: Tying quilts, cleaning the church, serving suppers, preparing food for picnics, outings, camping trips. I worked at a nursing home as a Registered Nurse for eighteen years. I'm retired now."

Agnes wrote that what made her most angry was the women who flirt with her husband and lead him on. She also wrote about what made her the saddest:

"Watching my husband hug the women and young girls and put his arm around them and the only hugs I can get is if I initiate them makes me feel angry inside," Agnes told us. "Having a husband who is attracted to certain women and he keeps running over to see them and confides personal matters to them.

Cleaving

"I know I sound rather bitter, but I have many hostile feelings to deal with. My husband must be addicted to women and girls, because he can't keep his hands off of them and I am treated like I have the plague. I have pretty much been pushed to the back burner and have felt like leaving many times but knew it would mean the end of his ministry. I felt I shouldn't do that. Now I feel I made a mistake but he is retiring this year so I hope to stick it out.

"He is a workaholic and it has been very hard keeping up with everything he dreams up to do. People think he is a great pastor and he really is, but a poor husband. I keep my mouth shut so they don't know that. Our children feel that he always paid much more attention to other girls than to them. They have resentful feelings." Agnes and her husband have four daughters.

"He is married to his parish. He is usually so exhausted when he comes home that there is nothing left for me. I have been served the leftovers and they haven't been great. We have hardly ever played together. When I try, he is always paying attention to some other woman or young girl.

"Sorry I have to feel this way, but I believe in honesty."

What's the solution to the lack of time and intimacy in ministerial marriages? Sparks' proposal for a community ministry pool would give these couples at least some uninterrupted time. Several wives, and authors of self-help articles and books, advised getting an answering machine to screen calls during family or marriage moments. Many noted getting out of town for the evening, day, or weekend. Jane and Penny, two other ministers' wives, mentioned that they plan their vacations to places where there are no phones. The most frequent advice given by the wives themselves was to intentionally schedule in time for each other and the family. Although it seems cold and calculating, making appointments may be the only way to get the quantity of time necessary to make it real quality time.

The obvious solution is for the minister to take his days

off and vacations and work less hours. It's high time the sixty to ninety hour ministry work week ended. When the long hours seem inevitable, some women develop a change of attitude. It's not the best solution, but for some women, it works.

"I think it's a privilege to be who I am but if I tried to stay in that traditional mold, I would have continued to become angrier and resentful," wrote Jessica, married thirty years to her husband who works in the Evangelical Lutheran Church of America denomination. "I went to a free class. It really helped me to see myself as an individual who could have control of her life. The turning point for me was to move here eighteen years ago and go back into nursing and do my own thing with my husband's full encouragement.

"I think some pastors' wives never find their own identity and function with an external focus of control—the church," said Jessica. "It's very sad when we never find out what real freedom in Christ is, to be comfortable with ourselves, in fact, to love ourselves so we are free to love others. That's what Christ is all about—and it feels great."

"For most of our thirty-seven years of marriage, I felt that I ran a poor second behind church priorities," said Karen. "Now I realize that I must own as much responsibility for that as my husband. Yes, congregations are demanding. Yes, we are both workaholics. Yes, other professions make equal, or even greater, demands on time and energy. We must be clear within our own minds what we can do: what we cannot, or should not do; what we must do; where we stand in the great scheme of things; and where we stand with ourselves and with our mate. Deep down I know that I am really important to my husband. And to my children. And to God. That's all anybody needs."

"My husband and I have very little time together," wrote optimistic Loisruth Chilton of Las Vegas. Loisruth's husband is a Baptist minister. "We're planning a wonderful holiday in Heaven: a special little island in the clouds somewhere there, with sparkling pools for swimming and a cool forest-covered mountain for hiking!"

But a good attitude may only go so far. How does it hold up when the ministerial couple finds themselves "owned" by a "killer" congregation? What happens to that good attitude when criticism leaves him, and his spouse, tumbling in its wake?

14

Clergy Bashing

"Petty people make me angry," said Mary Weaver. Mary Weaver is thirty-eight, has been married seventeen years to her Presbyterian minister husband, Dudley. They have a son and daughter. "I have not yet seen, or heard of, a congregation that did not have several whose primary role seems to be that of stirring up trouble. They generally behave like small children: If they feel they, or their favorite causes, are being ignored, they find something trivial to belabor. I pity them, for I see them as a people who usually are not taken seriously in any other areas of their lives. Because the church is by definition a family, these people are granted a hearing in their congregation. Unfortunately, while the church staff and officers are devoting themselves to resolving the problems caused by these selfish people, important programs and serious needs of the church must be put on hold. And many of them stay there! My husband is most frustrated by, and feels least effective in, his work when all he can seem to do is 'put out brush fires.'"

In the Mace study, thirteen percent of the pastors and nineteen percent of the wives listed "unfair criticism from church members" as a disadvantage of the ministry. In our study, we asked the women to whom we talked what made them angriest. Twenty-five percent said unfair criticism. Another eleven percent said unfair criticism was the saddest part of being in the ministry. In all, thirty-six percent of our respondents listed this aspect as a disadvantage in their lives. It is interesting to note the use of those two words together. They connote an emotional maturity on the part of these women toward their husbands' profession. Not one wife used the word criticism without unfair before it. They know criticism is a way of life, necessary in order to grow and improve.

Mary Weaver pointed out that criticism couldn't be avoided. "I have known ministers' wives who were so caught up in defending their husbands that they were unable to think of anything else," she said. "Anyone in a position of leadership is going to be questioned, criticized, and opposed at least some of the time. And the chances are good that any leader is going to make mistakes, or at least make decisions that don't please everyone. My own philosophy in this regard includes the fact that people cannot be led unless they chose to follow. No matter how good or right an idea may be, it cannot be carried out, at least in a congregational setting, without the support of a fair number of people. If the necessary support is lacking, then the idea needs to be abandoned, at least temporarily. I also keep in mind that every congregation we serve existed before our arrival and will continue long after we have gone. It is, in a very real sense, 'theirs,' not 'ours.' "

Ministers' wives also know that unfair criticism is an unnecessary and vindictive part of their lives. John, one pastor who wrote, said that he was fired for turning up the thermostat. His congregation accused him of being too involved. Emily, one minister's wife, told us that what made her saddest was watching her children's anguish over leaving a church, schools, and friends when their father was fired for "no apparent reason."

Ministers receive criticism from many sources on many subjects and in many ways. If new at a parish, the minister may be constantly compared to the previous pastor, reminding the

Clergy Bashing

new minister that he's not quite filling the shoes of the old minister. "That's how dear Pastor John would have handled it!" has scuttled many a new ministry.

Sermons are the pastoral duty most visible to the most members. If the minister injects a little humor into them, some feel he takes his position too lightly. One member of a congregation refers to his pastor's sermons as the comedy hour. If he's all fire and brimstone, he's accused of being too serious. And God help the preacher who "preaches" from the pulpit. He's accused of inciting boredom. More than one sermon a year on tithing can send members scurrying to a less financially demanding congregation.

Changing the order of the worship service can also get him in trouble. Fired up, eager, flexing his ministerial muscles, the pastor who breathes new life into the Sunday bulletin may be just asking for trouble. While the members of his congregation who welcome new experiences Sunday morning may applaud him, conservative members steeped in that congregation's traditions are more apt to start a holy war. One pastor wrote that he asked his board of deacons to cancel the evening service on Christmas Day as it would mean the third church meeting in twenty-four hours. The evening service was sparsely attended anyway, pointed out the pastor. On Christmas night there would be almost no one there. One deacon strenuously objected, accusing the pastor of a lack of commitment to his faith. The deacon only backed down when the rest of the board revealed they wouldn't be attending that service either.

In fact, changing anything at church can stir up so much controversy among the members that it keeps the minister practicing damage control for months, even years. A chance comment about ugly drapes, old furniture, or that strange blue paint on the sanctuary walls may be taken as a direct hit on the person, committee, or deceased member the drapes, furniture, and paint were donated by, arranged for, or in memory of. The unwritten rule among ministers is to wait at least a year before making changes to anything.

Not only does the minister have his own work to do, he oversees the work of the laity as well. In a September 25, 1989, *Fortune* magazine article titled "Turning Around the Lord's Business," Thomas A. Stewart estimates that all the volunteer labor in all the churches in the United States equals seventy-five billion dollars a year. With all those people working, the pastor's job should be easy. But as the overseer, he comes under fire when his volunteers fail to perform their tasks.

"I get peeved when congregation members neglect their responsibility towards keeping the church and property clean, mowed, and repaired," wrote Ida. Ida is thirty-two, married nine years to her husband who is a minister in the church of the Lutheran Confession denomination. "They just leave it for 'someone' else to do. That someone is always the minister and/or his wife. I don't mind helping, but I do resent it if we're the only ones doing this work."

". . . clergy often express the frustration and anger they feel toward parishioners who apparently have failed to do their jobs properly, or indeed to do them at all," wrote Anne Craig. Craig is project manager of the Sharing the Ministry conferences for the Alban Institute. Her article appears in a booklet, *What do you want your pastor to do?* "Developing norms under which laity hold each other accountable for completing agreed-upon work relieves clergy of playing policeman."

But play policeman he does. And he'd better play it well, because any fallout isn't going to hit the layman who fell down on the job. It's going to fall directly on the minister.

"In the anxiety of organizational tension, members cast about for a party to blame," wrote Speed B. Leas in a 1985 Alban Institute article titled *Moving Your Church Through Conflict*. ". . . they focus on the pastor as the one who has caused the mess or the one who should fix it." Reverend Sherry Taylor agreed.

Clergy Bashing

"The pastor is the easiest identifiable symbol of the church other than the building," she said. "He's like a lightning rod. Whatever right is God's doing—or the church; whatever goes wrong belongs to the pastor."

"It has been said that the clergy, particularly those in a parish setting, are the last remaining professionals who minister to the whole person," wrote Daniel B. Leavitt in *The Minister and the Mid-Life Crisis,* "and because demands placed upon the minister are so broad-ranging and omnipresent, it becomes impossible to satisfy them all. Thus an element of failure is built into every minister's role expectations."

You can't please them all, is how pastors put it. Neither his sermons, his changes in the order of worship or repainting the sanctuary will affect all his members the same way. It isn't only the things he does, or doesn't do, that cause controversy. The minister may take a pulpit unaware that it is already in the middle of a conflict as immense as differing philosophies on the inaccuracy of the Bible or as petty as how high the thermostat should be set. Differences in opinion within the congregation about its church's role in religion and the world may have already divided his parish.

"I am angriest when I feel my husband is being attacked unfairly for not stretching himself farther and for not taking stands that support the values and opinions of a very diverse congregation," said Shirley Skirvin. Shirley and her husband had a commuter marriage for a year when he transferred to Washington, D.C., from New York.

"The folks left of center want him to be more politically active; the folks right of center want him to stick with the spiritual and avoid the political altogether," Shirley continues. "It is incumbent upon the minister and his wife to be true to themselves and their own values, and to keep a steady trust that they are doing their level best to be true to the Ground of Being."

When members' differing opinions turn into a boiling

cauldron of controversy, he must play the Great Reconciler. It's the minister's job to court compromise, heal the divisions, and close up the ranks. When he can't, the minister becomes the focus of the problem. In many cases, he's also left with no way to defend himself. Any defense of his own position, no matter how right, will serve only to further divide the congregation. He's damned if he does, and damned if he doesn't. So most don't.

"I have discovered that it is very often impossible for a minister to defend him/herself," said our author Reverend Sherry Taylor who counsels clergymen. "Certainly it depends on the charges. However, if a significant number of people or people in leadership positions cease to trust in the effectiveness of your ministry, it doesn't really matter whether you are right or wrong. When things reach that point, it is clear that you can no longer be a pastor in that congregation. The enormous frustration for clergy is that they sometimes find themselves in positions where they believe they are being falsely accused. When they try to defend themselves, it only splits the congregation and makes matters worse. There are a lot of situations in which clergy wish to be vindicated, and it simply can't happen.

"Many ministers are people with a high need to please," she continued. "Their self-worth is tied up in pleasing people. Sometimes you don't have to do anything wrong and your effectiveness is just lost. I think it is really tough when that happens. It is a really nasty place to be."

The minister has a tough role to fill but then, that is his job. The challenge of a divided congregation may appeal to him. Because of what Reverend Sherry Taylor calls the halo effect, some of the criticism is directed at his wife instead of at him. Just as some members of the parish find it easy to criticize the minister, some people can't bring themselves to criticize the resident "holy man" at all. They have no such reservations about taking it out on his wife.

Clergy Bashing

"Just as I find it difficult to deal with attention that is given to me simply because of who I married," said Mary Weaver, "I also have trouble with anger or criticism that is directed at me because someone is angry, or disagrees with my husband."

"People say things to me they want to get back to my husband," said Jackie Haggin of Pierre, South Dakota. She's been married thirty-seven years to a United Methodist minister who now works at a church with a membership of one thousand. "Either behind my back, loud enough for me to hear, or directly to me. Also they make thoughtless remarks about my husband's abilities not realizing I also identify with him!"

The two-fer expectation is another area where the wife suffers the backlash of her husband's ministry. Jennifer Shew thinks it's time congregations recognized the two-fer attitude for what it is—financial clergy bashing.

"The time has come to hire and pay women who do the work of a full-time minister if the church is expecting, or accepting it," Jennifer said. "I do feel there should be increased awareness of role, function, etc. of clergy spouse on the part of the congregation.

"I am constantly resaying to people that I do not know details of my husband's schedule or calendar. Also, when appropriate, I talk about my experience as a clergy spouse, about men friends who are married to women clergy—all to raise awareness and counter outdated, prescriptive expectations for spousal behavior."

Marianne Bahmann was angriest over "the arrogance of people who presuppose that we are all like 'Church Lady' from Saturday Night Live, or Tammy Faye Bakker, or prudes."

Clare Smith of Charlottesville, Virginia, remembers an incident with a member of her husband's parish.

"When I was doing college teaching, I forgot a lunch once which I had been indefinite about attending," said Clare.

"The hostess, a rather mean-spirited old lady, was miffed. But then she was always miffed and eventually left the church."

Unfair criticism isn't leveled only at the minister. His spouse, in a church with a strong two-fer attitude, may come under fire too. Michelle, whom we met in Chapter Nine, made a list.

"I have been accused of being stuck up, because I didn't go around and speak to each and every one even though there might be five hundred people," she told us. "I have been criticized for not being a regular teacher in the Sunday school program. I have been criticized for being 'unsociable' because I didn't cater to the 'in' crowd. I have been criticized for my dress and my family's dress. I have been criticized for being outspoken and not hiding my feelings. I have been criticized for the type of work I did in order to help ends meet—manual labor, housekeeping. I have been criticized for my children's behavior, even though they were as well behaved or better than some who criticized." Even with all this criticism, Michelle said that being a preacher's wife wasn't totally negative. She had many wonderful memories, too, but she didn't list those.

Why does the criticism of the pastor and his wife seem incessant? As we've covered the aspects of the ministerial couple's life, we've found a severe lack of communication between the minister and the church, the church and the wife, and the wife and the minister. Problems arise because the pastor may be unaware of the expectations until he runs into them. These expectations, even if known by the congregation, are rarely stated during the interview process. Only after the minister accepts and the congregation hires, do they both discover there were questions that should have been asked.

". . . many of the problems that grow up between pastor and parish seem to have their origin in the implicit assumptions and unvoiced expectations of each about the relationships which were never expressed or checked out," wrote Richard H. Kirk in a booklet, *On the Calling and Care of Pastors*, published by the Alban Institute. ". . . it is important that vestry or board and pastor negotiate some kind of written contract or covenant which spell out these assumptions and expectations in very concrete and specific terms." A job description detailing the minister's duties and the expectations of the spouse would eliminate many misunderstandings. But it is a rare congregation that has studied its own needs and attitudes sufficiently to know what they are, or even to recognize that they have expectations at all.

The Ministers and Missionaries Benefit Board of the American Baptist Churches *Survey on Clergy Compensation* asked laity and clergy to rank what duties should be used to evaluate the pastor. Both pastors and laity chose preaching as the number one evaluator. The laity chose church growth as the second most important performance evaluation point. Pastors placed that item sixth. Third on the laity list was visitations. Calling was tenth on the clergy list. Pastors felt that the second most important evaluation should be on their amount of responsibility. Laity listed this item tenth in importance.

Clearly there are differences between the clergy and the laity on what's really important in the church. In this instance, they are in agreement on only one point: preaching. Where the pastor sees a long list of responsibilities that occupy his time, the laity wants him adding new members to the rolls. When asked to rank his duties in the order they were actually evaluated, the pastors listed the numbers crunch factors right after preaching: growth, attendance on Sunday mornings, budget, level of giving, visitation. They felt their congregations evaluated their level of responsibility as ten in importance out of nineteen factors.

Differences in expectations occur all too frequently. They lead to criticism of the pastor, the pastor's spouse, and their children if that congregation holds strong expectations of the two-fer philosophy. A minister in this situation needs to educate the congregation on what they can, and cannot, expect him and his family to do. Even then, they may not hear what he says. One wife wrote that even though her husband posted the same two days off each week in the church bulletin, they were still beset with petty phone calls at home. One couple, Jesse and Peter, received a phone call at 3:00 a.m. from parishioners saying that they had just taken their daughter to the hospital. The pastor told them he'd get dressed and be there soon. They told him it wasn't necessary for him to come down. The situation wasn't life-threatening. They just wanted him to know their daughter was in the hospital.

Sometimes criticism goes beyond conflicting expectations. Sometimes the ministerial family finds themselves the victims of clergy bashing installed in the pulpit of a "killer" church. Every church has its one or two members who create problems. Usually out of a sincere devotion to their congregation, or their job within it, they can make life hard for the pastor. But some churches defy all education, guidance, and patience. When constructive criticism turns into unfair criticism and involves more than just a few members, that's clergy bashing. Some churches seem born to eat their ministers up. Clergy bashing occurs when a church seems to go out of its way to demean a pastor.

Nancy and Michael faced their share of clergy bashing mostly over parsonage issues. The first incident occurred when they moved from Georgia to Massachusetts. In the South, at that time, ministers paid their own utilities. Electricity was cheaper there. When Nancy and Michael received their first electric bill in the Massachusetts parsonage, they paid it. And they continued paying the bills for three years. Then, while reviewing past budgets, Michael noticed that there was a line item for parsonage utilities. He brought up the bills to the trustees and they agreed to pay them. Michael didn't ask for reimbursement for the previous years' bills. The trustees didn't offer to pay them either even though they knew they always had before.

Clergy Bashing

"I felt funny about asking for it," said Michael. "I spoke to Nancy and we decided not to make waves. Today, if I had to do it over, I'd say, 'Remember the last three years? Let's take care of that, too.'"

"There's two levels that I think clergy work on being accepted: for themselves and being accepted as the leader of the congregation," said Reverend Norman Levinson. Levinson left parish ministry to become Associate Coordinator of Pastoral Services at the Institute for Living. "It was very hurtful when I realized that many times as far as I was concerned, they accepted me as a human being but when I wanted to exert the clergy authority (I hate that word, but I must use it), now all the little devils come up."

"A lot of my fellow clergy have run into this, that when the minister speaks in what they perceive as a clergy role, now that's a little bit different. Many people in the congregation are not willing to give that over even though they love the man. That totally confuses the man, hurts the man and that's going to affect the wife."

"Having my husband open to attack," said Mary-Jean Miner about what made her angriest. Her husband is a United Methodist minister. This is the second marriage for both of them. Mary-Jean and her husband found themselves assigned to a "killer" church and she worried for their health. Mary-Jean is hypoglycemic and tends toward depression under stress. She didn't want to be an added burden to her husband and went for counseling. When nothing helped, they requested a transfer. Distance gave them perspective and they recognized that they had, indeed, been abused by the former church. Their marriage, ministry, and health are still intact, in spite of what Mary-Jean describes as "unreasonable persons with serious problems sometimes, who manage to use power positions unfairly. One cannot respond in ways which may be divisive to the church community and many times the conflicts must be kept confidential. 'They' often never hear 'our' side, and the church grapevine tends to be swift, very involved, and not necessarily strong on facts. Sometimes we are *amazed* at the quotes attributed to us! It did help a bit to know that the church had a reputation as a 'killer' and that clergy bashing seems to occur to other nice people, too."

"It's like a family," said Catherine trying to explain the abuses that arise in a congregation. "Everyone in a family is different. We're all unique. I'm unique. Charles is unique. We don't always get along in a family. Then you have the congregation. You have all these different people with different personalities and they all come together and you're trying to keep peace and live together and be Christians. But we don't always get along. And we have to accept each other with all our faults. That's what it's all about. We're not perfect. I've made mistakes. Charles made mistakes. Can't they be forgiven?"

But mistakes when you are the clergy or his or her family are not easily forgiven or forgotten.

"I knew," said Beverly Kaiser, married thirty-five years to her United Methodist minister husband, "that my husband could lose his job if the children or I did anything that upset people very much." We heard one story where a Lutheran minister was told his wife must stop her political involvement in the community. It didn't reflect well on the church, its members, or on him. He told her. They are now divorced.

It isn't just church members who can make life hard for the ministerial family. The congregation's leadership, senior pastors, even denomination hierarchy can come down hard on a nonconformist minister's wife.

Melinda, who wrote us an essay describing her feelings about the church being the "other woman" in her husband's life, was a Baptist when she married her husband who is a United Methodist minister. She remained Baptist after their children were born and until he received his second appointment as a head pastor. But she joined only because of the expectations of the church and its hierarchy.

Clergy Bashing

"In our first church, my husband was associate pastor while he was still a student," said Melinda. "The head pastor called me in and told me that my attendance was too irregular and that I needed to take a more active role in the church.

"At our second church, my husband was doing his internship and the pastor called me in and talked to me about joining the Methodist church.

"In our third church, a leading member called me aside and told me that I should have my children baptized." Baptists dedicate their babies but believe that Christians should be older and able to choose baptism. Other Protestant denominations, including Methodists, baptize soon after birth. "Another member told me I should be more active and that I could make arrangements to help more since I didn't have a job outside the home.

"At our fourth church, I was told more than once what I should be doing by members. I should be part of the women's group. They thought I should help with teas.

"In our fifth church, my husband is head pastor," concluded Melinda. "I've been told by the administrative chairperson that I should attend funerals and weddings. I still do not attend them unless I know them personally and am friends with them."

How the hierarchy arranges her husband's schedule concerned Beth.

"Church bureaucracy drives me crazy," Beth said. "I have little patience with the hoops my husband has to jump through. There is little regard for the very little time we have alone. The church seems to feel very free to create a meeting on his one day off. Some months he goes three weeks without a day off. He still carries a twenty-five client counseling case load, so this means I rarely see him. I resent the constant intrusions for administrative and bureaucratic events. I never resent the real minister's calls—distress, sorrow, need."

For Annie, whose story of her depression begins in

Chapter One, the hierarchy intervened at an emotional and physical low point of her life simply because a Bishop felt Harvey needed some "mud on his shoes," the Bishop's euphemism for humbling Harvey. The Smiths were transferred from the suburban Georgia church that Harvey helped build to a small rural church in the hill country.

"We took Christian to Danielsville when he was two weeks old," said Annie. "I was very weak. I cried a lot. That move was tough. All moves are tough. I hate them. But that one! I couldn't see why they wouldn't let us stay another year so that I could get my strength back at least." For Lorraine and Jim, who we met in Chapter nine, the hierarchy created their commuter marriage when they transferred Jim to a church three hundred miles away from Lorraine's job.

Margaret resents that the hierarchy has passed over her husband for advancement during his thirty-five years as a minister.

"Failure on the part of our Bishop and cabinet to recognize my husband's skills," she answered about what made her angriest, "and the utter inability on my part to do anything about it!"

Clergy bashing is not just the province of church members and hierarchy. In our research, too many of the books and articles aimed at ministers and their spouses supposedly offering advice, encouragement and support, actually practice clergy bashing too. Too much of the advice does little more than perpetuate stereotypes, leaving the ministerial family with the impression they must live up to a myth of perfection. Although their final conclusions may be sound, the examples they use indicate that living up to the unrealistic expectations of the congregation is a job requirement. What they leave out of their self-help material, the denunciation of attempting God-like behavior, negates the advice they offer.

The saddest form of clergy bashing is when minister

and spouse do it to themselves through their own unrealistic expectations.

"A large majority of the ministers I have met are sensitive, spiritual people with a high sense of calling," wrote Mary La Grand Bouma in *Divorce in the Parsonage*. "They are conscious of being God's special representatives in the world. When people do not respond or things do not go well in the church, they often blame themselves. And because people expect so much from them, they try to live up to these expectations."

"My husband has never been able to spend much time with the family," said Karen. "Even when family activities were scheduled, church-related responsibilities always seemed to interfere. Sometimes I believe my husband was reluctant to say no to the intrusion; other times, in all fairness to him, the church duties did seem to need to take precedence. I say 'did seem to need to take precedence.' Maybe, in hindsight, some of that should have been changed. Even now, we still experience a good bit of difficulty in scheduling uninterrupted quality time for family."

"It's a work that is never done," wrote Marjorie Udall of the ministry. Marjorie and her husband are retired after more than forty years in his career as a United Church of Christ minister. They raised four children. "It's never completed, and I feel that I, personally, am not doing enough."

One woman told us she wanted to see the movie *Dirty Dancing*. She waited until it came to a theater in the next town so she could "sneak in and out without getting caught" by a parishioner.

Jacquie Reed said that the second thing that made her the angriest, after unfair criticism of her husband, was the complaints of other ministers' wives. Her answer underscored the dichotomy of philosophy among ministers' life: those who embrace it and those who live through it.

"It annoys me when I hear other pastors' spouses complain about their homes, congregations, etc.," she said. "Although we have lived in difficult places, our philosophy has always been to bloom where you are planted. You can choose to be happy and make the best of a bad situation, or be miserable. We have chosen the former and with God's help have found it hard to leave each appointment." Jacquie said what made her the happiest was that "by the love of God and his strength, I have been able to 'gut out' eleven years of difficult appointments."

Some wives are so blessed with Christian charity and cheerfulness that what another wife would call clergy bashing they call humor.

"There are humorous stories, too," said Gloria who told us in the last chapter about her celibate marriage. "Like our open house for the three congregations in our first parish. Three elderly ladies went on a self-directed tour of our parsonage which, incidentally, my husband and I spiffed up quite a bit with paint, wallpaper, carpeting, curtains, with money, blood, sweat, and tears of our own. When they went upstairs, they took it upon themselves to open my bathroom cupboards to inspect! I accidentally happened upon them, they looked so sheepish I pretended not to notice, smiled, and whispered a silent prayer of thanks to God that I had cleaned them too in preparation for the big day.

"I haven't done an open house per se since!

"We also don't make as many improvements either, only half the house now. And we don't pay for the stuff anymore either—the congregation does. We have a standing joke. If we wallpaper or paint the parsonage living room, we will be asked by the bishop to move on. Well, we just finished the dining room tonight . . ."

Most time the only way out of a horrific church situation is to move to another one. It isn't the only reason ministers change pulpits, but moving introduces yet another set of stresses and pressures for the ministerial family.

§15§

Get the Hell Out of Here!

"I am a very poor mover," said Betty Jean Souers, married thirty-three years to a United Church of Christ minister. Betty lives in Jacksonville, Florida, and has moved four times. "It tears me up inside. I am okay once I get to the new situation, but it is saying the good-byes that is so hard for me." Forty-seven percent of our respondents agree with Betty. Moves are tough to handle because they mean leaving friends, changing schools, and hunting for a new job. The only events more stressful than a move are the death of a spouse, divorce, or going to jail. It takes anywhere from a year to eighteen months to recover from the trauma of a move even if it goes smoothly. Before we discuss the reasons why a ministerial couple puts themselves through this trauma, we need to explore how ministers are hired for a pulpit.

The process a minister, or a church, takes to fill a pulpit differs slightly depending on the denomination. Although none of the protestant denominations use strictly an appointment process such as the Roman Catholic church, some come close.

Most denominations are broken down into conferences, or districts; geographic areas over which they have jurisdiction. Some denominations, such as the United Methodist, have more control over which pastor goes to which pulpit within their conference. In those denominations, when a pastor wants to transfer, a select list of possible pulpits is supplied based on the ruling body's perceptions of that pastor's needs and gifts. If a congregation requires a new pastor, another select list is supplied to the congregation of candidates picked because the ruling body found a match of congregational needs and pastoral gifts. From these lists, the pastor approaches the congregation, or the congregation interviews the pastor.

In other denominations, such as the United Church of Christ, the pastor notifies the conference that he wants a new pulpit, supplies a list of his wants such as location, size of church, salary, and the specific needs within a congregation he feels he wants to challenge himself with next. A church that needs a minister also notifies the ruling body of its wants. More often than not, the congregation is unaware of the real needs within it. Few address, for example, their expectations of the minister's wife. But the prospective minister does get a list of what the congregation *thinks* it needs.

Both systems have merit. In the case of the United Methodist minister, the advantage is strong job security. Even though the local church asks to have him transferred, he is not fired. He always has a job. It is the responsibility of the conference staff to find him another pulpit. Job security encourages pastors to be risk takers, to point out the spiritual and human faults of a congregation and work to correct them even if the congregation resists. A United Methodist minister cannot be fired merely for disagreeing with his congregation.

A United Church of Christ minister, on the other hand, *can* be fired for just such disagreements. Without the semiappointive process of other denominations, his job tenure is based squarely on his performance *as the congregation evalu-*

ates it. In essence, the U.C.C. minister does not have job security and this can reduce his desire to take risks and promote change in the congregation he serves.

Finding a new pulpit, or filling a vacant one, can take up to a year in those denominations that do not use the appointment process because the work is conducted by volunteers. Selected members of the congregation form a search committee to review applications, listen to sermon tapes, travel to hear the prospective candidate deliver a sermon and conduct a worship service, and interview.

Arranging all this around the time schedules of ten to twelve volunteers can eat up months.

The job market in the ministry *is* tight. In a *Time* article (December 1988), Richard N. Ostling wrote that in the Presbyterian Church there were fifteen hundred to two thousand ministers competing to fill only six to seven hundred churches. Ostling also noted that in the Episcopal Church, eighteen hundred ministers with secular jobs were waiting for pulpits to open up. The United States Occupational Outlook Quarterly states that competition in the job market for ministers is, and always has been, strong. There are always more ministers than there are pulpits to fill. But ministers still make moves.

"Leaving a church and the parsonage and driving to your next home, it is a very strange feeling," said Marylyn True. We have met earlier where she told us being married to a minister had no effect on how they raised their children. Marylyn's husband, George, is a Congregational minister. They have moved three times into church parsonages and have never owned their own home.

"You are stripped of any real material ownership, you are keyless, relying now on a relatively unknown congregation to which you have handed over yourself to—physically and spiritually. It is a chance to take, but I have always had some sense of God wanting us to be in a certain place at a certain time.

"It is very difficult to leave a church," said Marylyn. "In fact, in some unexplainable way, you never really leave. You touched lives, and distance and separation does not change that relationship."

In our survey, 34.1 percent of the respondents had moved less than three times. Forty percent moved three to five times and 25.7 percent moved six or more times during their husbands' careers. Four women moved twelve times. Our survey shows, based on years of marriage (our respondents total two thousand two hundred thirty-five years experience in ministerial marriages), ministers move every five and a half years. In fact, in the *Leadership* article, Donald L. Bubna estimates that twenty-five percent of all ministers moved every year. A study done by the Alban Institute and the New England Career Center showed that the most effective ministries lasted about eight years. The study also found that it took a minimum of five years in one pulpit for a pastor to gain the respect of a congregation. In fact, the study group defines a long pastorate as only ten years or longer.

A *Leadership* magazine article by Gary L. McIntosh, (Summer Quarter 1986) cited studies among Lutherans, Methodists, and Presbyterians that found a pastor's most effective years in a pulpit don't even begin until the sixth or seventh year.

Our respondents' length of employment in a single church ranged from a low of six months to a whopping high of thirty-five years.

Some reasons for this high mobility in the ministry is because of the appointment process in some denominations. A denomination steeped in itinerary moves its ministers more frequently than denominations that simply assist the local church in finding its pastor.

"Our family handles all moves (well, nearly all moves) the same," said Karen. "We always go into a church and truly make it our home. Then when it comes time to leave, we all fight it and want to stay forever. However, we know in our hearts that we need to go, if that is the plan of the Bishop and Cabinet." Karen and her husband are United Methodists. "We say our goodbyes and look forward to getting settled into the new place as soon as possible. Within a few weeks, we are almost as much at home in the new place as the place we have just been. Our children followed this pattern as well, and they have remarked on more than one occasion that moves, though painful, helped them learn how to cope in new situations and enriched their lives many times. We feel good that they were always able to adjust." Karen and her family moved twelve times. Eight of the moves were to new pulpits, the other four were to new homes within the same community. Three of the moves occurred in one six-month period when they moved out of the old parsonage, into a rental home, and then into the new parsonage. Karen's youngest child was six months old for the first of these three moves.

But the itinerant system doesn't explain all moves, especially in those denominations where the local church hires and fires. The statistics on the number of ministers waiting for the relatively scarce number of pulpits suggests that most ministers should hunker down and stay put. Why do they expose themselves to the intense competition for another pulpit?

"Only twice did we move to get away from a bad situation," wrote Jean M. Parker of Seattle, Washington. Jean's husband is an Episcopal minister. "Then other times we moved from one church to a better situation. We usually anticipated new, exciting adventures: a new city to know, new friends, etc. We expect to be here until my husband retires in eight years."

The Ministers and Missionaries Benefit Board of American Baptist Churches *Survey on Clergy Compensation* asked pastors what prompted them to leave their prior church and accept their current pulpit. Almost fifty-five percent responded that they were attracted to the new church's leadership or congregation. Over forty-four percent said they moved for personal or family reasons. Thirty-five percent said they no longer felt motivated at the prior church and went in search of a more challenging pulpit. The fourth most selected reason was getting away from specific problems at the prior church. The fifth reason pastors moved was for an increase in pay and the sixth was to move to a larger congregation with more ministry options. The final two reasons were to move to a more attractive church with better facilities, or to a better parsonage or housing market.

When the Baptist survey asked the laity respondents why they thought any pastor moved to a new church, almost seventy-three percent thought it was because of loss of motivation at the prior church—the third reason the pastors chose. Sixty-seven percent of the laity chose specific problems at the prior church as the reason a pastor changes pulpits. Almost sixty-two percent of the laity feel that moves occur for personal or family reasons. Both pastors and laity chose a larger congregation or wider ministry as the sixth most important reason a pastor leaves a pulpit. The laity put financial considerations higher than the pastor, placing more money fourth while pastors place it fifth. And in a strange twist on their own assessment of the local church's leadership and congregation, the laity selected their own attractiveness to the minister as fifth important while the pastor put it first.

Obviously, the congregation's perception on why a minister moves is different from the pastor's, and once again we encounter opposing expectations just as we've encountered them on every other issue between clergy and congregation. As discussed in the last chapter, clergy and congregation only agree on the importance of one of the clergyman's duties: preaching. Everything after that varies in importance by who's expressing the expectation, minister or member. Probably the shortest ministries come early in a minister's career. As in secular employment, on-the-job training may be the only real way

Get the Hell Out of Here!

any of us learn the pros and cons of the profession we chose. It takes time and practice to discover our strengths and weaknesses, which aspects of the job we like best and which we are best at. A minister's first church may not fit his conception of his ministry after he's been there a year or two. With a better understanding of his own style of ministry, and after discussions with his peers, he realizes another church is more suitable for him. So the attraction of a different church's leadership or congregation becomes the number one reason to change churches.

"The excitement of a new church wanting Bob to come and be their pastor," wrote Peggy Ostenson about her happiest moments as a minister's wife. Peggy and Bob are Presbyterians and have been married for forty-one years. They moved six times during Bob's career, and each time, both agreed that the move was God's will for them. One of those moves was from Los Angeles to Woodville, Mississippi, a small town with a population of only thirteen hundred.

"The large church in Coral Gables, Florida, contracted him out of the blue," said Peggy about their last church. "They flew us down from Mississippi. We were in awe over the beautiful church and almost afraid to step into such a position. Bob really prayed several days before he accepted. It was an exciting ministry during which twenty-six young people went into full-time service. We saw lives change."

Personal and family considerations was the second most important reason that pastors gave for moving from one church to another. Some ministerial families find it difficult to live far from their extended families and relatives.

One wife pressed her husband to transfer from a rural to an urban area because the schools were better. Ministers also move, as do laypeople, because their spouse receives a better job offer. As the number of dual career couples in the ministry increases, the spouse's career will become even more important in the decision to change churches. The ministry also offers families the opportunity to live in a different part of the country, expanding both their horizons and their life experiences.

Loss of motivation at the present pulpit was the third most important reason for changing churches. As a minister grows and gains experience, he becomes more comfortable with his role, learns how to handle it and discovers what challenges him. Many ministers accept a call to a church with specific goals in mind. They want to concentrate on evangelism, help build a new church, or increase a congregation's awareness of their own spirituality. The minister may see a church unaware of community needs and, like Harvey, want to increase their awareness. Another minister might see a church so active in the community that they've let their spiritual growth lag behind. Armed with his goal, the minister accepts the call, rolls up his sleeves and gets to work.

Once the minister perceives that he has met the goals he set for himself when he accepted the pulpit, he begins looking elsewhere for a new challenge. If he doesn't find it in his present congregation, he looks to other ones. The minister who finds his goals have changed midstream, which happens more frequently to new ministers fresh from seminary, also searches for a new congregation. Sometimes the goals are simply impossible to achieve within the present congregation, so the minister leaves that pulpit to another pastor better suited to the task.

Ministers do leave churches over specific problems. Infighting can ruin the effectiveness of a ministry even though the pastor has done all in his power to clear up differences. Problems that existed before he took over the pulpit contaminate his ministry. Because he is, many times, powerless to defend himself, any action he takes can be misconstrued by the opposing faction and may goad them on to sabotage the good that might come from his efforts.

Seminary students are warned to come into a new

church with their own attitudes, expectations, and ministry style firmly in place.

Six months, a year, even six years into a pastorate, is not the time to change his personal style. Although he's decided to preach minus his clerical collar, drink beer at parties, or get active in local politics; his congregation is used to the "old" minister, the one he was before he made what are, to the congregation, startling lifestyle changes. The desire for change is the first indication that it's time to move on and let his growth, maturity and new ideas bask in the reaction of a new congregation.

Sometimes the specific problems that drive a minister to a new church are part of his negotiated pay package. Eager to start in the ministry, the pastor may have settled for much less in money and benefits than are healthy for his family. Congregations are traditionally wary of starting stewardship campaigns to bring a pastor's salary up to par with either the community, the congregation, or his professional colleagues. One congregation refused to raise their minister's fourteen thousand dollar annual salary. His resignation forced them to increase it to twenty-seven thousand dollars. It proved impossible to replace him at the salary they paid.

Marital problems also precipitated moves. One Congregational church search for a year to fill their pulpit and settled on a minister from another state. He arrived, but within a month, sent a letter to the Board of Deacons and the entire membership of the congregation announcing his resignation.

The pastor had accepted this call, because he wanted to get away from the woman he'd had an affair with in his prior congregation in hopes of saving his marriage. But his lover followed him to the new church, and they decided he would leave both his wife and his ministry.

It isn't only the husband who can wreak havoc on the ministerial family. Wives participate in extra-marital affairs, too, although in lesser numbers. One wife's solution made it impossible for her minister husband to stay at the church where he worked.

In a *Leadership* magazine forum article titled *How Pure Must a Pastor Be?*, panelist Charles Swindell, a pastor from Fullerton, California, told of a member of his staff whose wife left him. Some of the marital problems were because of the pastor's tendency to workaholism.

The couple divorced and later she remarried. Swindell told the pastor that, at some point, he'd probably want to date and remarry. Swindell didn't think the congregation could handle it. He recommended that the pastor transfer to another church.

"For many months we tried to keep him in our ministry," said Swindell, "but eventually the difficulty and awkwardness of the situation became too much for the congregation—even our great flock—to handle."

"Of course, any big change in a minister's life is difficult for the congregation to cope with," said Donald Njaa, Executive Secretary of the Ministry of The Evangelical Covenant Church, and also a panelist. Njaa stated that his church would probably have allowed that minister to stay. "Things get disrupted, and that minister may have to relocate simply because people can't cope with the change." Relocating seems a high price to pay for someone else's actions, even if it was his wife's.

Ministers' wives also pay the price for their husband's infidelities. Usually she forgives and, faithful to scripture and her own needs, follows.

"Many ministers' wives will not risk joining the 'other woman' in exile . . ." wrote Ann-Janine Morey in an article for *The Christian Century* (October 5, 1988). ". . . many marriages still operate on the assumption that the male minister's vocational identity will determine his wife's identity as well. If she fails to defend him, even when he has clearly betrayed her, she risks doubting the value of her own life dedication, and she calls into question the efficacy of her husband's entire ministry

Get the Hell Out of Here!

as it is exemplified in his loving, forgiving wife." So time and time again, ministers' wives are the ones to forgive and try to forget, but who still suffer the traumas of moving on in the midst of marital problems.

Looking for a new pulpit can solve these problems. The minister who is blocked by a board that won't increase his pay, give him a housing allowance, or increase his benefits, can negotiate those items into a new contract with a new congregation.

When they move on, now a little smarter, a little surer, and just a little suspicious, the minister and his wife clearly state during the interview process what they will live up to in the way of congregational demands. By learning, before he accepts a pulpit, that a church has high expectations for his wife, or unrealistic demands for its minister, he is free to decline that pulpit.

Like everyone else, ministers move to better their situation, work in more attractive surroundings, make more money, achieve new goals, and to challenge themselves. The changes are exciting. The new church is like an African safari with an amazingly rich and diverse jungle to explore, unknown and mysterious. Moves, however, are stressful and studies show they are more stressful for the spouse than for the minister. The minister's role is better defined than his wife's. Because of the long hours associated with the ministry, it usually falls to the wife to plan and execute the move, get everyone settled and find all the new doctors, dentists, babysitters, dance and piano teachers, dry cleaners and drug stores her family needs. Then, according to our survey results, every five years she starts over again from scratch.

"I guess the biggest disadvantage for me is the frequent moving," said Margaret who has moved "eleven or twelve times." She and her husband are United Methodist. "I have finally come to the point of really WANTING my own home and a long-term friendship circle." Margaret is fifty-nine.

"Sometimes I've moved with joy and expectation, sometimes reluctantly." Margaret and her husband originally planned to serve a church for a few years after he graduated from seminary. Then, both would return to college for advanced degrees. "Our subsequent changes of plan were mutually agreed on." Both Margaret and her husband completed their degrees then returned to the midwest and itinerancy. "I can't *really* say I wanted that, but we did agree that it was best for him. How I feel about it is a mixture of joy, disappointment, and knowledge that we have very often been in the right places at the right times."

In *Married to the Minister,* Roy M. Oswald points out that while the minister gains a support group quickly in the congregation, ". . . his wife needs to move more slowly and cautiously, attempting to ferret out those relationships which will be understanding and caring, but not lay too heavily projected expectations upon her."

While these new relationships form, the minister's wife rarely has the readily available support of her, or her husband's, family.

"Seldom does a minister live within a hundred miles of either his family or his wife's family," wrote Robert W. and Mary Frances Bailey in *Coping with Stress in the Minister's Home.* "As a result they do not have the opportunity to enjoy the companionship of their parents—especially since they do not have any 'long weekends' to go and visit them."

"Moving isn't the easiest thing, especially with children in school," said Nancy. Nancy's husband accepted the challenge of healing a church hurt by the past abuses of both its pastor and music director. "I never moved as a child. I grew up in a town where my ancestors started the church and the fire department, drove the first school bus. My children don't have that, or relatives nearby—some would say that is no loss—but I grew up with a great sense of extended family. So for my children, we substituted with 'adopted' church folks who serve as Grams and Gramps, Aunts, or Uncles.

"The hardest part of handling each move has been with the children, when they talk of wishing we hadn't moved, or what would it be like if we still lived in a particular place," continued Nancy. "Mostly we use these as the beginnings of good discussions about how moving makes us feel. But as the ones who made the decisions to move, we feel responsible. On the plus side, it has given us a chance to learn about different areas and build lasting friendships in each place, and that's something we want the kids to experience, that even though you move, you can nurture a relationship."

"Both of us attended college and spent our first year of marriage three hundred fifty miles away from our homes, so we were fairly well adjusted to being away from our families," said Mary Weaver, married seventeen years to a Presbyterian minister. "We returned to my hometown for Dudley's seminary years. During our first three years, my father's sudden, tragic death and my mother-in-law's equally sudden and tragic death made us more aware of our love for and reliance on our families. We also felt much more responsible for our surviving parents. Moving far away for a year's internship was very hard on both of us; our son was born that year, and we needed, and missed, the support of family and friends. After the final year of seminary, we moved to a parish comfortably close to my husband's family. Two years later, we moved to his hometown and enjoyed six and a half years of being able to be with, and call on, my husband's father and stepmother, sisters, grandmother, aunts and uncles! When we moved again, almost four years ago, leaving them behind left a tremendous void in our lives.

"We have never really *had* to move (in the sense that Methodist ministers *have* to move, or Presbyterian ministers who run into trouble *need* to move)," said Mary. "We had to decide each time a call was issued and have turned down several which seemed to be good opportunities but did not give us the gut feeling that they were right. God's will is often very hard to grasp!"

For Darlene, leaving her family was so difficult, she mourned as though a death had occurred.

"Our last move took us away from my parents and a sister to whom I am very close," said Darlene. "It was terribly difficult. I handled and experienced it as a death with a great many of the same grief reactions. I felt I was still in mourning. This is our third church in eleven years. I understand and can accept the reasons for the moves, but it is very difficult."

Sixteen percent of the pastors surveyed for the Presbyterian study said that leaving their families was an area of stress for both of them, but forty-nine percent said saying goodby to friends was the most stressful aspect of their moves.

"We have moved three times so far," said Olivia, married twenty-four years. "Moves are difficult emotionally because each time, friends are left behind. I find it takes a minimum of one year to get acquainted and accustomed to the peculiarities of a new location. We try to maintain family ties, especially at these difficult times when other ties are broken."

David Augsburger, professor of pastoral care at the Associated Mennonite Biblical Seminaries, wrote in a November 20, 1987, article for *Christianity Today* that "the healthy person needs from twenty to thirty significant others or so each drawn from family, church, work, play, neighborhood, and relatives." As noted, it can take more than a year to adjust to a move. But adjusting isn't the same as rebuilding a close circle of friends. By the time the minister's wife re-establishes her personal network, it may be time to move on again. Over twenty-five percent of the pastors responding to the Presbyterian study said that making new friends was an area of stress for both partners in the marriage.

Thirty-nine percent of pastors found that adapting to a new job created tensions for both themselves and their spouses: many of whom *must* find a new job. Job opportunities

Get the Hell Out of Here!

for ministers' wives with careers may be slim at the new location. Even without professional careers, our respondents complained that they left a job they loved and that it took a long time to find anything comparable in the new area. For some of the women, leaving their jobs was also a blow to their self-worth and independence.

"As a preacher's wife, I've move eight times in nineteen years," said Jeanette Paulson. Jeanette is forty-one and wrote an article for *Spice-a* newsletter for clergy spouses on the subject of moving.

"I move poorly," Jeanette continues. "This last move was particularly hard emotionally. I was working part-time as a writer at a weekly newspaper—just finishing five years at it. I did a good job, earned respect for my work, made wonderful friendships with my co-workers and, in fact, had higher visibility in the community than my husband. Now, I'm back to being 'the pastor's wife' and struggling mightily with my loss of personal identity."

One wife, who moved six times in twenty-five years, wrote "shifting careers on each move has presented challenges that I have not always welcomed." Jacquie Reed, who has her own speech therapy practice, thought moves hampered her career.

"Every time we have moved, I have been at the peak of my profession, and then we go. I must say though, opportunities for employment have opened up wherever we have lived. Some have been out of my profession, but rewarding personally."

"My biggest problem emotionally is finding a job," said Diana Kemp. Diana is a Presbyterian married for eight years. She is a nurse and has worked, at least part time, throughout her marriage and their two moves. "Deciding when and where to start. You apply and wait in anticipation, hating to leave the house in case they phone. I tend to get crabby and impatient with my family during this time. I know deep down that God will open doors when the time and right place come along, but it's tough!! We just moved this past July, so I'm going through this job searching now."

For one wife, previously married to a career military man, marriage to her Episcopal minister husband meant staying put for the last fifteen years. She moved nineteen times as a military wife.

"I have need to work in order to have enough to educate the children and save for retirement," wrote Rosemary Todd of Cheyenne, Wyoming. "I am fortunate to have a good education and the opportunity to stay in one spot so I could advance in my job." Rosemary is the Nursing Director of the County Public Health Department.

Other aspects of moving also produce stress. One woman told us that when they moved from the southeast to the northeast and changed denominations, the culture shock was too much to handle. They quickly moved to the southeast, although to a different state, and back to their original denomination. Jennifer Shew wrote that the transition from seminary in New York City to their first congregation in Ithaca, New York, was so stressful that her husband began to have back problems.

Shirley Skirvin told us why she decided to have a commuter marriage for a year when her husband accepted the call of a Washington, D.C. parish: "My more painful move was the breaking up of our home in New York where we had raised our children," said Shirley. "My son had already left home, but our daughter lived with us all through her college years and we had to leave her behind when we moved to Washington. It was good for her but very hard for me to 'abandon the nest.' We have moved, altogether, about ten times since we were married."

Forty-one percent of the pastors responding to the Presbyterian study noted that leaving their present congregation was an area of stress for both themselves and their spouse. When the pastor's resignation comes as a surprise to the con-

Get the Hell Out of Here!

gregation, they may react with anger. Lyn Cotton of Lakewood, Colorado, has been married seventeen years to a Disciples of Christ minister. She also compared a move to experiencing a death.

"Moves are always difficult, mainly leaving friends behind. They are also exciting—an adventure," wrote Lyn. "But mostly they are kind of like a death experience. Death of relationships can hurt a lot. We were called to his current church. Many people at the prior church were actually angry and felt he was moving just to hurt them. 'Why are you doing this to *me*?' they would ask. I just couldn't understand that, and it made me kind of bitter toward some."

Why compare moving to death? Many people move—the national average is, after all, twelve moves in a lifetime. But unlike other professions, ministers are advised to sever most, if not all, ties to their former church and community. The rule of thumb here is to wait at least two years before returning to a former parish for any special event or visits. Trips back to a former congregation undermine the work of the current minister to win the confidence of the congregation. He'll hear about "dear Pastor John's" way of handling things for longer than he cares to, even if Pastor John does wait the two years to return of a visit. If the previous pastor makes a habit of returning often, and sooner, the new pastor may never assimilate his ministry style into the congregation. So, the minister and his family cut themselves off from associates and friends in former congregations. Some friendships flourish only after the minister has moved on. Several wives noted they struck up relationships with members of prior congregations because they could no longer be accused of playing favorites. It is more likely, however, that the ministerial family will sever all ties with a former congregation, yet another aspect of this profession that is like no other.

In Marshall Shelley's research for *The Healthy Hectic Home,* he found that seventy-seven percent of the pastors strongly considered family when accepting a call to a new church. Some of the factors they mentioned were moving closer to relatives; to areas with better schools; better job opportunities for their spouse; a church with families and children closer to their ages; and the desire to live in a particular city or area of the country. Some members, denominations, ministers, and their wives, still feel the decision to move rests solely on the minister's understanding that it is a call from God that both he and his family must obey. That is changing, and more ministers than ever consult their wives on this important decision.

"We are contemplating our second move," said Cathy who is forty, married eighteen years to a United Church of Christ minister. Although he attended seminary when she met him, Cathy's husband did not feel the call to a local-church ministry until they'd been married for twelve years.

"When my husband decided to go into the ministry, we were living in our own home, in a city with rather few UCC churches, in a section of town without any," said Cathy. "We were at a crisis point in our life, and did not discuss much about what we wanted in a new situation. I was anxious to make a move, but did not examine what I wanted in a new situation. I assumed that we had to take whatever came along, which was true to some degree, because my husband had not had a church job before; but my resignation and denial in dealing with the situation we moved into took me years to face.

"I am handling this move much differently. I was convinced of the need for it long before my husband was. We have tried to talk about many aspects of the new situation we hope for." Cathy's husband now works for a church in rural Michigan with one hundred fifty members. Cathy told us in Chapter Five she felt forced to shake hands with parishioners at the close of Sunday service. She's learned, the hard way, as most new ministerial couples do, that the time to find out about a congregation's expectations of the minister's wife is during the interview

Get the Hell Out of Here!

process. Her comments show that there's more to accepting a pulpit than just acceding to the strength of her husband's call.

Several wives mentioned that they knew it was time to move on before their husbands decided to look for another pulpit.

"We have moved four times in thirty-two years, which isn't bad," said Lois Farina, married to a United Methodist minister for thirty-three years. "I was rather glad to move each time. I was more ready than my husband. We were seven years at our first charge, thirteen at the next, and nine at the last. We're now going on our fourth move here in Madison (Wisconsin). Actually I looked forward to the move 'cause it got me out of things I was tired of doing or wanted out of."

Ministers don't always choose to leave a church. Sometimes they get fired. Our research didn't uncover statistics on the number of ministers fired from congregations. The recent scandals of Jim Bakker and Jimmy Swaggart in the Assembly of God denomination, and the year's suspension of InterVarsity Christian Fellowship president Gordon MacDonald, among others, show that churches are serious about punishing the unethical, abusive, or illegal activities of their ministers. Sometimes, though, the firing is for reasons that are less clear cut. A firing may be the climax of difference of opinion in theology that escalates into a holy war, or it may be the result of a pastor tinkering with a thermostat.

On May 2, 1991, just days before the deadline for this manuscript, we received a letter from one of our respondents. It was unsigned with no return address. We tried matching the handwriting and the distinctive hand-stamped shell design on the back of the envelope. But there's no way of knowing, for sure, which of our respondents sent this letter:

"Shortly after I filled out your questionnaire, my husband was fired!! No reason given—at least none that holds water: e.g., one of the rumored reasons was that I was a working wife, however, at the time he was fired, I was not working and had not worked since we arrived in that assignment. Naturally, living in church-paid housing, we had to get out. (They generously gave us two weeks to pack.) Being underpaid church workers, we had barely enough savings to rent a moving van, not enough to rent an apartment to move into. The Church is investigating my husband's firing—till they complete the investigation, he can't be hired for any church position. No outplacement services were offered—no loan toward relocation—no severance pay—nothing. The only assistance we were given was that one of the church employees bought us one bag of groceries. Fortunately, we had a relative with a guest bedroom who was willing to let us stay indefinitely; equally fortunately, that relative lives in a city with good job prospects for a good secretary, and I was able to get a job inside a week. My husband was terribly upset about the firing. We had no medical insurance until I'd been working three months. Then he was diagnosed with severe depression and prescribed medication at $60 a month. He *did* finally agree to look for work, but had so little self-confidence he'd only look at part-time, minimum wage jobs. Calls to the Church about the investigation result in only the report 'we're working on it and will let you know.'

"So now the big thing I hate most about being a minister's wife is that if an accusation is made and the church board believes it, he gets fired, is guilty until proven innocent, and these people who claim to be Christians show no charity. The faster they could wash their hands of us, the better. The worst is that no one will tell us what the accusation was. How can we disprove it if we don't know what the problem is? Any reasons we've heard are either ridiculous or outright lies."

Unfortunately, our respondent practices the very habit of which she accuses her husband's former church: withholding information. She did not list what the ridiculous or outright lies were.

"Normally, this type of action (decertification) would not be taken unless he were having an affair, having marital problems, or abusing drugs or alcohol. They can't prove any of those, so we're certain that wasn't the problem. (I don't think either of us drank anything stronger than Pepsi in front of any member of the congregation and in the whole time we were there, our total consumption was two bottles of white wine and one six-pack of beer.) There were never any complaints about his performance, at least not to us. So, who knows what accusation was made? Or how they intend to make it stick?

"To fit more easily in the space on your form, I guess we should call my complaint about ministry 'tenure uncertain and based on board's whim.'"

Whether they choose to leave or are fired, moving is traumatic. When they choose to leave, even if the new church turns out to be worse than the last, they can choose to leave again. But a firing such as the one just described can inflict a greater trauma: leaving the ministry altogether.

16

Take This Career and Shove It!

"Over the years I have suffered from stress-related ailments—digestive problems and mild (nonclinical) depression—which I am sure are related to my husband's work. In a very real sense, ministry is a family profession: we are all bound up in and aware of problems and tensions within the congregation," said Mary S. Weaver. We first met Mary Weaver in Chapter Four when she shared her feelings about not having a pastor to turn to in her times of need. "Because my husband is never really 'off duty,' I am always 'on duty' as far as the family goes. All trips and vacations are planned and carried out tentatively. 'We're going to see Granddaddy next week if nothing comes up,' is the only way of life my children know. I can understand why more and more clergy marriages are ending in divorce and why many ministers' families have emotional problems. It's a tough way of life, and one that most 'outsiders' seem to feel should be all sweetness and light!

"If I did not truly believe that my husband is doing the work he is meant to do, I would beg him to find another way of using his abilities rather than just teasing him about it occasionally. The same thought enters his mind from time to time."

How often does a minister consider leaving his profession? According to the Baptist Survey on Clergy Compensation, 11.7 percent of the pastors responded that they very seriously considered leaving the ministry. Another 34.5 percent said they considered quitting somewhat seriously. Over fifty-one percent said they never considered leaving the ministry.

Members, on the other hand, have an overinflated view of life in the pulpit and 84.4 percent of them said that their pastor *never* considers leaving the ministry. Only 9.3 percent thought their pastor considered quitting very seriously (1.7 percent) or somewhat seriously (7.6 percent).

The reasons a pastor leaves the ministry are the only area that they, and the laity, agree on. Both pastors and members said that conflicts with the congregation, goals, or expectations were the primary reason for seeking secular employment. Thirty-three percent of the pastors chose this answer while 27.9 percent of the laity picked it. A little less than a third of the pastors placed financial considerations as the second motivator. And 13.9 percent of them said a personal reason such as burnout, health, no personal growth or career considerations was the third reason for leaving the local parish, or the ministry, behind. Laity had those reasons reversed. Over nineteen percent of the members said personal reasons were the deciding factor and only 14.8 percent said money drove their pastor from the pulpit. Clergy placed family considerations fourth on their list (7.2 percent). Almost ten percent of the laity felt their pastor left the ministry because he had a loss of God's call or a loss of faith in God's word. Another ten percent of laity said age or retirement were the reasons their pastors left the ministry.

It is interesting, that while ten percent of the laity choose a loss of faith as the reason a pastor leaves his profession, that reason didn't appear on the ministers' list and neither

Take This Career and Shove It!

did age or retirement. The laity obviously fails to understand the depth of devotion a minister feels to his work. The ministry is not just a job. It is a calling—a powerful one. Even after they've chosen to leave the ministry, pastors still feel like pastors. Even in secular employment, many still feel the call to minister. The pastor who told us that being called to the ministry was like having a wart on his nose that he couldn't get rid of, reminds us that the call to serve God exists for a lifetime, not only through one's working years. To leave it behind, to fight such a strong pull, can diminish self-worth, create bitterness, and cut deep emotional scars.

If the aftereffects are so bad, why do pastors leave the ministry? For some, it's purely a question of money, or rather, the lack of money. Most laity feel their pastor is better off financially than they are themselves. Of the members responding to the Baptist survey, 47.5 percent felt that their pastor's salary was higher or much higher than the members of their congregation. Only 17.2 percent of the pastors agreed. In the same study, forty-eight percent of the pastors felt they were falling behind inflation while 53.8 percent of the laity thought their pastor's salary was keeping up with the rising cost of living. As their children get older; as they compare what they don't have with what others at their age and income level do have; as college bills loom in the future and they realize they have no equity in a home for their retirement, the minister may choose to leave the profession. One pastor noted that while he never expected to get rich, he didn't think his children had to settle for second-rate colleges, because he couldn't afford to send them to one of their choice. He left the ministry for secular employment and a bigger paycheck.

There is still the feeling among laity and churches that paying the pastor a paltry salary keeps him humble enough to lead them on their spiritual journey. Instead, low pay drives a dedicated, devoted pastor out of the ministry, because he must meet the needs of his family. So steeped are some ministers in following the biblical example of Jesus, that they fear even asking for an increase because they will appear greedy. Rather than demand they be paid what they're worth, they desert the profession.

Vern was a United Presbyterian Church of America minister for almost sixteen years. Ordained in 1950, he left his last church in 1966. Socially conscious, Vern traveled to Selma and participated in the Alabama Freedom March with Dr. Martin Luther King. Vern's ministry style was to push his congregation into social awareness. As a Presbyterian, Vern worked for a denomination that had semiappointive powers to place ministers in churches. With this secure base, armed with his social conscience, he used his bold and antagonistic style to prod his churches into social activism.

"In fairness, I must tell you that my husband is somewhat of a radical in his approach to the church," said his wife Carol. "His plan was always to 'shake people up and make them think' and his ministry was unconventional. This always led to conflicts with the 'old guard' in each congregation and he finally gave up." Vern was often proud of the fact that he divided the churches he served because, by holding up the mirror, he forced them to look hard at themselves.

Vern's abrasive style wasn't his only problem in the ministry. He received his share of clergy bashing.

Once, he moved the communion table a few feet away from the wall where it normally stood. People in the congregation were furious. Vern proved, using biblical texts, that the Lord's supper was served *around* the table, not just in front of it. Tradition prevailed. The table was replaced.

In another parish, where the parsonage was next door to the church, Vern's sons played basketball in the parking lot. A parishioner, the wife of a former minister of the same church now retired, told the boys to play elsewhere. She took Vern to task for allowing his sons to play games on sacred ground. Pointing out to her that it wasn't sacred ground, it was a parking lot, did no good. She complained to the church board and they voted to prohibit all games from any church grounds.

Because of his aggressive style, built on his belief that the church's responsibilities went beyond the spiritual to the community, Vern was asked to leave all of the churches he served except for the last one.

Even at home, his social consciousness met barriers. Vern's wife didn't want him marching in Alabama, placing himself in danger, possibly leaving her, and their four children, without a husband and a father. But it was the strain of low pay in the ministry that dealt the final blow for Vern's ministry. Deeply in debt, he left the church for secular employment and enough income to support his family. Then, Vern's wife revealed an affair with another minister, a close friend of her husband. Vern went to the church for help. He wanted counseling to save their marriage. He also expected some justice from the church hierarchy, some punishment for his best friend's moral lapse. Vern got neither.

"My problem is distinguishing between his personal problems and the problems in the church," said Carol, Vern's second wife. Although Carol met Vern after he left the ministry, she lives with the aftermath of Vern's experience in the church. "Vern is very bitter. He blames the church for his loss of ministry and his divorce from his first wife. He doesn't think they gave him the support he needed. He's physically ill, emotionally ill and punishing himself, too." Although both Vern and Carol tried psychiatry and therapy over the years, Vern resists change. He has a heart condition, severe arthritis and has attempted suicide several times. At age sixty, he was fired from his secular job. Because of his expertise, therapists advised him to start his own business. For a year and a half, Vern told Carol he was writing brochures and developing proposals to start the business when actually he wasn't doing anything.

"I've asked him on a number of occasions if he would like to have a church again and the answer is always a resounding *no!*" said Carol. Carol learned not to ask too many questions about Vern's past. The questions only escalate his bitterness and aggravate his hypertension. Although he left the ministry, Vern never stopped being a minister.

"I used to cringe when I woke up and found it was Sunday morning," said Carol. "Vern sat in front of the TV flicking the remote control through all the channels with religious programs. He ripped every show, every minister apart. His analysis of their style, message, and religion went beyond sarcasm to vitriolic diatribe." Finally, Carol took control of the remote. "I just couldn't take it anymore. When he asked for the remote, I just said 'I'm watching this.' Then he'd leave the room.

"I'm not a Pollyanna thinking everything is wonderful all the time." said Carol. "But I do believe that negativism begets negativism. My attitude towards life is to remove myself from as many negative things as I can. Not him." Vern has isolated both Carol and himself from the world. As a couple, they have no friends, belong to no clubs, and never entertain.

"I've given up entertaining," said Carol. "It's too nerve-wracking," Vern dominates all conversations with the same aggressive style he used in the ministry. Carol remembers one dinner party where Vern so antagonized the host by monopolizing the conversation and putting him on the spot for his religious beliefs that they have never been invited back.

"Vern is always right," said Carol. "He's incredibly well read. He doesn't open his mouth until he's read about something and he knows he's right. But, it's the way he talks to people. Sometimes you can be so right that you turn people off. I don't bring anything up about religion any more and on the few occasions my friends and he are together, they know not to bring the subject up either.

"It's like he's punishing himself for some reason," said Carol. "One of his doctors told me that Vern needs his pain. He is in considerable physical pain as well as emotional pain." Over the years, Vern never gave up his ministerial voice or style.

Take This Career and Shove It!

Eight years after leaving his last church, Vern was called to fill a pulpit for one Sunday while the pastor was away. Carol didn't feel comfortable going. She isn't a Presbyterian, in fact, she says she's "a very lapsed Catholic." She's twenty-five years younger than Vern and knows from experience the age difference upsets people. She didn't want to make waves even for one day. Vern returned home to tell her he'd blasted the congregation but good. Situated in a poor part of town, he railed at them for their pretty stained glass windows and carpeted floors. Without knowing anything about their mission program, he condemned them for not being more socially conscious with their resources. He seemed pleased he had upset them. He's never been asked to fill a pulpit in the twelve years since. Now he uses his ministerial voice only on Carol. She has given up hoping he'll change and leave his bitterness behind.

"When we moved to our first home, there was a church nearby," said Carol. "I was very lonely. I thought why don't I go there? Sure, I'd be using the church, but if I volunteered to help somewhere, they'd be using me too." She and Vern attended one service. "All through the sermon and the service, he criticized the minister's message, his theology. Vern also made sarcastic comments about the church itself and the members. By the time the service was over, I was in tears. Vern said he'd go with me every Sunday, but I just couldn't take the chance. I couldn't stand to go through that every Sunday.

"I'm not the same person I was twenty years ago when I met him," said Carol. "I've grown, but he hasn't. The doctors advise me to make him help me more, to make him more sensitive to me. But how do I do that with a sixty-year-old man? Send him to his room? Take away his allowance? How do I do that?" Carol wasn't ready to divorce Vern. She felt if she left him, he'd try suicide again. If the attempt was successful, Carol didn't think she could live with herself. She's slowly learning that what Vern does with his life is not her responsibility.

"I think ministers are trying to find perfection in an

unimproveable area," said Carol. "And I think the congregation expects him to find that perfection, too. But I wonder if Vern was working for the greater glory of God or the greater glory of himself. And, how can you believe in anything if you don't believe in yourself?" Carol admits that much of her husband's frustration is based on the peculiarities of life in ministry. Vern obviously had a strong call to be a certain kind of minister, one that makes parishioners aware of their own higher calling in life. Compromise and acceptance don't appear to be aspects of Vern's personality. But the most crushing blow of all to his self-confidence must have been leaving the ministry, not over differences in theology, civil rights, or community activism, but over money.

"I would really like to know why people become ministers if this is what it does to them," said Carol. The argument that Vern felt a divine call and that leaving the ministry convinced him he's a failure, doesn't quite answer it for her. "He doesn't ever mention God in his diatribes," she explained. "He talks about the history of religion, the ceremonies and traditions but God does not come out. He's always criticizing churches for spending money putting in new floors, rugs, redecorating, adding on. He's right, maybe the church should spend that money on the poor but I can't believe that all those people were bad people. You can't keep laying guilt on people. A soft touch does more than a sledge hammer."

Vern's self-imposed isolation is almost complete. Carol stays because she still can't quite handle the possible consequences of her leaving him. Even twenty years after he's left the ministry, Vern's ministerial voice is strong. Soon the conflict within him between his own conscience and leaving the church will drive Carol away, too.

One of our authors, Reverend Sherry Taylor, is Placement Officer for the United Church of Christ Connecticut Conference and handles requests from both ministers and churches to find, and fill, pulpits. "There are some family moti-

Take This Career and Shove It!

vations for leaving pulpits; one of the concerns is financial. There are clergy who simply discover that they can't raise a family and meet their family needs on the money they are making in the ministry. This doesn't happen often, but it does happen. Another reason that clergy sometimes leave the ministry is because their wives are grievously unhappy in the role of minister's wife. I have known of several clergy who have left the ministry primarily to save their marriages."

Mary Weaver addressed this issue: "One of my husband's seminary professors once remarked to a group of seminary wives that 'so many ministers are married to real obstacles to the Gospel.' That is a hard saying, but one that I think has a great deal of truth in it. It has certainly stayed with me for fifteen years or more! When you love and admire the man to whom you are married, it is not easy to be objective about his work, especially when you are right in the middle of that work. I often think to myself: At least a surgeon's wife doesn't have to watch him operate!"

Mary is correct. It's hard to blame the minister's wife who is unhappy with the unrealistic expectations of her husband, the congregation, or church hierarchy for his parish problems. Some find it easy to do so. Some of the self-help literature for pastors and their wives does blame her. Although they encourage her to be her own person, to do only what she wants to do within her husband's congregation, they still impose upon her the stereotype of the traditional minister's wife. If she presses him to spend more time home with his family, she takes him away from doing God's work. When she insists on taking a full family vacation, out of town, if not out of state, she deprives the congregation of his time to fulfill their needs. When her concerns are compared with the work of the Lord, she's typecast as petty, uncooperative, and an "obstacle to his ministry." Many wives handle the demands of the congregation on her husband, her family, and herself. Through sheer force of will they carve out identities of their own even when that identity is as closely tied to the church as their husbands'. Probably just as many cannot or will not. Whatever the reason, their inability to conform to or adjust the role of minister's wife to themselves, can wreak such havoc on the marriage that the only way up is out. Some wives feared that even before they married.

In his autobiography, *And the Walls Came Tumbling Down,* the late Reverend Ralph David Abernathy, civil rights leader and president of the Southern Christian Leadership Conference, wrote about two women in his life. One he called Jackie, the other was Juanita. Though they had an understanding that they would marry, Jackie was adamant about not marrying a preacher. If she gave specific reasons, Abernathy didn't share them in his book. Jackie never relented, and when Abernathy announced his decision to enter the ministry, the relationship ended.

On his second date with Juanita, he found that she was also determined not to marry a minister. Abernathy persisted and finally Juanita Odessa Jones became his wife and shared in his life-long ministry.

For some wives, the decision to enter the ministry comes after they've fallen in love with the man, many times after years of marriage. John and Jane celebrated their tenth anniversary before he decided to become a minister. Annie and Harvey already had the first of their six children when he felt called to change careers.

Another minister's wife, Cathy, explains it this way. "He was considering the ministry among several options," said Cathy. We met Cathy in Chapter Four when she told us she felt forced to shake hands with departing parishioners after Sunday service. "In fact, he enrolled in seminary for a trial 'theological reflection year' while I finished college and we figured out how serious we were about each other. His interest in the ministry was a tremendous obstacle to me before we married. My image of the ministry was colored by my fear that there would be no family time. I was so angry and upset over this issue and some others in our relationship that I broke up with him and thought I was better off. We got back together and were married during that seminary year.

"He did not feel prepared to go into the ministry right away after seminary and did not seek a church. I was quite happy with that. I wanted time alone with him. I wanted a family. I wanted to go to a church where we both felt comfortable/challenged. He found a job as director of social services at a hospital.

"After finishing a pastoral counseling training program some twelve years after seminary, my husband felt called, rather unexpectedly, to enter the parish ministry rather than full time counseling. What could I say? 'No, you don't feel called?'

"My husband started looking for a church and was eventually ordained and called to a church in this community three and a half years ago. It has been an enormous struggle for me to try to articulate what is wrong and to begin to make a different way of life possible. We are now looking for another church situation for him in a different community where I hope life will not seem so hostile to my individuality."

"Ministers sometimes walk away because they feel isolated and because they feel like they are living in a fishbowl, and they attribute these needs to themselves," said Reverend Sherry Taylor. "Usually, when a pastor leaves for these reasons, it is expressed as personal needs; but I think the needs of the family often parallel that of the pastor." Sherry also noted that warnings from seminary on the pitfalls of life in the pulpit don't have the same impact as actual experience.

"We are reminded that the work can eat up all our time if we let it and leave us no time for family or friends or ourselves. We are reminded that our spiritual life can end up on the rocks if we don't take time for it, and that is true. I think seminary professors also warn us that we are not going to have the time to spend at study that we had in seminary, and we are going to need to be sure we have time for that. And the pitfalls are the ones we've identified in this book: low pay, isolation, enormous demands. I think now when I look at the ministry that we expect clergy to be amazingly emotionally and psychologically sound; and we don't give them a lot of help for staying that way." People to minister to ministers and their families is an issue only recently addressed. Too many times even denomination hierarchies come down hard on a pastor with problems. One conference supervisor told a minister that if he was unhappy it was too bad. They could always get a new minister. They couldn't get a new congregation.

Ministers also get so tired of fighting with "killer" congregations that their lack of energy makes parish work impossible. In-fighting over an issue that places the pastor in the middle can convince him enough is enough. Many times the bone of contention isn't the real issue at all—rather, it's the manifestation of a deeper problem within the congregation.

"In some cases, the public issue isn't the real issue," said Sherry. "It's probable that there are people who don't like the pastor or the pastor's leadership style or who support an associate pastor and want him to be in a position of leadership. That's a tough situation because no defense works. Pastors in a denomination like this one (United Church of Christ) where we can't really keep them in the church if the congregation no longer wants them, get bitter when they find themselves in this position. It feels like nobody will come to their defense."

Burn-out is another frequent reason clergy leave active ministry. Some of this is their own fault. Rather than educate their congregations to reduce unrealistic expectations, the minister bounces from church to church trying to change himself to meet demands that may be radically different in each one. Much of the self-help literature is devoted to teaching pastors the art of negotiation, not only for salary and benefits, but also for an adequate job description. The Baptist Study on Clergy Compensation found that only forty percent of the responding pastors had a written job description. The laity, who are so used to having one in their own jobs, assume that their pastor does too. Over sixty-one percent of the members surveyed said that their church had a written job description for the pastor.

Only 17.4% of the pastors responding said their performance was evaluated annually. Over sixty-seven percent said there was no procedure at all to review the pastor's job. Over sixty percent of the laity didn't even answer the question. We can only assume that if they don't know, then there probably isn't.

In one article, a pastor said that each minister should give away a piece of his soul in every sermon. If he didn't give away a piece of his soul each Sunday morning, he was shortchanging his congregation. But when all the pieces of his soul are gone and the pastor is left empty, he may choose to withdraw from the profession that drained him. Without adequate support systems that defend, encourage, and rejuvenate him, the pastor simply has nothing left to give. The entire ministry is diminished by the loss of yet another sensitive nurturer.

Some ministers leave for health reasons. Heart attacks and serious illnesses take their toll in the ministry, too. Just being a minister doesn't give clergy an escape hatch from the same debilitating life blows we all suffer.

Delbert and Shirley Keltto are Evangelical Lutherans who accepted a call in Springfield, Illinois, after serving twelve years in an Ohio church. Six weeks after they arrived, Del was diagnosed with hepatitis type B and hospitalized. For three and a half years, he took the drug prednisone and suffered its side effects: hair loss, irritability, weight gain, and loss of stamina. Few in the congregation know how ill Del was. He pushed himself to accomplish the goals of the large downtown church with eight hundred members. Always a reconciler and negotiator, on the medication Del's personality completely changed and he snapped over the smallest issues. Shirley described it as a nightmare. Finally, he couldn't push himself anymore.

"I remember when he told me," said Shirley. "I was lying in bed, ready to go to sleep. The lights were out. He said he just couldn't go on any more, he couldn't work even one more hour. I was shocked, just shocked. I thought what do I do now? To me it seemed like the end of the world.

"For Del it was like an admittance of failure. We came here in August of 1986 and six weeks later he was in the hospital. He was called here. He had a job to do. If this had happened in our other church it wouldn't have been so bad. He'd finished what he had to do there. He wasn't finished at this church. He'd just started.

"The church was very supportive when Del was sick," continued Shirley. "But I would have wished the parish was more understanding. They just kept demanding, pushing him. They still expected him to perform miracles. They saw he was in the hospital. They knew he was taking medicine so they thought he was all better. That's the way we are, we want instant gratification, we expect instant cures. We had the feeling that if we didn't produce, they'd get someone else. So Del also felt fear over losing his job. So he pretended. But finally, he just couldn't go on. Even though he felt he hadn't completed his job, he couldn't go on.

"It was such a lonely time for me. My prayer support and emotional support was all back in Ohio. I hadn't had time to make those contacts here. And, because of the drug, he wasn't the Del I knew." A new test revealed Del did not have the type B hepatitis, but a rarer form, type C. Even worse, the prednisone was ineffective for treating type C. What he needed was rest. He consulted with his bishop and decided to stop working.

"When Del announced at the annual meeting that he had to leave, it was the hardest thing I've ever had to watch him do," said Shirley. "Yet, it was a load off both our shoulders." The Kelttos received physical and emotional support from both the congregation and their church's hierarchy. Their bishop told

Take This Career and Shove It!

them about the denomination's disability program, and they received two-thirds of Del's pay. The church where Del worked paid his full salary for an extra two months.

Del didn't know if he'd ever be able to go back to work. The disease is chronic and treatment lasts a lifetime. His energy level will always be low and pushing himself, as he used to, is impossible.

But, five months into their "retirement," Shirley discovered she liked being out of parish ministry.

"Being away from the demands of the parish has been a real eye-opener," she said. "When you're in it, you don't realize or know any different. But I can't believe how much time and energy, both physical and emotional, the church requires. I don't know now if I want to go back to that schedule, although I would want my husband's health back." Shirley described herself as being picky in what she chose to do or not to do in the church. Even so, she spent three nights a week in church activities, singing in the choir, joining women's fellowship, and the community issues of the large, urban church.

"You get home at 9:30 and you're all wound up. You don't go to bed until midnight. The next morning I was dragging. Now, I have my evenings to myself. It's amazing how energetic I am in the mornings going to work."

Shirley did miss contact with parishioners. "There's something about the minister's wife," said Shirley. "People come to you with their confidences and their prayer support. I miss that. There must be a need for me to have that, too." The primary advantage to Del's absence from the ministry was joining another church. They didn't attend their prior church to make it easier for the new pastor to be accepted by the congregation. At their new church, a smaller one, they noted that the pastor, female, was not as demanding of herself as Del had been.

"And the church didn't fall apart, Del said," Shirley explained. "We realized we didn't have to place those heavy demands on ourselves."

A year later, Del Keltto is rested and ready to return to work. He's aware of his limitations. Eight-hundred-member urban churches with ministries to the poor, the elderly, and the community are out of the question. Del is looking for a less demanding church and will control his schedule better.

"We need to find an understanding congregation," said Shirley. That congregation will not be in the Springfield area. Del's Bishop has already told them there is nothing available there. The Kelttos are looking for a church in Minnesota, Shirley's home state, or Ohio where Del was born.

Shirley has been Business Manager for the *Illinois Times* for the past five years. Going back into the ministry means she must leave the job she loves. She clings to the hope that their transfer will move them close enough to a city where job opportunities will be open for her.

When the Kelttos find a new church, one with fewer members, fewer demands, it will mean a cut in pay. The ideal congregation meeting Del's needs for a less hectic schedule might even pay less than he's making through his denomination's disability program. But Del would be back in the ministry. Now that he feels better, Del is chomping at the bit to return to the vocation he loves. It was hard to walk away from his job, but the time away has made both the Kelttos realize that some things are out of their control and that they are not failures. Del realizes that the old days are gone.

"I feel I'm going to have to keep reminding Del not to get involved morning, noon, and night," said Shirley. "He knows intellectually that he shouldn't push himself, but I think, once he's back, I'll have to keep reminding him to slow down.

"Yet I'm excited about the move," said Shirley. "Maybe the nomad-ness of this life has affected me, but over the thirty-one years we've been married, each place was a different adventure. I'm ready for a new challenge."

Reverend Ralph Abernathy also wrote in his autobiography that from the time he knew his name he knew he was going to be a preacher.

"The preacher, after all, was the finest and most important person around, someone who was accorded respect wherever he went," wrote Abernathy. Reverend Norman Levinson doesn't believe that's true today. Levinson, who, as Associate Coordinator of Pastoral Services for the Institute of Living, counsels clergy, sees as reasons pastors leave the ministry the current lack of respect for the profession and the loss of identity.

"Our society has totally changed in their outlook on the clergy," said Levinson. "I remember as a kid when I saw the Roman Catholic priest walk down the street, even though I was not Roman Catholic, that there was a kind of an aura about him. I'm running a group with priests in therapy, and that's no longer true, and I think this has spilled over into the ministry, too. I don't think people look upon the clergy in the same vein they used to. Ministers used to be usually among the most educated people in the community. They never were highly paid for their education, but at least they had the respect of the community. Now they have neither.

"I just don't think we live in a religious society. I think we live in a secular society," Levinson continued. "Since I've been ordained, I have seen the role of the clergy and the mind of the laity change tremendously. Why? I suppose there are 1001 reasons. Attitudes, for one. People are not as locked into religious thinking or church doctrine as they once were.

"Many times, the congregation hurts both the minister and his wife either unknowingly, or if knowingly, in a cruel way. If it is a deliberate act, I think there is still a symbolism of clergy and their wives. I think that a lot of people are very angry. I think we're in an angry society, and that anger will grow, especially as a deepening economic recession forces us to deal such problems as professional people who lose their jobs after giving so many years to a company. Where's that anger going to go? One safe place is mother's womb. Well, mother's womb is the church. They can go in there and they can yell and scream and holler and let out all this anger toward the clergy person and then leave, go outside, look at the stars and say: 'By God, I feel great!'"

"For the poor clergyhood who may not know what's going on, is devastated. People feel they can dump on the clergy more than they used to. Clergy take more dumping than they used to.

"There's a sense of 'what am I worth in a secular society? I'm not worth much.' That hurts. So he's got to find his compensation in other ways, doing the work of God, accepting a call, serving people, healing, teaching, baptizing; but, even that is not held in the high degree that it once was in the general populace.

"It's their loss of identity," said Levinson, describing the primary reason pastors leave the ministry. " 'Just where do I fit in? My role is not as clear as it used to be.' When you take a risk, it's dangerous. When you step out of the norm, they put you back into a norm—you and your wife; you step out of that, you place yourself at high risk; and it's dangerous.

"I'm not sure even that clergy as a whole know exactly where they're coming from. That anxiety is also put upon the wife. Where does she fit in? At least back in the 1950s, and the 1940s, they had a role to identify with whether they liked it or not. I'm not so sure that's clear any more. I don't feel they get the strokes that they used to get or the respect." Levinson left local church ministry when he no longer wanted to deal with being, as he put it, an ecclesiastical fireman.

"I found that I don't care if the candles are taller than the flowers or if the flowers are taller than the candles, or that the stained glass windows are dirty. That is not where the church is for me. I gain more satisfaction out of hands-on with people having problems. I can see results helping people get back into ministry, or to help them make a choice not to go back into ministry, but to be a healthier human being. I feel that's more rewarding.

"I think it's an exciting time in which to live and be in the church. I think that there are a lot of things that are going to be even more unstable than they are now, in the church's definition of its role in society. I'm going to be honest with you: marriage to a minister must be horrendous. I think there are more problems there than being the minister himself of herself. They can expect it. But the wife didn't ask for this."

Unfortunately, the very actions ministers take to promote their humanness and reduce unrealistic expectations, contribute to the lack of respect they receive from their congregations and the community.

"Clergy have colluded in their own eroding support process by insisting on emphasizing their humanness," wrote G. Lloyd Rediger in an October 1988 issue of *The Clergy Journal.* "Pastors typically wear open shirts, drink beer, and joke about themselves now. This may help them feel more 'authentic,' but it also removes the strong, loyal, and traditional support reserved for pedestal figures in a society."

"That is a problem for some laypeople, not all," said Reverend Sherry Taylor. "The pastor should know who is who. The problem is some people want the pastor on a pedestal. Some don't. Hopping on and off gets tiring and confusing." Reverend Levinson's comments about the state of uncertainty over the minister's role in society confirms this. Until its redefinition is complete, clergy will remain confused on whether to promote their humanness or preserve themselves as the symbol of God.

As in other issues, lack of respect is also a two-way street in the ministry. Although some ministers leave the profession because they simply don't get the strokes or the money for the job they do, they also leave because they see a lack of commitment on the part of the congregation. As ministers painfully raise their calling to a profession, the laity assumes that all the responsibilities of the church belong to the pastor. Not only is he the pastor, he's also the CEO of a large organization, the janitor, carpenter, plumber, and chief cook and bottle washer. He's their evangelist, their mission director. He's their voice of conscience in the community. The congregation forgets that it isn't the pastor's church, but their church.

Jennifer Shew mentioned that the lack of vision and courage to try new things and worship in new ways made her angry about sharing the ministry with her husband. She also noted a pettiness within the church on many of its program points.

"I do not appreciate full-time sponges—people who want to soak up everything," said Cindy Chenewerk of Salem, Oregon. Cindy and her husband are Southern Baptists. "They soak up all the time, yet never do their share of the work or ministry in the church." Peggy Ostenson said that what made her saddest was "when hearts are hardened and lives aren't changed. When church officers disappoint us for different reasons."

"The apathy towards growth through open-minded learning," was what angered Gloria most. "Most people are so preoccupied with earning money, leisure time activities, and what they've 'earned in life,' looking forward to relaxing in retirement, etc., etc., and acquiring more and more material possessions. Most people give precious little time to nurturing their soul, growing in faith, sharing with others to create a *solid* church family."

"Visiting the dying parishioner daily before death," is the saddest aspect for Frances. Frances is married to a United Methodist minister and is in seminary to be a minister herself. "All know the person has been 'playing church' all these years and is not 'right with God, ready for the judgment.' It's sad to know they attended for years, heard the gospel over and over and never really 'got it.' I'm not making a judgment—just a very sad observation."

Contradictions, conflict, confrontation, lack of commitment, and compromise. Over and over again, ministerial couples and families are faced with difficult choices. Confined to a role that no longer has a set definition, clergy are encouraged to isolate themselves from their congregation, their hierarchy and their peers. The peculiarities of the ministry seem to push clergy to cut themselves off from every available source of support. When the stresses and loneliness become too great, they may face the final choice: divorce. Unfortunately then, their isolation will be complete.

17

Divorce

"I've had few flashes of clarity in my life," said Beverly. "The night my husband told me he is a homosexual was one of those moments of clarity. I knew we had a problem in our marriage but being a typical '50s' kind of wife, I figured it was my fault. I didn't know we had *that* problem."

Beverly and Neil were married in 1971. Neil works in a denomination that would decertify him as a minister if the church hierarchy discovered his homosexuality. Beverly divorced Neil in 1982 but told no one but her own family why.

"We had just moved to a new church—a very nice one—from a difficult church," explained Beverly. "It all happened on his day off. I found him crying in the bedroom. Sobbing. I asked him why he was crying. I thought he suffered from burnout from the previous church. But then he told me he was a homosexual." Beverly was so distraught and angry that at four in the morning, she walked around the parsonage dividing up the furniture.

"I knew immediately that I wanted a divorce. I was also sick of being second, third, eighth on his list of priorities." Beverly describes Neil as a very private person—even with his wife. He was distant, not approachable. Neil wore a clerical collar, like

Roman Catholic priests. That, and his own personality, projected an arm's length approach to the congregation as well.

"I know he suffered, too," continued Beverly. "It must have been hard for him to live with a woman who expected intercourse, not just sexual, but emotional; and communication. Our relationship was distant in all respects. Sexually, I know we made love four times because we have four children but sex was rare."

What makes Beverly's story unique is not that her husband was a homosexual minister, but that she's kept his secret ever since the divorce, almost ten years.

"Neil didn't tell his parents why we divorced," said Beverly. "His mother didn't think I was a good enough minister's wife anyway so I think she was relieved. She and I made our peace later. The only people I told were my parents." Beverly's four children still don't know. Neither do the churches Neil has served since his divorce nor the church hierarchy.

"The Bishop at that time would have had Neil out on his ear if he knew," said Beverly. It was January when Neil upset Beverly's world. She knew that night she was leaving and she told him so. Neil begged her to stay, not because he still loved her or wanted her, but so he wouldn't have to face the congregation with a separation and divorce during the Lenten season. Beverly stayed.

"It was the worst time of my life," she said. "I had to find a place to live. I rented an apartment and I'd go and paint and fix it up. Then I'd come back to the parsonage and cook for him, wash for him. I didn't tell anyone. But someone saw me in the real estate office and then people heard rumors." Neil had wanted to be the one to find a place to live. He wanted privacy; out of the parsonage, out of the fishbowl. But Beverly was determined to live on her own. Because the church would lose its tax-exempt status on the house if the minister didn't live there, Neil was forced to stay.

Through it all, Beverly attended her husband's church.

Divorce

When her repressed anger became too much, she turned to one friend in the congregation. She was a true friend, it turned out, for she also kept Neil's secret.

"There was a time, I was so angry, when I wanted to tell everyone," said Beverly. "I wanted everyone to know how much it hurt. I wanted him to feel even just ten percent of what I felt. I had to come to terms that I just didn't love him. But my feelings ran the gamut: Hate him, hug him, kill him, love him, hate him. There were times when I sat in church listening to Neil preach about the spiritual life and my friend had to virtually hold me down in my seat. I never took communion from Neil again. I couldn't take communion from him."

When Neil's superiors in the denomination asked him and Beverly to go for counseling for their marital problems, Beverly agreed.

"I wasn't going to say anything," said Beverly. "I was going to go wearing my hat and gloves and not say a word, just look beautiful. Struck dumb, but beautiful. I felt the Bishop would be on Neil's side. I wanted to look so good the Bishop would turn to Neil and ask him how he could leave such a perfect wife." Beverly and Neil drove to the appointment together determined to be civilized through the ordeal. They even planned to stop for lunch on the way home.

They were the sixth out of twelve couples that the Bishop interviewed that day. Along with counseling, the denomination was searching for reasons why so many ministerial marriages faltered.

The Bishop asked Neil if he'd consider a reconciliation. Neil answered: maybe. Surprised, Beverly listened as the Bishop scolded her husband for being so tentative. When the Bishop asked Beverly if she would consider a reconciliation, she answered with a determined and deliberate no.

On the drive home Beverly and Neil waged a vicious verbal battle.

"I had anger and pain and he wouldn't deal with it," said

Beverly. "He had anger and pain, too, because I wouldn't continue to be his cover." Beverly never told the Bishop or her husband's immediate superiors that her husband was a homosexual. The Bishop who interviewed them kept in contact with her for several years after the divorce, checking to see that she was all right.

Easter weekend, Beverly and the four children moved out of the parsonage into their new home. Neil sent a letter to the church boards and to every member of the congregation. Beverly insisted on a letter rather than an announcement from the pulpit so that she could see it, and more importantly, edit it. Without telling them the real reason, Beverly and Neil reassured the congregation that their separation and divorce had nothing to do with the church.

Still Beverly attended the church where her husband worked.

"Some of that was for continuity for the kids, so they'd have the same church, same Sunday school, same friends," explained Beverly. "And some of it was to show the congregation that I wasn't the one running away." Her silence about the real reason she and Neil divorced made Beverly the victim.

"Some people in the congregation want someone to blame for what goes wrong and they can't blame the ministerial one," said Beverly. "So a lot blamed me. Years later a woman from the congregation came to me and apologized for being so unremittingly opposed to me. Of course, this was after Neil had transferred to another church. When she realized it wasn't something I'd done, she apologized. Neil was perfectly happy to let me take the bulk of the blame."

About three years after the divorce, Beverly drifted away from the church and most organized religion. She attends the Catholic church on the major holidays because she finds the rituals so moving. Neil stayed at the church where the divorce occurred for several more years. He took a leave of ab-

Divorce

sence and then re-entered parish ministry. Beverly still kept his secret.

"I kept it secret because I needed the financial security," said Beverly. "If I told, he'd lose his job and then there'd be no child support. I'd be up the river." Beverly returned to college, got her degree, and started a career.

"The other reason was I worried about the congregation," said Beverly. "If they knew Neil was gay, they'd worry if that negated their weddings, baptisms. And, in the end, it was better for the kids. They aren't scarred by a messy divorce.

"I don't have any problem with gays," said Beverly. "But Neil was also compulsive about being all things to all people except his family. That didn't help our marriage either. But he's basically a decent human being. I don't really want to hurt him. I always took it as a mark of my healing that I no longer had that feeling that everyone should know he is gay. I don't think we would have lasted as a couple anyway. I had a chance to start over. I've found an inner peace I wouldn't have had otherwise.

"Yes, I would still keep his secret."

Homosexuality among the clergy is as controversial now as it has been for centuries. Contrary to public belief, and no matter how much we want to ignore it, there have always been ordained homosexuals. Denomination conferences debate the issue heatedly. Will they or won't they ordain homosexuals? The question is moot. Whether or not they chose to recognize it, churches still ordain homosexuals.

According to G. Lloyd Rediger of the Office of Pastoral Services, homosexual pastors perform their duties within the church with the same competence, sensitivity, and dedication as heterosexual ministers. The only difference between them is that the secret homosexual pastor adds one more layer to the role: fear. Fear that he will be found out, fear that he will lose the job he loves because of something he believes is out of his control, his sexual orientation.

There is no doubt we live in a homophobic society and

without casting stones at either side, homosexuality creates heavy pressures for a minister simply because, as church members, we want our pastors married. When he is married, the laity has a large stake in that marriage. As we've already seen, the pastor's marriage must appear perfect even if it isn't.

In David and Vera Mace's book, *What's happening to Clergy Marriages?*, their research groups listed as the number one disadvantage of clergy marriage the expectation of the congregation that their marriage be a model of perfection. Pastors felt this more strongly than their wives. Eighty-five percent of the pastors surveyed felt their marriage was watched as a model by the congregation while fifty-nine percent of the wives agreed.

Many members, ministers, and denomination officials feel that a minister's marriage and family life are part and parcel of this job; one of the "tools" of his profession. To them, keeping up the illusion of a perfect marriage seems imperative and adds more stress and strain to an already difficult situation.

This attitude removes from view the one thing members need to see: the work involved in creating a successful marriage. By hiding all the conflict, communication, and compromise required to make a marriage strong, the ministerial couple's mask of marital harmony hides the very steps we need most to see. It is ridiculous to assume that the minister and his wife never have an argument, never disagree, never yell at their kids; but we do assume just that. Once again, what we see is what we know. Based on what we see, the mask the ministerial couple wears to hid any faults in their marriage, leads us to believe that they do have a guardian angel protecting them from the same pitfalls we face in our marriages.

Our need to believe the minister's marriage to be the example of wedded bliss is so great that a divorce can cause deep wounds in a congregation. Such was the case for Beverly. Keeping her husband's secret turned church members against her. They assumed the divorce was her fault. Although in most

Divorce

denominations, divorce is no longer grounds for dismissal from the ministry, many churches still lose faith in a divorced minister and look for a new one to fill their pulpit. So, though he doesn't lose his profession, the divorced minister may lose his current church.

The divorce rate is on the rise in the ministry, just as it is in the general population of this country. Current Population Survey statistics compiled by the U.S. Bureau of the Census show that 7.6 percent of all residents in the United States over the age of eighteen are divorced. Statistics compiled by Rediger show that fifteen percent of ministers will seek divorces. Comparing only percentage of populations, there are twice as many divorced ministers as there are divorced laypeople. The social acceptance of divorce does reach to ministers and more of them are taking this option out of an unhappy marriage despite expectations of some of the laity.

Over nine percent of our survey respondents either divorced their minister husbands or are in second marriages with previously divorced ministers. Three of these women divorced ministers.

One example among the women with whom we talked is Tina. Tina met Jeff in college. Tina was happy she fell in love with a prospective minister. As the daughter and granddaughter of ministers, she had always been active in church and felt that clergy wives made a special contribution to the lives of the congregation and the community. Tina is forty-four and was married to Jeff for thirteen years. During those years Tina helped with youth groups, church school, and choirs. She dealt often with members in crisis situations. Tina held conference leadership positions. She entertained extensively in the parsonage, inviting in all the church organizations. Tina and her husband also opened the parsonage to the homeless, taking in people for periods from one night to three months.

"The anger, unhappiness, and despair I experienced was related to the man and not the ministry," said Tina. "We began our marriage in a different state and always lived at least two hours from my family. This was not a problem. We moved four times in six years. I finally put my foot down and refused to move, as the reasons he wanted to move were not healthy and too disruptive to the family. It was flight behavior, looking for utopia rather than working through the problems at hand.

"Our oldest child had a health problem that required several serious operations when he was young. The problems associated with this were related to a very self-centered, non-supportive husband rather than the ministry. The same was true when our second child was born prematurely. The parish was very supportive and helpful, which was good for me."

For Tina the disadvantages of the ministerial marriage were the lack of family privacy and time. She described the poor salary, especially with children, as very stressful for her. What made Tina saddest was "seeing the needs of my children to share time with their father always coming second to his church responsibilities." Tina's children were aged ten and younger when she left her husband.

"Most of our friends were from within the parish. As the years went by his areas of interest became so parochial he was unbearable to anyone else and, finally, unbearable to parishioners. However, I did have some friends of my own from outside the parish.

"I hate to lay the problems of our family entirely at the feet of the vocation. Interpersonal dynamics are complex," said Tina. Tina left because of her husband's workaholism, his neglect of his family and his flight behavior pattern. Jeff's problems stemmed from his own personality quirks but were compounded by a unique aspect of the ministry.

"The ministry is a very lonely, isolated profession in that most clergy are not working with a team of their peers on a daily basis," explained Tina. "Furthermore, the person in their profession who is above them is very removed. There is no inherent system of checks and balances for ideas, perceptions,

Divorce

or behavior. When a clergyman runs into trouble with his work or mental health, there's no peer there feeding back reality or providing support or identifying the problems. The wife may do this but if the clergyman is using denial, the wife has no 'credentials' behind her observations. Little problems are seldom addressed in time so they grow and grow. And finally not only the minister, but the church and the family are in *big* trouble.

"The fallout of these problems obviously has a serious effect on the children. The family puts all their energies into appearing normal so that the husband has some credibility to carry out his job. The whole family is in a great deal of pain and conflict. It's very difficult to live this way for an extended period of time.

"In my case, there was no way to put Humpty Dumpty together again," said Tina. "I left and the church fired him and a once brilliant man with a very good wife alongside him has gone down hill ever since. My point is that his psychiatric and work-related problems would have been identified and addressed in a more normal work environment with daily peer and supervisor contact. Also, historically it has been difficult for clergy families to have enough privacy and money to access counseling and psychiatric help. Our denomination has made some effort to address this problem but there is a long way to go.

"I think the system of one minister in one church for a whole career has failure built into it, in that it is very difficult for the minister to remain healthy in such a parochial, isolated setting. If the system is to remain as is, then the governing bodies larger than the parishes, such as the diocese or conference, need to recognize this isolation and provide conference and socializing for the clergy couples to foster a sense of community for them. Salaries also have to be adequate for families if you have married clergy. In many realistic respects, I think the Roman Catholics have the right idea in single clergy living in group housing.

"Quite frankly, I know very few healthy clergy families. They are at great risk for failure. I also know very few clergy children who elect to enter the ministry, another barometer of the hard life.

"In many respects, church people are more bonded to supporting their buildings than clergy families." said Tina. "This occurred to me a few winters ago when oil prices were sky high. I looked around the center of town at the three big churches. One church could have been heated on Sunday and everyone could have held their services there. However, all three oil burners were fired up each Sunday. They would pay for the oil before they would pay a living wage to their clergy or hire a second minister to share the load. The system is self-destructing and some very fine people are being chewed up in the process!

"I have never regretted being a minister's wife," said Tina who is now remarried and not to a minister. "I was exposed to a great variety of people and living experiences and opportunities to help my fellow human beings. However, I doubt that I would ever do it again. I would not be interested in living that hard life again."

We met Barbara in Chapter Ten where she told us about the arm's-length distancing, in both directions, between ministers' wives and church members. Barbara has been divorced since 1983. Her happiest moments as a minister's wife were watching religion work.

"Seeing Christ become a reality in a person's life is a joyful experience," said Barbara. In a poignant reflection, Barbara added two other things that made her happiest as a minister's wife: "to be proud of your husband when he's preached well; to be the person he turns to in all the vagaries of life." Barbara, very committed to the ministry, said her anger rose when members "refused to open up the Word." Barbara and her husband have four grown children. They ended a twenty-nine year marriage.

Divorce

"This questionnaire has been answered in the past tense as I am not currently involved in ministry," wrote Barbara. "My husband and I broke up. Part of the reason for his mid-life crisis was maladjustment to the job. He viewed the congregation as many individual bosses rather than as a more singular responsibility to God. He left the church, and has adopted a 'worldly' lifestyle replete with live-in girlfriend.

"Although there were problems along the way, I felt the advantages outweighed the disadvantages," said Barbara. "My husband and I were close at the time, so I thought. I felt mostly fulfilled.

"As I look back on our life as a ministerial couple now, I feel unsure of what was real about it. I thought it was real at the time. It was real to me."

One wife revealed to us that she was the other woman in a clergy affair. Cyndie met Don at their denomination's annual conference. She was a delegate from her church and he represented his.

"I came into the position of a clergy wife by way of the back door," said Cyndie. "We were both married when we met, but our friendship turned into an affair which caused him to take a leave of absence from the church until his divorce was cleaned up. My marriage ended in divorce also.

"It was a horrible mess," said Cyndie of their affair and divorces. "It caused a lot of pain to us and each of our spouses at the time. I've forgiven myself, but Don still feels guilty at times. It's made us more sensitive to each other and taught us how fragile a marriage can become if you don't take care of it.

"Only a few friends know of this secret and we don't tell anyone else, no matter how much we think we can trust them," said Cyndie. "We want to reach out to other clergy couples when this kind of thing happens to them, but we're concerned that we may be found out and it would really damage his career." Cyndie and Don have been married for ten years. She is forty-seven years old.

"What we're seeing with ministers is that they divorce, then find a new pulpit," said a minister who requested anonymity. "Within a year after they transfer, they remarry. Sometimes that second marriage is to a woman from the previous congregation. That's when you start believing the rumors. It's a dicey situation, very dicey." One of our questionnaires returned with a note from the woman's husband. She couldn't answer the survey, he explained, because, after twenty-five years of marriage, she had run off with another religious professional from his church.

Cyndie and Don are correct in feeling that widespread knowledge of their past affair would wreak havoc on his career. Attitudes toward divorce have softened. According to the 1988 *McCall's* reader poll on "Faith, Values and Morals," only eleven percent of the more than eighteen thousand women who responded thought divorce was sinful or immoral. Attitudes towards extramarital sex have not softened. The number of respondents who thought extramarital sex was immoral increased ten percent in the ten years since *McCall's* first took this survey. In the 1978 survey, seventy percent of the respondents said extramarital sex was immoral. In the 1988 survey that figure increased to eighty percent. Not all second marriages among clergy are the result of an affair with a parishioner. Affairs, though more frequent among clergy than we'd like to believe, are still relatively rare. Statistics from the Office of Pastoral Services show that thirty-seven percent of ministers seriously contemplate divorce, and as already noted, fifteen percent will follow through. In the *McCall's* survey, almost fifty-six percent of the respondents said there were situations where divorce was justified. Because divorce, under certain circumstances, has become more socially acceptable, divorced ministers don't suffer the stigma as much from their congregations.

Mary DeHaven of Cut Bank, Montana is forty-five and has been married to her Presbyterian (U.S.A.) minister husband for seven years. They met when he filled the pulpit of the church where she worked as a secretary. He had been divorced for six years. He had three grown children, she had four, the youngest aged sixteen. The marriage had little effect on her children although they weren't "sure about me marrying a minister. But it worked out fine."

"We enjoy being together," she said. "Quality for us is different than for others. Most likely squeezed in, but fun: riding in the truck for meetings, kissing in the elevator at the hospital, walking through a mall or a closed car lot, a good movie on television, reading in bed." Mary feels her husband balances church and family well. In fact, Mary noted that it's more apt to be she who does too much church work and may neglect her family because of it.

The DeHavens live in a parsonage and Mary likes it that way.

"We gave our home away to move here," she said. "We had put too much money into our last home. The depressed market would not let us sell it. We gave it to my parents."

Mary said she was proud to become a pastor's wife and she believes she received a call also. She told us she loves the church, and her questionnaire was peppered with happy faces after her positive and upbeat comments.

"Being in a poor marriage for twenty years, believing divorce would mean not being able to be active in ministry" were the things that made Mary saddest in her life. "Then going through a divorce, remarriage, gives a greater compassion for hurting people." Mary's husband had been married twenty years also.

"He tried not to make the same mistakes he had when he was young and married (unhappily) the first time," said Mary. "We were both allowed to have a blessed second chance."

Some churches actively support their divorced or divorcing minister.

Nancy met her husband in church. A neighbor, active in

the congregation, invited the recent college graduate to a church service and to meet the minister.

"I attended that first service to find that it was Layman's Sunday, when each part of the worship was handled by a different person. I had no idea who the actual minister was. Two weeks later, when I returned, the same person led the whole service and I made the identification. My vocation at the time was in Safety Education and he asked if I would talk with his youth fellowship. That led to a hiking outing within weeks and basically we both knew of our commitment.

"Here the dynamics become interesting as he was married at the time although officially separated and in the process of divorce," said Nancy. "That congregation was, and continues to be, a whole family and in this instance was very supportive of Ed. When he knew he would face a divorce, he met with the church to tender his resignation. The church had just come through a messy situation with the previous pastor (Nancy told us of her husband's work in the scandal-scarred congregation in Chapter Twelve). Ed did not want to subject them to it again although his situation was not 'messy.' The church refused his resignation and became a source of great support and provided many opportunities for us to be together, from dinner invitations to joining families at lakeside cottages. Since the divorce wasn't final until November and this was late May, we courted until the new year and were married the following April. It was a wonderful courtship.

"I was glad that our courtship took almost a full twelve months, because it gave me a chance to see how the church calendar affected him: like the stresses of budget building and stewardship, the energy of the holy days and the drain they produce. I was glad to have experienced that with him, to know that the changes during the year were not something I had caused or was responsible for. When our engagement was announced, the congregations response was, *'finally'* and nine

Divorce

months later when we announced my pregnancy, they felt it was about time!

"I have no problem with his vocation. I just remind folks that if he were a plumber, I would be a plumber's wife. The issue isn't what he does. The issue is that we are partners in life.

"I have been asked by search committee members how I view my role as the minister's wife. My response has always been that my first commitment is to my family, the nurture of my husband and now three children. I explain that when kids are sick, I stay home. Sometimes I suggest that my spouse stay home, take time out, because he has no reserves. I tell him that by caring for himself he is in better shape to serve them."

Though only twenty-three when she met Ed, Nancy had an opportunity few clergy wives get, the chance to see the demands of his job on her fiancé's personal life. It was just the training she needed, and one that most minister's wives don't get until it's too late. Odds are Nancy would have married Ed anyway, even if the demands of his job seemed high. But at least she learned that the pressures of the ministry cause periods of stress for which she didn't have to blame either herself or her marriage.

In a survey done by the Task Force on Women of the Synod of the Trinity, United Presbyterian Church of the United States of America, clergy wives were asked what the Task Force could do to support them. Half of the responses dealt with aspects of educating the minister's wife to the expectations she'd meet; educating the minister on what, and what not, to expect from his wife; and educating the congregation that the minister's wife is not an appendage to the pastor but a person in her own right.

Out of thirty-eight specific requests, seven requested fellowship opportunities between themselves and other ministers and their wives; support groups at seminaries; including spouses in minister conferences and retreats; and, establishing a clergy couple, both ordained, to serve as pastors to pastors and their families. Three requests were for denomination counseling services that were more readily available, confidential, and not a threat to their husband's jobs. Four answers dealt with money issues including more pay to the minister; better pension plan; personal finance courses; and providing secretaries to small parishes so that an inadequate budget or the twofer attitude doesn't force the minister's wife into the position of unpaid second staff member. Better parsonages was another request. One woman requested promoting the right of clergy wives to join a different church so they can fully participate in Christian fellowship and have their own pastor to turn to.

As obvious as it is that the role of the minister's wife is changing dramatically through the influences of women's liberation and the necessity and desire for the dual career marriage, it is also apparent that there is a long way to go. Choices abound in all our lives. Some stagger us and leave us confused. Some just become a part of the constant "noise" of some decisions that surround our relationships. One factor in our choices is that our decision affects only ourselves. Choosing a path to follow may hurt us, may affect our immediate families, but seldom does it cost our husband his job, our children their security, and home, and leave anywhere from one hundred to three thousand people shaken.

What's the difference between the average wife and the minister's wife? Not much, maybe. Some of us are married to workaholics. Some of us are married to people in other emotionally draining professions. Some of us leave our marriages and get divorces and for some of us, that also means losing our homes, status, and identity. But most of us make those decisions based on a real freedom to choose. Because of the unique demands of the ministry and the laity's approach to ministers, that freedom of choice is diminished for the minister's wife merely from the sheer numbers of people who feel they are a part of her life. There is no doubt that life's decisions are harder for the minister's wife.

18

If I Knew Then What I Know Now . . .

Although Annie, the wife whose story of attempted suicide began Chapter One, survived, her marriage was troubled and she asked for a divorce. Soon after Annie told Harvey she was leaving him, she admitted herself back to Ruble 1, having attempted suicide again. Almost exactly two years after Annie entered Ruble 1 for the first time, she returned. This time, there was no hesitation. This time she went willingly, without guilt over how her admittance to the hospital might affect Harvey's ministry. This time she knew the problem wasn't her childhood.

"I was dying in private, he was dying in public," said Annie. "Harvey would not have lived if he stayed in the pulpit. Or, he wouldn't have been able to enjoy his retirement. I was angry about him not taking care of himself." Annie described Harvey's skin as ashen; he looked as old as Methuselah. His back problems flared up. Annie ran interference again, taking time to assemble papers or clear tables when they were at church functions so Harvey had time to stand up and straighten up without falling down from the stiffness and pain.

Private Lives of Ministers' Wives

Sometimes, Harvey looked like death. But he never missed a Sunday service, never missed a day of work.

Annie never felt that she came first. She believed that Harvey placed the church first and her, second.

"I never felt our time together was enough," said Annie. "Harvey did. He always thought the few hours—one hour here, three hours, tucked in, always tucked in—were enough. I didn't. I always said to Harvey: We're cheated. I feel cheated as a couple. I fought desperately to hold on to what we had, a deep love and concern for each other. A marriage. I wondered if God wanted us to have marriage. That's what he brought us together for wasn't it?"

Back at Ruble 1, Annie shared her room with another patient. Exhausted, emotionally spent, once again she learned how to take care of herself. Back she went each morning to the group meetings. She attended her small group sessions dealing with depression. She talked to her counselor, and to Dr. Glück, her therapist.

Annie's spirit was broken. Always spunky, goal-oriented, strong willed, she remembered the days before her marriage when she worked to get what she wanted and usually succeeded. Now she was weak. She just wasn't strong enough to save her marriage. Weak. The sense of failure further devastated her spirit. Weak and broken.

"What do you like to do?" asked the young, female counselor in Annie's private session.

"I take care of my children, the parsonage," said Annie.

"But what do you do for you?" said the counselor folding her hands on the desk and staring at Annie. Annie looked down at her own hands clenched tightly in her lap and considered the question. Too quickly, she answered:

"I like to spend time with my husband. We don't have too much time but I like . . ."

"No, Annie," the counselor interrupted. "I want to know what *you* like to do."

If I Knew Then What I Know Now . . .

"I have my church work," said Annie. "I visit in the nursing homes, I put on special programs, I teach . . ."

"Annie, that's what you do for others," the counselor interrupted again. "What do you do for you?" This time the answer was a long time coming. The counselor waited.

"Nothing," whispered Annie, finally, her head lowered.

"What did you do before? Before you were married? When you were younger?" the counselor persisted. This silence was even longer. Annie raised her head and looked at the counselor.

"I used to dance," Annie said tentatively. "I used to play tennis. I used to sing."

Annie sat in the small group session that met to discuss depression. A Ruble 1 staff member talked but Annie wasn't listening. Distracted, Annie reviewed the meeting with the counselor. What did she do for herself? Nothing. Where was the Annie she knew? Gone.

The group leader went to the blackboard in the front of the room and drew a diagram. In the center she wrote: Anger. Annie thought about Harvey.

He'd told her, during the first depression, that he foresaw it. The problem was her childhood. Annie heard his voice in her head repeating it. Your childhood. Your childhood. His voice wasn't malicious or callous. Harvey said it calmly, with concern and love, because he believed it. Her problems stemmed from her unstable childhood. Harvey referred to it as Annie's problem.

Not true, thought Annie. Not true. Annie knew her childhood could no longer be the sole blame for her depressions.

The group leader's voice seemed louder and Annie's attention focused on her. She had completed the diagram on the blackboard, a circular web around the word anger. Annie came out of her reverie and listened.

"Depression is unexpressed anger," said the group

leader as she turned from the blackboard and faced the patients. "Depression is repressed anger." That made sense.

Annie had planted a small seed of anger while she lay on the gurney, minutes after the birth of her sixth child, gasping for air. Over the past six years, that small seed had grown. It felt like it took up all the space within her chest. Annie's heart ached, literally ached. Suddenly, the seed bore fruit. It exploded.

Annie couldn't wait to see Dr. Gliick. In the hospital counseling room, she ranted and raved. She screamed, cried, yelled. Every emotion and resentment came to the surface. Annie's anger spewed out of her like a volcano erupting. She'd seen too much, heard too much, done too much, suffered too much.

The doctor just sat there.

"God didn't bring us together just to make us miserable," Annie screamed. "We had something dynamite going. I resent the church for what it's doing to us." Annie paced around the office, angrily swiping away the tears from her face with the back of her hand.

"But why suicide?" he asked.

"The church always came first," screamed Annie. "I was always competing with God. Oh, the guilt was terrible. How could I compete with God?" She calmed, for a moment. "If I died, it would be over quicker. A wake, a funeral, soon the talk would go away. Harvey would be free to devote all his time to God and the church. But, if I went to counseling, I'd be a reminder, every Sunday, that I was weak. I'd always be there, tainting Harvey's ministry. Death was better." Annie sat and covered her face with her hands as though hiding shame. A small spark of the old spirit returned and she was up and pacing again. "I didn't want to die! I just wanted Annie back, my marriage back!"

Annie yelled, screamed and cried for her full fifty-minute session. She had come to Ruble 1 exhausted but that was

If I Knew Then What I Know Now . . .

nothing compared to the fatigue she felt now. Annie was spent, used up, as squeezed dry as a dish cloth.

The doctor expelled a sigh of relief. Annie slept for a whole day.

"Do you know what jogging is?" said the counselor later. Annie shook her head.

"I think maybe you should try it." said the counselor.

"Show me how," said Annie. The counselor jogged around the room. Annie stood up and tried it.

Annie was used to moving. At the hospital she roamed the corridors of the hospital walking back and forth, up and down. She'd sign out and walk the grounds of the hospital. When she returned she'd sign back in, take off her coat, sit for a minute. Then, she'd put her coat back on, sign out again, and walk and walk and walk. Being in the hospital was for Annie like a long nightmare. The two weekends she stayed, while most of the staff was off, were the longest days of her life.

Taking the counselor's advice, Annie started jogging to manage her stress. She started easy. First one block. Then two blocks. Then half a mile. With each step, Annie nurtured a new seed in her chest: health. Her heart ached less.

Annie's healing began.

Healing wasn't easy.

"It was such hard work," said Annie. "It was laborious. Everything I did it seemed that I had to put my hands behind my back and push myself." At Ruble 1, Wednesdays were field trip days. "Instead of going on the field trips, I talked the doctor into letting me go to work on Wednesdays." Annie has worked at the Hilltop Steak Restaurant for more than twenty-four years. She continued jogging, gradually increasing the distance she ran. She learned, again, how to take care of Annie. She let go of her childhood and concentrated on her life in the present. Annie's entire family attended group sessions at Ruble 1. Shane, only six, didn't like to go. "We talk about such miserable things," he said. They all disliked it because the issues were hard, their emotions raw.

"You don't heal until you get it all out," explained Annie. "That's why you have to live there, be in residence, so all those emotions come to the surface and then out. The garbage in me had to come out. That's why I was slowly dying, because I kept it all inside me." Thirteen days after she entered, Annie went home.

It is her second stay at Ruble 1 that Annie remembers most vividly. Her first depression and first admittance is foggy in her memory. She remembers only a few sharp images, her face in the mirror, giving herself over to God. Perhaps it's because the first depression treated the wrong problem: her childhood. Perhaps Annie just wasn't ready to face the real conflicts in her life. Whatever the reason, her first hospitalization, though it cleared up some issues from her shaky beginnings, didn't help.

It was the second depression that finally brought to the surface what being in their kind of ministry, with their kind of personalities, did to Annie's emotions and strength. It was the threat of Annie leaving him that finally convinced Harvey that Annie's childhood wasn't the only problem that overshadowed their life together.

"We were feeling more in that first depression that this was Annie's problem," said Harvey. "It wasn't until the second depression that I began to realize this was *our* problem. A lot of it was the fact that I wasn't learning to set limits.

"I over-extended myself for years." Harvey continued. "I prided myself that every time the children needed me, or Annie needed me, I was there. But it was only for emergencies. I put my family first but it was just for a small period of time, to get through that emergency, and then I was gone again. I was only there for crisis time.

"But it had to come to Annie saying she'd leave me before I could come to the point where I was willing to say:

If I Knew Then What I Know Now . . .

Look, I feel when I married you that this was God's will. If I have to, I'll give up the church to hang on to you. It was only then I began to change.

"Up until that point, I never believed I came first," said Annie.

Annie and Harvey are still married.

"Harvey is a wonderful man, a wonderful husband," said Annie. "He's a dedicated man. He loves me. When I see him, sitting down, relaxing, with his shirt collar open; or, when he's all dressed up in his suit, that really turns me on. I just love seeing him that way." Annie giggled like a bride, enjoying the thought. "That's what I fought for. Harvey and my marriage."

Even though he was close to retirement, Harvey left that difficult assignment and transferred to another church. Secure, now, that she was first in Harvey's heart, Annie stayed. At their new, and last, church, Harvey and Annie were intentional about taking time off to be together as a couple and as a family. They scheduled mid-week "weekends" away and Harvey learned to set limits. Deaths, illnesses, and weddings still ate into their time, but Annie didn't mind anymore. When she saw Harvey overextending himself, she spoke up. Harvey listened.

Just before they left the horrific church situation, Annie and Harvey's dream for a home of their own came true. A parishioner gave the Smiths the last lot in a recently developed housing tract. Mostly hill, it was a difficult building site. Annie and Harvey's son, Keith, designed a three-level house to fit the contours of the lot and then built it.

Annie and Harvey are still in the ministry, but it's a different kind of ministry. When Harvey was close enough to retirement, he requested a sabbatical and immediately following that, he retired. Harvey is back in college studying gerontology and he and Annie perform a nursing home ministry. It's an ecumenical pilot program. One Sunday a month they travel to the facility where Annie's mother lives.

After almost forty years, Annie and her mother are reunited. It isn't exactly a comfortable reunion. She was only two when her father took her away, so Annie doesn't remember her mother. But, Harvey and Annie agree, if they can perform their nursing home ministry for strangers, they can also do it for Annie's mother. Annie regrets that she never got the chance to talk to her father about why he divorced her mother and took her away. Annie met her two sisters when she was eighteen. As difficult as her childhood was, Annie discovered that she is, in a way, Cinderella. Her two sisters stayed with their father. Annie now realizes that she was the lucky one. She escaped.

Annie sings and plays guitar to entertain the elderly residents of the homes they visit. After she and Harvey lead a short ecumenical service.

"This is how we'd like to do our ministering as long as we're able."

"In my mind I remember the Boy Scout days," said Harvey, "when we sat around the campfire. The nursing home ministry is what we want to do all across the country. Maybe we'll only travel to a home once or twice in our lives but we just want to go and be involved with the people for a few hours, lift their spirits and be on our way."

Annie and Harvey are still in therapy. They see their doctor about once every six weeks or when they feel they need to.

"It's something we'll do for the rest of our lives," said Harvey. "It's a way to take inventory. Every once in a while something happens and you get emotionally involved. You need to work it out in a way that makes us feel good about ourselves and enables us to help others.

Still married, still ministering, and still very much in love, Annie and Harvey talked with us one last time in their home built snugly into the side of a hill. Downstairs is a veritable jungle of plants. Former parishioners know who to ask when they need cuttings for their next plant sale and Harvey always obliges. Harvey's indoor garden is augmented with outside gar-

If I Knew Then What I Know Now . . .

dens on the three landscaped areas in their front lawn. He is landscaping the steeply sloped hill behind the house.

On the second floor, the kitchen, living room, and dining room blend together in one open space. Large windows frame an attractive view of rooftops and blue sky as the hill lifts their view over the top of a Boston suburb. Jet planes drift down and float up from Logan Airport in the distance. An exercise bike stands in the corner beneath the windows, ready to pedal into the marvelous sunsets.

Annie is still jogging, still using running as exercise, enjoyment, and stress management. On the refrigerator hangs a picture of Annie, beaming with accomplishment, crossing the finish line of her first marathon run. She placed first for her age division. At sixty-two, Annie has a runner's body, lean and tight, but not overly muscular. She still has her long hair. She smiles more now and she's still spunky.

At sixty-seven, Harvey is trim from swimming. His back problems no longer flare up. Although still a crusader (some things never change), Harvey set limits. When asked to substitute for three months for a pastor who had a heart attack, Harvey accepted, making it clear that it was up to the members of the church to handle all the administrative work. Harvey would only do the pastor's work: preaching, visiting, marrying, baptizing, burying. It worked perfectly. Harvey and Annie both agree that's how the ministry should be. The laity takes care of the church; the pastor takes care of the laity. They wished they'd known it sooner.

Because of the "never go back" rule, the Smiths were reluctant to return to their previous parish. They did, however, consult the current pastor of the Medford church, their longest assignment, about making that their "home" church. Since it had been over eight years since they worked there, and the pastor was firmly established, he agreed. The Smiths would have found another church if the pastor objected. They attend once a month. "It is good, after all these years of ministering to others, to be ministered to," said Harvey.

"After the second depression, I think we were about to separate the church and God," said Annie. "God could not have planned this. Things happened to us that were not God's will. I don't want to lay all our problems on the church. The church is a beautiful place. You can't blame the church because we overextended ourselves."

"Ruble 1 was a very positive experience," said Annie. "It was good for me. It helped me. When I came out of there I would tell a lot of people: Everybody should go to Ruble 1 because you find out who you are. You find out what makes you tick. You're different. You have a deeper understanding of yourself.

"I wasn't willing to give up on Harvey. I knew I loved Harvey and I knew he loved me. I knew we had something good going here. In everything anybody does there are going to be those things that aren't pretty—disadvantages. But, there's gotta be hope. I'm still functioning. I'm kind of proud of me. I've come through thick and thin. We both have, Harvey and I. But we both always knew, we loved each other. And I'll be damned if I'll let anyone take that away from us.

"My bone of contention with Harvey was that nobody cares about him the way I do. And I needed to know, to feel, that he cared about me the way I cared about him.

"In the ministry, you listen to people's pain. That's not a complaint. I'm not complaining. That's the way it is. But, then you hurt too. The problem is, in the ministry sometimes that comes in bunches. It all piles up. It's overwhelming. Harvey and I are very people oriented, very brotherly, yes. In the ministry you get out of yourself a lot. But in getting out of yourself you have to remember yourself, too. You have to in order to function.

"We are two human beings with a heart and a soul. Some people think we have angels that watch over ministers

If I Knew Then What I Know Now . . .

and their wives and that bad things don't happen to us, but we're no different. We're just like you."

Would they do it all again? We asked that question over lunch at the Hilltop Restaurant where Annie still works. Annie deftly sidestepped the question and let Harvey answer. Harvey thought he would do it over again. But differently.

"I wouldn't do it again," Annie said quietly but with conviction. There was no doubt that Annie wouldn't relive the past no matter how much she learned from it. We sat once again on the modular couch in the Smiths' home. The house is the sanctuary they've looked for all their lives, their own private space. Harvey had left to pick up Shane from college and bring him home for the weekend. It was just Annie speaking now.

"We'd have to be more professional if we did it again," said Annie. "We'd let the church members do more instead of taking it all on ourselves. We made it difficult for ourselves taking on all the work and the issues, forcing some congregations to be more socially active then they were ready to be. They were only protecting their church, their home.

"But Harvey and I treated each church like our family. We're open people, very open. Very human. We're sensitive, perceptive. We jump in with two feet, our whole selves. Even though some congregations didn't like the issue-oriented part, they knew we loved them.

"I wonder, though, if we could be truly professional. We're not geared that way. It would be against our natures. That's probably why I said that I wouldn't do it again."

Annie is happy and at peace. The church is still a big part of her life but now it's on her terms. She doesn't subjugate herself to it anymore. Harvey is as socially conscious as ever and still ministering but he sets limits and doesn't forget the hard lessons of the past. Although Annie says she probably wouldn't do it again, she is still in the ministry. Their shared ministry, in their style, is probably what they've been waiting a lifetime to accomplish. Annie's life is, in the final analysis, a success story. She saved her marriage, their ministry, and her mind by refusing to allow their own unrealistic expectations to devour the love they share. Painful as it was at the time, this was Annie's choice.

"Weariness is part of their fabric of the ministerial life," wrote Robert W. Bailey and Mary Frances Bailey in their book *Coping with Stress in the Minister's Home.*

Other professions are as demanding of time as the ministry: accountants closing in on April 15th; retail businesses; the self-employed; lawyers; doctors; factory production line workers frantically filling a last minute order. Other professions are as demanding emotionally: psychiatrists; social workers; therapists; nurses. Other professions make demands on spouses: the banker's wife at a community dinner; the businessman's spouse at the annual Christmas office party or company picnic; the politician's wife campaigning for her husband; the doctor's spouse at the annual hospital fund raiser. There are always times when we work so hard and so long that we neglect our families. There are always times that we don a role to help our spouse or he dons a role to help us. There are always difficult things we do to support our spouse. In these respects, the ministry is no different than any other job. Weariness is a part of the fabric of all our lives. Returning home drained, exhausted with nothing left to spare for the most important people in our lives happens to all of us.

What makes life in the ministry harder than our lives is that few of us feel 'owned' by our employers anymore, whereas parishioners have a proprietary feeling about their pastor. Usually this comes from a sense of love and respect for either the minister himself or the role, but the perception of hundreds of hands clutching at him for help and support can devastate even the best loved minister. People seem to need the minister as their father; as a friend, counselor, teacher, leader, even, in a nonphysical sense, as their lover. Certainly they need him to be, at least, the symbol of God if not God himself.

If I Knew Then What I Know Now . . .

Pastors are primarily care-givers, nurturers with strong needs of their own to please people. Out of a sincere love of his congregation, and a strong desire to help them, he may destroy his marriage, himself, and his ministry.

There can be others within a congregation who feel they "own" the minister because their donations to the church pay his salary, maintain the parsonage, and finance continuing education. These are the people who want an accounting, who require numbers. It's as though ten more visitations this month over last month, five new members, or double the number of baptisms, somehow means they've gotten their money's worth out of the pastor.

Some members of a congregation, rare but still there, seem to delight in pulling the pedestal out from under their pastor as though by doing so, they get to punish God himself. And there are those with their own agenda who fight change out of a deep need for tradition and continuity. Rather than explore their own feelings, they attack the current symbol of change, the minister. Even if change came as the result of a laity board, the minister faces the repercussions.

Standing with him is his wife. Those members of the congregation who love him simply because he is the minister will criticize her first, so she suffers the fallout of the halo effect. If the pastor is having problems getting his work done (getting the laity's work done), it must be because she is not keeping up her end of things at home. She must not be as supportive as she should be.

Members expect her to be active in the church. They don't analyze why. Most can't express their expectations when asked. Most will deny they have expectations at all. But they are there. Unless she makes it clear from the beginning, the minister's wife who isn't in church every Sunday, who doesn't participate in church in some way, may find parishioners aloof, cold, and vaguely or even overtly disapproving. We can argue for years, and ministers' wives have been, that it shouldn't be that way, but it is.

For the rest of us, when we face our moments of overwork, exhaustion, or emotional disarray, we have a sanctuary. We have a place where we can relax, unwind, clear our minds, be off duty, be ourselves. Some ministerial families have no such sanctuary. Even if they own their own homes, they are on duty all day. Drop-in visits occur there as they do at other parsonages. They can always be reached by phone and frequently are. Part of their job is accessibility. Unlisted phone numbers for ministers are rare. In fact, no other profession would have provided us the ease with which we found our list of ministers' wives. In the white pages of the phone books, they are easily identifiable. Other professionals have unlisted phone numbers or list the phone in the spouse's name. We would not have been able to find three hundred and thirty-three doctors' wives or lawyers' wives by simply checking phone books. Home, where we can be ourselves and know we can enjoy some hours of peace and privacy, is not the same sanctuary for ministers and their families.

On those few occasions, relatively, that most wives must play banker's spouse or doctor's spouse or politician's spouse; we steel ourselves for our time in the spotlight. We may dislike it, may even hate it, we may love it, but we do it because that's what marriage is about: supporting each other. Few of us play that role on a daily basis. As one wife put it earlier, a surgeon's wife doesn't have to watch her husband perform every operation. The plumber's wife doesn't go on his calls with him. The lawyer's wife doesn't sit in the courtroom for each case her husband tries. Role playing is very different for most ministers' wives. Sometimes the minister's wife isn't supposed to just be there to showcase her husband. In a church with a strong two-fer philosophy, the minister's spouse is expected to work, to add her own two hands to the task, to add her mind,

If I Knew Then What I Know Now . . .

emotions, and sensitivity listening, advising, and counseling the congregations along with her husband.

The minister's wife doesn't have options. While most wives put on and take off their roles perhaps only several times a year, the minister's wife dons hers weekly, if not daily. She wears her role for a lifetime whether or not she wants to, and whether or not it fits.

There is a feeling, wherever it comes from, that she must always be nice. Nice is part of the territory and it is also part of the weariness. Annie remembered a parishioner telling her she had to be nice all the time. That parishioner felt nice was part of Annie's job as a minister's wife.

"That isn't very pretty, is it?" said Annie.

"The hypocrisy of constant 'Niceness' eats at you," our author Sherry Taylor observed. "Because you can't be honest, you begin to resent people and the church and then you can't minister. Boldness is great. Martin Luther said, 'Sin boldly—but love God more boldly.'"

For the women who answered our survey, boldness means having the courage and strength to be themselves. The advice most often given by our respondents to their sisters in ministerial marriages is to carve out identities for themselves even if it means some criticism from the congregation. They also advised a strong dose of common sense. You simply can't please everyone, they said, but you don't have to go out of your way to antagonize people either. Choosing the appropriate battleground seems dependent upon some experience in the ministry. Finding yourself so you can be yourself takes time and is also not a problem unique to the ministry.

So how do they cope?

"Maintain a positive attitude," said Jacquie Reed who told us in Chapter Ten about how she found friends. "Difficult circumstances in an appointment cannot last forever. My experience has been that no matter how hard your life may be, there are always small moments to rejoice."

"Your first ministry obligation is to your husband," said Evelyn Roberts, whose marriage to evangelist Oral Roberts is the longest marriage of all respondents. "Let him pour out his heart to you. Then you pour your heart out to God and forget it. You can't solve every problem your husband has, but you can listen, be sympathetic, and pray with him.

"You are called upon to do many things as a minister's wife that you might escape if your husband were a business man," continued Evelyn. "I do them as unto the Lord, reminding Him that I am planting a seed of faith. This helps me to put the things I don't necessarily want to do in a different perspective. Then I do them joyfully, rather than grudgingly, because I'm expecting something good will happen to me as a result."

"I think being a minister's wife is the same as being married to anyone," said Evelyn Johnson Moore of Cranston, Rhode Island. Evelyn has been married twelve years to her husband who works in the United Methodist denomination. "There is a need to balance who you are as a couple, as individuals, as parents, as citizens of the world. As long as one's self-esteem is healthy, a woman married to a minister can do and be what she chooses. As in all relationships, it is important to support, nurture, and prod one another. The nice thing for me is that since church is an integral part of my life I volunteer there so I get to see and be with my husband. At the same time, it is important for me to have other interests.

"The key for me is not to be pegged as the minister's wife but to be Evelyn. So when introduced as 'our minister's wife,' I always say: "Hello. My name is Evelyn."

"Share in the church in the way you would if you weren't the preacher's wife," said Dianna Higgs, a minister's wife from Las Vegas. "Don't try to be who you aren't. It will kill you, or, at least, your marriage."

"I think one of the secrets of good ministry is longevity," wrote Linda. Linda is thirty-three and has been married for fif-

If I Knew Then What I Know Now . . .

teen years. Her husband has changed churches only twice. "It took awhile to learn this. But I see congregations left without a shepherd and confused because the majority of pastors changed churches so often. I know some have very valid reasons for leaving. But people are people and are the same just about everywhere with the same joys, problems, etc. Pastors wives, or I think women in general, tend to take things more personally or harder than their husbands.

"Don't expect a perfect situation anywhere or in any church," continued Linda. "Make up your mind to invest your life in one congregation and one place, if possible. The fulfillment of being a part of these peoples' lives will be indescribable, growing together, laughing together, crying together, watching children grow. This is not always possible, but if it can be achieved, would be very rewarding. As pastors' wives we must learn to try to look at situations as objectively as we can and not always with anger and defensiveness. Take time to think and pray before speaking. People do not necessarily mean to criticize when they express an opinion and we should be careful not to take it as a personal affront."

"Be natural and accept the many joys and keep trying to overcome the negatives," was Joanne Gillis' advice. Joanne is a thirty-four year veteran of ministerial marriage. "Never play minister. Participate as a layperson where your talents can be used. Accept some of the demands of the congregation that you can live with and gracefully reject the others. Do not be naive, there are demands on your life. You will live a public life. Work out a way to live that is comfortable for *you and your family.*"

"Overall I am content with my 'role' because I feel I have established my own identity," said Donna Lee Fowlie. "I used to be 'the minister's wife' or 'Charlie's wife.' Not too long ago we were at a meeting and someone approached my husband saying, 'Oh, you must be Donna's husband.'"

Change is coming to the role of the minister's wife. Even though abuses and expectations linger, more than ninety percent of our respondents said they'd do it all again. Many wives who divorced their minister husbands said they divorced over his personality not because of his job or the demands of the congregation. Even with the expectations, insensitivities, demands, workaholism, loneliness, too little money, and inadequate parsonages, the vast majority of ministers' wives we met are happy. They faced the choices, made their decisions. They have few, if any, strong regrets. They are fiercely loyal. They married a man, not a minister. He's their husband, not their pastor. She isn't a minister's wife, she's a woman. He isn't a man of the cloth, he's a friend and a lover.

As one woman wrote: "I would marry *this* man again no matter what he did for a living because I love him."

For most ministers' wives, anything outside that core of love, anything placed in competition with it, just isn't relevant.

And that *is* by their choice.

Epilogue I

"A dismayed and somewhat dismal-looking clergy couple sat across from my desk in late fall," observed Reverend Sherry Taylor, "and outlined the gruesome schedule of their lives. It had been a typical fall in the life of a clergy family. Despite the fact that they were Protestant, it was quite clear the Jewish calendar was right: the new year really did begin in September. For this couple and for many like them, it had been an exhausting time of start-up in the church year. Gloomily they looked at me and said, 'In September things are so busy, it is impossible to even have sex.'"

When we tell this story to people, they think we're kidding; but we're not. When we tell this story to other clergy, many of them roll their eyes and say, "Tell me about it." For some clergy, all we have to do is say, "No sex in September," and they know exactly what we mean. There are times in the church year that are so busy, if your spouse is working as a pastor, that about all he comes home for is to sleep. It is not a pretty picture.

On the other hand, a number of years ago a group whose name slips our minds did a survey of clergy wives asking them to list the pros and cons of being married to a pastor. The responses paralleled those you have read about in this book, including this interesting addition. One poor woman answered a questionnaire and didn't have much good to say about the situation, but then, as an afterthought, she wrote, "Well, the one good thing is that sometimes we can have sex in the middle of the day." A flexible schedule does have its benefits. We assume, however, that this woman wasn't talking about September—maybe she had in mind that wonderful period of time that falls between Epiphany on January 6th and whenever Lent begins.

There was a time when being married to the minister was considered by many folks to be a career in its own right. Not only did churches have expectations of their pastors' wives, but the wives had expectations of themselves. Many of them talked about being in ministry with their husbands; of having a partnership; of being the unpaid additional, unofficial member of the church staff. Many wives with those expectations were happy to enter that career. Some folks of the persuasion thought of themselves as being "called" to the position of pastor's wife. They were a team. Their marriage was made in heaven and they went together about God's work in this world.

For better or worse, that teammate definition of a minister's wife no longer goes unchallenged. While some wives still subscribe to the notion that their ministry is being the pastor's spouse, there are as many women who simply fell in love with the man and had no real commitment to his profession. In fact, many of these women were completely unaware of the rigors of being a pastor's spouse. They were under the impression that they were entitled to lives of their own that would not be held up to scrutiny by their husband's congregations.

The old saw about, "If you can't stand the heat, get out of the kitchen," is often applied to women who find themselves living in a parsonage, married to a pastor, and unhappy about the expectations people have for them. It is not that these women don't want to have anything to do with the church, it is

Epilogue I

simply that they want to have a relationship with the church on their own terms. They don't consider themselves to be half or a two-fer. They consider themselves to be a whole person who makes choices just like any other member of the congregation. Some of them may choose not to be members of the congregation at all. Telling them that all these expectations simply go with the territory, while perhaps historically correct, is no longer accurate. The truth is that there are many congregations who do not have these expectations of the pastor's spouse. And more and more, as women create careers for themselves outside the home, the notion that the wife comes along as an adjunct employee is simply no longer valid.

The issues never are simple. It is rarely a matter of a wife refusing to participate at all in the life of the congregation her husband serves. It is more often a case of a woman who wants to meet some of the expectations but not all of them; who has some expectations for herself that she wants to meet. The tension is not simply between the wife and the church, but also the wife and the husband. Perhaps his expectations are the ones she is having trouble meeting. Perhaps she resents the fact that she should have to meet them at all. These are contemporary questions that affect lots of marriages, not simply the marriage of a pastor and his wife. But a pastor and his wife are no different. It is just that often their options seem much more limited.

For those folks who persisted in believing that the role of the pastor's wife is not appreciably different from that of other public figures, we would like to present the Bathing Suit Test. If your pastor lives in a town where members own swimming pools or where there is a municipal pool or even where there is a local beach that many of your congregation visit, sooner or later the wife will be confronted with the Bathing Suit Test. Do not confuse this with the test all women go through when they stand in the dressing room trying to decide if there is any bathing suit they dare wear in public. This is the test that says, "If I wear this in public, how will members of my husband's congregation react?" Trust me, most members of his congregation don't want to see his wife wearing a string bikini. Well, maybe they do, but they'd never admit to it. What they are more likely to say is that this is an inappropriate wardrobe choice for the wife of a minister. Even if she is twenty-five years old and the star of the aerobics class, a pastor's wife knows better than to appear in public in anything *anybody* could consider revealing. Sex appeal is not one of the qualities we value in the minister's wife. Princess Di can wear a bikini and Jackie Kennedy Onassis can sunbathe in the nude, but a minister's wife had best be less daring. The Bathing Suit Test is more revealing than the bathing suit she chooses; it exposes just how much her life is affected by his job.

The church, as one of our wives has said, is a seductive mistress. But it is too easy to blame the church for its high expectations and its demands on your husband's time. It is also safer. It is far less threatening to sympathize with your husband about how busy he is and how demanding the congregation is then it is to confront him with his own behavior. Just as it is easy to blame a husband's infidelity on the other woman who pulled out all the stops to get him, it is also easy to blame the congregation for your husband's lack of availability. Clergy wives need to separate the issues.

In her book, *Working Ourselves to Death,* Diana Fassel tells of a clergy wife who says that she learns more about her husband when she listens to him preach than she does in all the time they spend together at home. Fassel's conclusion is that her husband's intimate relationship is really with the church and not with her. He can control the relationship he has with the church, but he can exert much less control over the relationship he has with his wife. Blaming the church does not put the blame in the right place. In truth, sometimes it is the husband

Epilogue I

who uses the church as an excuse to be absent from his family and to avoid an intimate relationship with his wife. But confronting that is scary. It is so much easier to take his side and blame the congregation.

The "blame the congregation" solution may make the situation bearable or palatable, but it doesn't solve the problem. If he continues to be really involved in the church, she's going to continue to be unhappy with him and with his profession. Things won't get better. When a wife reminds her minister husband that the work of God and the work of the church are not always the same thing, she is doing him a favor. Demanding time for herself and for her children may finally provide the church with a pastor who is not exhausted and overly involved, but instead is healthy and human. And as in Annie's case, those demands may even save her life.

Even when wives choose to be very involved in their husband's congregations and walk into the marriage knowing what is to be expected, the children don't have that luxury. The tenderest most sensitive area for most ministers' wives who are also mothers is the vulnerability of their children. Imagine the delight of one pastor's wife when, after having left the church and heard that the new pastor's children were well behaved, (unlike hers) she learned that the new pastor's son had dyed his hair orange. Hearing people criticize your children for being children—for doing things that everybody else's children do—is the hardest part of the arrangement. Keeping your mouth shut when you would like to say, "Oh yeah, did you see what your kid just did?" is not a piece of cake. We all want to come to the defense of those we love. The problem is when you are a pastor's wife, sometimes you can't.

I recall an anonymous letter I received berating the behavior of my six-year-old son on the school playground. Did he throw anything? No. Did he hit anybody? No. Did he say anything obscene? No. He made a face at a teacher he didn't particularly like. The letter castigated the child for his willful, undisciplined, evil behavior. Then it went on to charge the parents with a full list of inadequacies for having raised such an ill-mannered child. The letter clearly stated that there was no excuse for a clergy to have such an unmanageable son. "At the time I was devastated," observed Reverend Taylor, "I couldn't believe anyone would do anything so vicious. And, it upset me to think that somebody who worked in the public school system in my town was spying on my child."

Some of the stories we have told are funny and some are not. Some will sound like sour grapes—as if these wives protest too much. And much of what we have written may convey the idea that life as a pastor's wife is a pretty sorry state.

In many ways being a part of the minister's family is a wonderful experience. The real gifts of clergy wives are very often used and celebrated in a church where they might have been ignored elsewhere. The opportunity to touch people's lives in such a unique way is a real blessing. For children to have so many surrogate grandparents and be fussed over by a whole congregation is a dream come true. And to know that your husband does work that he finds fulfilling and that others need and appreciate is very satisfying. Most ministers' wives wouldn't trade the experience for anything in the world. Most ministers' wives feel fortunate.

It is just that none of them feel fortunate all of the time. The loneliness, the expectations, the need to be the person someone else thinks you are can be mildly irritating or overwhelming. The joys of this kind of life do not diminish the difficulties. And we find that what clergy wives are asking for is a realistic look at who they are and what life as a minister's spouse requires.

Often when clergy wives begin to tell some of their stories to other women in the congregation, the response they get

Epilogue I

is, "I never knew you felt that way." While some people are dismayed, most folks are surprised that they feel as isolated or as unappreciated or as overworked as they do. The folks at the Alban Institute have said that ninety percent of the congregation doesn't know ninety percent of what the pastor does ninety percent of the time. That's fairly accurate, and the same could be said for clergy wives. Folks have no idea what kinds of demands are being placed on you by other people in the congregation. And they have no idea of what life in the fishbowl is like. What we hope we've done is to say out loud some of those things that clergy wives aren't yet ready to say. And because we know the church as a supportive, loving, and receptive institution, we imagine that when people hear what we have said, they will respond with kindness.

If you are reading this book as a clergy spouse, there is only one piece of advice that we want to give. Be yourself. God created each of us as an unique and peculiar individual. We are not all cut from the same piece of cloth. No matter who you are, or what your relationship is to the church, you are called to be the particular person God intends for you to be. Sometimes you can't sort out who that is with so many conflicting opinions, but each of us is asked to discover just who it is we are. Discovering that person and being authentic may not make everyone in your husband's congregation happy, but it will allow you to be sane and whole.

If you are reading this as a member of a congregation, we would ask you to remember that you call a pastor, and not a pastor's wife nor a pastor's family. If you give your pastor's wife the room to be herself and discover what particular gifts she brings, you may not always be delighted, but believe it or not, you will go a long way to insure the success of her husband's ministry. It will also create an attitude of genuine acceptance that is the hallmark of the church.

Remember those familiar words of Paul in his letter to

the church at Corinth, "Now there are varieties of gifts, but one Spirit . . ." Let the Spirit flourish.
    To each her own.

The Reverend Sherry M. Taylor
Area Minister, Connecticut Conference
United Church of Christ

Epilogue II

I am not a minister nor am I married to a minister. I refer to myself as a Reformed Ministers' Wives Bigot. In the four years it took to research, interview, and write this book, I learned some unpleasant things about myself and how I treat my minister and his wife. I recognized myself too many times as I read the survey answers and listened to the women in this book. The first question I'm asked is: why write about ministers' wives? It started in a church fellowship group.

Spectrum is a couples' club. Each Mother's Day, the men make dinner for the women. While they cook at one house, the women meet at another house for cheese and crackers, and yes, some wine, even beer. The first year I attended the gathering turned into a good-natured gripe session. One thing led to another and we were soon sharing stories of watermelon seed-spitting contests in living rooms and other embarrassing competitions involving bodily functions. I even chimed in with the one occasion when my husband forgot my name. As we hung our husbands out to dry relating their worst past misdeeds, I found myself enjoying the evening immensely. I must point out that these were good marriages. We just wanted to complain a little. If truth be told, we all went home thinking our own husband wasn't half as bad as the other women's. I enjoyed it.

For me, the evening turned sour when the last woman to speak started on her husband. She said he'd been crabby all day. He waited until the last minute to get the groceries he needed for the dinner. He'd snapped at the kids. In retrospect, she didn't say anything about her husband that was any worse than what the rest of us had said. Compared to seed spitting in the living room and forgetting your wife's name, her comments were pretty mild. My reaction wasn't. Vague feelings of disappointment, even shock, replaced the warm feelings of camaraderie I'd felt only moments before.

She was talking about my minister! The fact that he was a man, a father, a human being, didn't seem to matter. Apparently, the fact that she was married to him also didn't matter. She had done the unthinkable. She said negative things about my minister.

It took a while after that for me to discover that I was a bigot, that I clung to am impossible stereotype: I wanted my minister perfect. Some deep-seated need within me dictated that there must be someone in this imperfect world to turn to for the shining example of what life should be. I chose my minister, his wife, and family. I'm embarrassed over my abuses: I called the minister at home after hours with petty problems. I gave messages to his wife to take to him because she was more accessible. I didn't know how to talk to someone perfect. I went out of my way to talk to the minister's children although I didn't make the same effort with other children in the congregation. I went to him for counseling when I should have gone to a therapist. And I, like many members in many churches, let him down on more than one occasion, saying I'd do a certain job and then not following through.

I've learned too much writing this book. I learned it from Annie and Harvey; from Carla Neggers and Joe Jewell; from George and Marylyn True; and, from the women we inter-

Epilogue II

viewed, read about, and who answered our survey. This book is written exactly the way I learned about my bigotry: through the stories, in their own words, of the ministers' wives I've met.

Theirs is not an easy life because of its many contradictions and hard choices. The fact that most are happy is a credit to their own tenacity, common sense, and immense capacity to give. Theirs is not an easy life because they have to deal with people like me.

My bigotry was so strong that I was surprised to find that ministerial families suffer the same terrors and tragedies the rest of us do: seriously ill children, parents and spouses; divorce; giving up the work we love because we simply can't do it anymore; emotional illness; lack of support groups, friends and family; pressure; stress; collapse. I thought, by the nature of their work and faith, that they were immune to these things.

I like to think of myself as honest, caring, and aware of the needs of others. I'm reasonably intelligent and when I learn something I remember it forever. I have a college degree, my family enjoys a middle-income lifestyle. I don't think people would describe me as petty, dictatorial, or insensitive. Yet I perpetrated many of the small, annoying acts that the women in this book spoke about.

Most church members would describe themselves as I have described myself: sensitive, caring, aware. But we are the people who perpetuate the myth of perfection for the minister and ministerial family. We are the ones who continue the subtle and mild abuse, born of ignorance, that confuses the minister's wife.

Because her role has no current definition, the minister's wife holds us, too, at arm's length. As she works within her husband's church, doing what needs to be done to help him; protecting herself from our prying eyes; not relaxing enough to show her humanness; she also, unwittingly, perpetuates the myth of perfection. As parishioners, we only know what we see. Too many times what we see is the traditional minister's wife, because it simply costs her too much energy and time to educate us that she is a unique personality with her own needs. So she shares, with us, part of the blame for perpetuating the stereotype.

My actions rose out of an ignorance that is now gone. Hopefully, through what these women shared with us, this book can eliminate ignorance elsewhere. There are mean-spirited people in churches who this book will never touch. They won't recognize themselves in these pages.

Other people, those like me, will continue to say they treat their minister, his wife, and children as real people but will then go on to perpetrate more acts that make life in the ministry feel like a walk on hot coals.

The single most unpleasant thing I've learned about myself while working on this book is that I am really not completely reformed after all. Even after four years of researching, interviewing, writing, I still want my minister to be perfect. I still want that shining example of what life could be and should be and I have still personally elected my minister, his wife and children to be that ideal. I recognize my deep-seated need to be close to God and apologize for selecting another human being to be the symbol of God; to be the only God I can see, hear and touch in a physical sense. I need that and it appears I'm unable to give it up.

But I don't have to act on it. I don't have to continue subtly or overtly abusing my minister and his family. I am aware of their needs even while I secretly wish for perfection.

They have a tough job and I wish them well for I suspect that even Reformed Minister's Wives Bigots will continue to try their patience.

Liz Greenbacker
Meriden, Connecticut

Appendix I

The Survey

I wish to remain anonymous (circle one) Yes No
Age:
Years Married:
Is your husband's church (circle one): Rural Suburban Urban?
How many members, approximately, are there in his church?
1. In what denomination does your husband work? Do you belong to the same church? If you don't, has this caused any problems?
2. How did you meet your husband?
3. Did you know, before you married, that your husband was, or was planning to be, a minister? How did you feel about it?
4. How did you prepare yourself to be a minister's wife? What advice or suggestions did your husband offer?
5. What is your definition of the traditional role of a minister's wife?
6. Does your own life match that of your definition? How is it different?
7. Have you ever had to act the role of the traditional minister's wife with members of your husband's congregation? How and why did this happen?
8. Have you ever received a negative reaction from your hus-

Appendix I

band's congregation for not following the traditional role of the minister's wife? How and why did it happen?

9. Please describe your activities inside and outside your husband's church. Do you work outside the home?

10. Has being a minister's wife hampered or helped your career? What is the reaction of your co-workers and supervisors when they learn you are a minister's wife? How do you feel about this?

11. What are the advantages to being a minister's wife? What makes you the happiest? Please explain.

12. What are the disadvantages to being a minister's wife? What makes you the saddest? Please explain.

13. What makes you the angriest being a minister's wife?

14. How many times have you had to move? How did you handle the move emotionally?

15. Are your friends mostly from inside the congregation, or, are they mostly from outside the congregation? Why is this and how do you feel about it?

16. Do you have children? What affect did life in a fishbowl have on raising your children? Were there any problems because they were 'preacher's kids?'

17. Do you and your husband share child-rearing duties, or, do you handle most of it? How do you feel about this?

18. How much time does your husband spend with the family? How do you feel about the amount of family time he has available?

19. How difficult (or easy) is it to get 'alone' time—intimate time—with your husband? Please explain.

20. When you are together, is the time quality time or is it squeezed in between his commitment? Please give examples of how you get and use time with your husband.

21. If you don't feel your husband can spend enough time with you, is it because of the demands of the congregation, or, is it his personal demands? Is he a workaholic? Please explain.

The Survey

22. Do you feel your husband is paid adequately for his level of education and the job he performs? Why?
23. Have you ever had financial difficulties? How did you handle them?
24. Do you live in a congregation-owned dwelling or do you have a housing allowance? Which would you prefer and why?
25. What would you have done differently if you knew as a bride what you know now about marriage to a minister?
26. Do you have any advice, or tips, to offer other ministers' wives?

Appendix II

The Survey Results

We sent out 464 surveys to ministers' wives. Most of the ministers' names were taken from phone books. We received 119 responses. The women who answered our survey referred 131 other women to us. We received 101 completed questionnaires for a response rate of almost 22%. Eighteen responses were polite refusals. One woman's husband had recently died. One woman had been married only two months and felt she wasn't qualified to answer.

Age: Ages of those responding ranged from 29 to 73.

Years Married: Timespan of marriages ranged from 3 years to 51. Evelyn Roberts has the distinction of being the longest-lived ministerial marriage veteran!

Residence: 16% Rural
32% Suburban
42% Urban
10% Other

Number of Congregation Members: Ranged from 95 to 3,600

Appendix II

0–200	12.7%
201–300	14.5%
301–400	9.1%
401–500	5.5%
501–700	3.6%
701–1,000	7.3%
1,000 and over	18.2%

Summary of Accumulated Data

1. In what denomination does your husband work? Do you belong to the same church? If you don't, has this caused any problems? Denominations: United Methodist; Presbyterian (U.S.A.); United Church of Christ (includes Congregational); Evangelical Lutheran Church of America; Lutheran; Episcopal; Southern Baptist; American Baptist; Baptist; Assembly of God; Disciples of Christ; Church of the Lutheran Confession; Unitarian Universalist; Christian Church; Church of the Brethren; Independent Lutheran; Interdenominational, Roman Catholic.

More than 90% of the respondents are members of the same denomination. Ten percent changed denominations to their husband's church. Five percent are Roman Catholics.

2. How did you meet your husband?
A variety of responses are covered in depth in Chapter Two.

3. Did you know, before you married, that your husband was, or was planning to be, a minister? How did you feel about it?

Almost 80% of our respondents knew their husbands were, or were training to be, ministers.

Forty-nine percent said they were pleased/happy and 10% said they felt called to be a minister's wife. Of the rest 14% didn't like the idea, and, 13% said it didn't make any difference.

The Survey Results

4. How did you prepare yourself to be a minister's wife? What advice or suggestions did your husband offer?

Answered in Chapter Two.

5. What is your definition of the traditional role of a minister's wife?

All the women described the traditional, stereotypical wife.

6. Does your own life match that of your definition? How is it different?

Very few women said their life matched that of the traditional minister's wife. Yet, they included extensive lists of jobs and responsibilities they assumed within their husband's congregations that were also listed under their definition of the stereotypical minister's wife. Some pointed out that their attitudes were different. They performed those tasks because they wanted to, not because they had to.

7. Have you ever had to act the role of the traditional minister's wife with members of your husband's congregation? How and why did this happened?

Most answered yes. Chapter Four covers the instances.

8. Have you ever received a negative reaction from your husband's congregation for not following the traditional role of the minister's wife? How and why did it happen?

Answered in Chapter Fourteen.

9. Please describe your activities inside and outside your husband's church. Do you work outside the home?

Seventy-six percent of our respondents work outside the home. Sixty-eight percent of those said they had careers, and, 12% said they worked, at no pay, in their husband's church.

Appendix II

10. Has being a minister's wife hampered or helped your career? What is the reaction of your co-workers and supervisors when they learn you are a minister's wife? How do you feel about this?
Answered in Chapter Eight.

11. What are the advantages to being a minister's wife? What makes you the happiest?
The number one advantage cited was having a ready-made community of friends and church family (51%). Other answers included: seeing people touched by husband's ministry (25%); sharing in the joys and sorrows of the laity (19%); pride in her husband's work (12%); the opportunity to meet all kinds of people (9%); parish members' generosity (12%); the opportunity to serve with her husband (11%). Other items mentioned were flexibility of schedule; clergy discounts at stores; parsonages; recognition and respect; and, their husband's happiness.

12. What are the disadvantages to being a minister's wife? What makes you the saddest?
The answer given most often was no close friends/loneliness (16%). Also listed were: hurting with people in the congregation during their troubles (12%); lack of privacy (11%); moving (11%); substandard salaries, family needs second to church; no weekends off in the usual sense (all at 7%). Other answers included unfair criticism of husband, herself, or her children; no regular pastoral care for themselves; being judged. Fourteen percent listed lack of time.

13. What makes you the angriest being a minister's wife?
Twenty-two percent mentioned unfair criticism here. Other answers included interruptions on their day off; petty attitudes of people in the church; invasion of privacy; lack of commitment of members to the church; children's suffering;

The Survey Results

their husband putting the church before them. Four percent said nothing about being married to a minister made them angry.

14. How many times have you had to move? How did you handle the move emotionally?

Never moved	6.2%
One move	9.3%
Two moves	18.5%
Three moves	11.3%
Four moves	13.4%
Five moves	15.5%
Six moves	10.3%
Seven moves	3.1%
Eight moves	2.0%
Nine moves	3.1%
Ten moves	3.1%
Over ten moves	4.1%

Forty percent said they handled moves well; 25% said they handled moves poorly and 22% said, though they didn't like leaving a congregation, they adapted well at the new church.

15. Are your friends mostly from inside the congregation, or, are they mostly from outside the congregation? Why is this and how do you feel about it?

Twenty-nine percent said their friends were from inside the congregation; 21% said their friends were from outside, mostly from work; 42% said both; and, 6% said they had few, if any, friends.

Appendix II

16. Do you have children? What affect did life in a fishbowl have on raising your children? Were there any problems because they were 'preacher's kids?'
Eighty-seven percent had children.

One child	4%
Two	36%
Three	22%
Four	13%
Five	4%
Six	7%
Seven or more	7%

Two women took care of foster children; one had eleven, the other had twelve.

17. Do you and your husband share child-rearing duties, or, do you handle most of it? How do you feel about this?
Forty-nine percent of the respondents said they were the primary care-givers for the children; 42% said they shared child raising duties.

18. How much time does your husband spend with the family? How do you feel about the amount of family time he has available?
Thirty-eight percent said they did not have enough family time together. Twenty-four percent mentioned loneliness.

19. How difficult (or easy) is it to get 'alone' time—intimate time—with your husband? Please explain.
Answered in Chapter Twelve.

20. When you are together, is the time quality time or is it squeezed in between his commitments? Please give examples of how you get and use time with your husband.

The Survey Results

Sixty percent said getting 'alone' time with their husbands was difficult. When they did get together, 63% said it felt like it was squeezed in. Most wives mentioned that they had only one night a week free with their husbands. Some mentioned that they had one day twice a month or once a month. A few mentioned that they got only one weekend every three months.

21. If you don't feel your husband can spend enough time with you, is it because of the demands of the congregation, or, is it his personal demands? Is he a workaholic? Please explain.

Forty-six percent said their husbands were workaholics, and of them, 62% said it was his fault and not the church's expectations. Thirty-five percent said the workaholism was a combination of both his expectations of himself and the demands of the congregation.

22. Do you feel your husband is paid adequately for his level of education and the job he performs? Why?

A whopping 79% agreed that their husbands were not paid adequately for the level of education, experience, and duties within the church. Eight percent said they did think their husbands were paid adequately.

23. Have you ever had financial difficulties? How did you handle them?

Covered in Chapter Five.

24. Do you live in a congregation-owned dwelling or do you have a housing allowance? Which would you prefer and why?

Forty-two percent of our respondents get a housing allowance and own their own homes. Fifty-eight percent live in parsonages. Of those, half would prefer a housing allowance.

Appendix II

25. What would you have done differently if you knew as a bride what you know now about marriage to a minister?

Nineteen percent of our respondents said they wouldn't change anything about their lives. The balance of responses were single answers: not knuckling under to congregational expectations; finishing college; waiting to go into the ministry until they were financially able to do so; limiting the number of children; establishing support systems; moving more; and, moving less. One woman said she wished she'd gone on to seminary and become a minister too. Another said she would have returned their wedding gifts and banked the cash. Only one woman said that maybe she wouldn't marry a minister again.

26. Do you have any advice, or tips, to offer other ministers' wives?

The number one answer here (22%) was to "be yourself." The advice was to be the person you'd be if your spouse wasn't a minister. Other answers included making, forcing, or encouraging the minister to take time off to be with spouse and family; a good sense of humor; be supportive of your spouse; keep your faith strong and love people; know what you're getting into; watch finances closely; try not to let criticism bother you. One woman said that each minister should read the questionnaire for this book; and, one woman wrote: Just say NO!

Bibliography

BOOKS

Abernathy, Ralph David. *And the Walls Came Tumbling Down.* New York: Harper & Row, 1989.

Bailey, Robert W., and Mary Frances Bailey. *Coping With Stress in the Minister's Home.* Nashville, TN: Broadman Press, 1979.

Bouma, Mary La Grand. *Divorce in the Parsonage.* Minneapolis, MN: Bethany Fellowship, Inc., 1979.

Coble, Betty J. *The Private Life of the Minister's Wife.* Nashville, TN: Broadman Press, 1981.

Fortune, Marie M. *Is Nothing Sacred? When Sex Invades the Pastoral Relationship.* New York: Harper & Row, 1989.

Hadden, Jeffrey K., and Anson Shupe. *Televangelism. Power and Politics in God's Frontier.* New York: Henry Holt & Co., 1988.

Holck, Jr., Manfred. *Making it on a Pastor's Pay.* Nashville, TN: Abingdon Press, 1974.

Hughes, Kent, and Barbara Hughes. *Liberating Ministry from the Success Syndrome.* Wheaton, IL: Tyndale House, 1987.

Kirk, Richard J. *On the Calling and Care of Pastors.* Washington DC: The Alban Institute, 1973.

Leas, Speed B. *Moving Your Church Through Conflict.* Washington DC: The Alban Institute, 1985.

Mace, David, and Vera Mace. *What's Happening to Clergy Marriages?* Nashville, TN: Abingdon Press, 1980.

Merrill, Dean. *Clergy Couples in Crisis. The Impact of Stress on Pastoral Marriages.* Waco, TX: Word Books, 1985.

Oden, Marilyn Brown. *The Minister's Wife, Person or Position?* Nashville, TN: Abingdon Press, 1966.

Rassieur, Charles L. *The Problem Clergymen Don't Talk About.* Philadelphia: Westminster Press, 1976.

Shelley, Marshall. *The Healthy Hectic Home: Raising a Family in the Midst of the Ministry.* Waco, TX: Word Books, 1988.

Sinclair, Donna. *The Pastor's Wife Today.* Nashville, TN: Abingdon Press, 1981.

Truman, Ruth. *The Underground Manual for Ministers' Wives.* Nashville, TN: Abingdon Press, 1974.

U.S. Department of Commerce, Bureau of the Census. *Statistical Abstract of the United States, 109th edition* (1989): Table #622: Employment status of the civilian noninstitutional population 60 years old and older by sex, race and Hispanic origin: 1955–1987.

U.S. Department of Commerce, Bureau of the Census. *Statistical Abstract of the United States, 109th edition* (1989): Table #640: Labor force participation rates for wives, husband present, by age of own youngest child: 1975–1988.

ARTICLES AND PAPERS

Augsburger, David. "The Private Lives of Public Leaders." *Christianity Today* (November 20, 1987): 23–24.

Berkley, James D. "Turning Points: Eight Ethical Choices." *Leadership* (Spring Quarter 1988): 32–41.

Brice, Heather. "After the Affair: A Wife's Story." *Leadership* (Winter Quarter 1988): 58–65.

Bibliography

Bubna, Donald L. "How to Bid a Healthy Farewell." *Leadership* (Summer Quarter 1988): 118–123.

"Clergy Compensation Guidelines." Hartford, CT: Connecticut Conference of the United Church of Christ, 1990.

Craig, Ann. "A Pastor's Lament. . . ." In "What Do You Want Your Pastor to Do?" Washington DC: The Alban Institute (December 1976): 3–4.

"Forum: How Pure Must a Pastor Be?" *Leadership* (Spring Quarter 1988): 12–20.

"Forum: Pastoral Counseling: Benefit or Burden to Ministry?" *Leadership* (Spring Quarter 1987): 128–137.

"Forum: Private Sins of Public Ministry." *Leadership* (Winter Quarter 1988): 14–23.

Holck, Jr., Manfred. "Clergy Compensation Planning for 1991: Part I." *Church Management—The Clergy Journal* (July 1990): 48–51.

Jacoby, Susan. *McCall's* Readers Speak Out: "Faith, Values and Morals." *McCall's* (May 1989): 69–73.

Johnston, Eldred. "What is the Minister's Job?" *Church Management—The Clergy Journal* (April 1987): 6.

Leavitt, Daniel B. "The Minister and the Mid-life Crisis." *Action Information* (January-February 1979): 9–11.

McIntosh, Gary L. "Is it Time to Leave?" *Leadership* (Summer Quarter 1988): 70–75.

Maeder, Thomas. "Wounded Healers." *The Atlantic Monthly* V. 283 (January 1989): 37–47.

Morey, Ann-Janine. "Blaming Women for the Sexually Abusive Male Pastor." *The Christian Century* (October 8, 1985): 866–869.

Muck, Terry, and Marshall Shelley. "Forum: When Pastor is Also Parent." *Leadership* (Fall Quarter 1987): 130–136.

Oden, Marilyn Brown. "Stress and Purpose: Clergy Spouses Today." *The Christian Century* (April 20, 1988): 402–404.

Osborne, Larry W. "Negotiating a Fair Salary." *Leadership* (Winter Quarter 1987): 84–88.
Oswald, Roy M. "Married to the Minister." Washington DC: The Alban Institute, 1980.
———. "Why do Clergy Wives Burn Out?" *Action Information.* Washington DC: The Alban Institute (January-February 1984) 11–15.
———. "Part II: Why Clergy Wives Burn Out." *Action Information.* Washington D.C.: The Alban Institute (March-April 1984) 1–5.
Rediger, G. Lloyd. "Affairs." *Church Management—The Clergy Journal* (October 1986): 34–35, 42.
———. "Supporting Clergy Systemically." *Church Management—The Clergy Journal* (October 1988): 32–37.
Reilly, Robert T. "How Interfaith Couples Make the Most of Their Differences." *U.S. Catholic* (May 1989): 23–28.
———. "Mixed Blessings: Ten Lessons Learned from Interfaith Couples." *U.S. Catholic* (March 1990): 34–39.
Robbins, Paul D. "Clergy Compensation: A Survey of Leadership Readers." *Leadership* (Spring Quarter 1981): 35–45.
———. "Forum: Laymen Talk About Money and the Local Church." *Leadership* (Spring Quarter 1981): 127–138.
Ross, Charlotte. "Summary of Survey of Clergy Wives, Clergy, Lay Persons. Role Expectations of the Pastor's Wife." The Task Force on Women, the Synod of the Trinity, United Presbyterian Church, U.S.A., Camp Hill, PA, 1979.
Sparks, James Allen. "How to Get Away Without Leaving Town." *Church Management—The Clergy Journal* (April 1987): 9–10.
"Special Report: How Common is Pastoral Indiscretion?" *Leadership* (Winter Quarter 1988): 12–13.
Stewart, Thomas A. "Turning Around the Lord's Business." *Fortune* V. 120 (September 25, 1989): 116–128.

Bibliography

"Survey on Clergy Compensation." New York: The Ministers and Missionaries Benefit Board of American Baptist Churches, 1985.

Taylor, Carolyn. "Letter to the Editor," *The Witness*. In "Married to the Minister." Washington DC: The Alban Institute, 1980.

"The Role of the Pastor's Spouse in the Local Congregation." Questionnaire results. New York: Research Division of the Support Agency, United Presbyterian Church, U.S.A., February, 1977.

Whybrew, Lyndon E. "Minister, Wife and Church: Unlocking the Triangles." Washington DC: The Alban Institute, 1984.